Warwick Mare

THE EVOLUTION OF THE SAILING SHIP

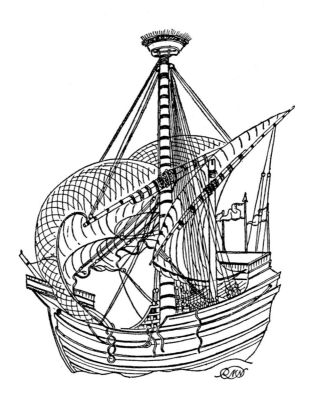

The Evolution of the
SAILING SHIP
1250-1580

Selected and arranged by Basil Greenhill

Keynote Studies from The Mariner's Mirror

Series Editor: David J Starkey

CONWAY
MARITIME PRESS

Introduction © Basil Greenhill 1995
Text © *The Mariner's Mirror*

Published by Conway Maritime Press 1995,
an imprint of Brassey's (UK) Ltd,
33 John Street,
London WC1N 2AT

The material in this book first appeared in *The Mariner's Mirror*

British Library Cataloguing in Publication Data
Evolution of the Sailing Ship
I. Greenhill, Basil
623.820309

ISBN 0 85177 655 8

Typeset by Dorwyn Ltd, Rowlands Castle, Hants
Printed and bound by Bookcraft (Bath) Ltd

CONTENTS

CONTENTS

PREFACE

The Mariner's Mirror (MM) is the international journal of the Society for Nautical Research (SNR). Established in June 1910, the SNR published the first issue of the *MM* in January 1911. Save for one prolonged interruption (October 1914–June 1919), occasioned by wartime, the journal has been produced regularly ever since, on a monthly basis until 1924 and quarterly thereafter. The *MM* is currently (1995) in its eighty-first volume.

In launching *Keynote Studies from The Mariner's Mirror*, the Publications Committee of the SNR has two principal objectives. First, by focusing on the material published in the early volumes of the *MM*, it is intended that the series will reveal something of the interests and scholarly contribution of those who founded the SNR and established the *MM* as a forum for the discussion of matters maritime. Second, and perhaps more importantly, the series is designed to make accessible to modern researchers the work of previous generations of historians, much of which is still of relevance to contemporary debates on maritime history and archaeology. With this aim in view, each volume in the series will comprise material selected from the *MM* and arranged so as to address a particular theme. As well as articles long and short, editors will draw upon the notes, queries and answers which the editor of the first *MM* accurately forecast would 'form by no means the least interesting or least valuable part of the Journal' (Vol I, 1, p. 2). By these means, it is hoped that this *Keynote Studies* will rescue from obscurity and render useful the substantive arguments and nuggets of information contained in the early volumes of *The Mariner's Mirror* 'wherein may be discovered his Art, Craft & Mystery after the manner of their use in all ages and among all nations'.

The first volume in the series concerns one of the themes that dominated the early issues of *MM*, the evolution of the sailing ship in the medieval and renaissance world. Our knowledge of this important topic has, of course, developed considerably since the early twentieth century. However, the material presented in the pages that follow formed a considerable part of the base upon which such developments have been made. It therefore remains of great value to those concerned with ship technology, a vital, but still misunderstood, aspect of human history.

DAVID J STARKEY
Series Editor

INTRODUCTION

The Society for Nautical Research came into existence on 14 June 1910 as a result of the enthusiasm of a small group of men whose leisure interests had led them to study the development of the sailing vessel, and more especially of her sails and rigging, in the medieval and post-medieval periods. This was not a fashionable subject and these men were not historians. The Society and its journal were originally intended to provide a vehicle for discussion inside the founding group and the early volumes of *The Mariner's Mirror* show this very clearly.

These prime movers in the formation of the society were, in alphabetical order, Harold Brindley, Leonard Carr Laughton, Alan Moore and Robert Morton Nance, together with Gregory Robinson. Dr R C Anderson, later to be the President of the Society, was the younger contemporary of these men and in 1959 he wrote, '. . . it was the bringing together of Nance and Laughton with Moore as an intermediary that led to the foundation of our Society'.[1]

The story was told in detail by Alan Moore himself in 1955 on pages 267 to 280 in No. 4 of Vol. 41 of *The Mariner's Mirror*, though he probably understates the importance of his own role. Of these men Harold Brindley was a distinguished zoologist, a fellow of St John's College, Cambridge, of whom Moore wrote, 'He was a large and massively built man with a fine head and thick brown hair. His marked features bore a kind look that reflected his mind . . . He had the best point of view for an antiquarian, that which sees the past as part of the present and does not regard something which has gone out of use as necessarily done with'.[2] It might be added that Brindley appears to have been an indefatigable researcher and, as far as the development of the ship in medieval times is concerned, he was the leader of the group.

Leonard Carr Laughton was the son of Professor Sir John Laughton, a distinguished and very influential naval historian of King's College, London. Dr Anderson wrote of Carr Laughton Junior that he had, 'a vast store of knowledge on almost any subject connected with the work of The Society for Nautical Research, a store he was always ready to share

1 *The Mariner's Mirror*, Vol. 45, No. 4, (1959) §267–8
2 *The Mariner's Mirror*, Vol. 41, No. 4, (1955) §269

with others.'[3] Nevertheless, though a journalist by profession Carr Laughton published relatively little on maritime history but his *Old Ship Figureheads and Sterns*, published in 1925, has, at the end of the twentieth century, become a collector's volume.

Alan Moore himself was the son of a distinguished medical practitioner and in due course inherited a Baronetcy. He studied medicine at St Bartholomew's Hospital in London. His interest in the history of the ship, and particularly in seventeenth-century rigging, developed very early in life and, he was to say later, conflicted with his medical studies. I remember him personally from the meetings of the Society in the 1940s as a man who combined great charm with immense knowledge of his special subject. He took a particular delight in the building at Brixham in Devon of a hypothetical reconstruction of the *Mayflower* of 1620 which now lies at Plymouth, Massachusetts. Both his vast knowledge and his personal charm come through in the pages of his book *Last Days of Mast and Sail*, Oxford, 1925, reprinted, Newton Abbot, 1970, a classic of scrupulous record of informed observations of the detail of the masting and rigging of vessels which Moore had himself been able to study at first hand on his travels, particularly as a temporary naval surgeon during the First World War. This is the very best of what I suppose we would now call amateur maritime ethnography, but which he rightly described as nautical comparative anatomy. It was characteristic of Moore that in the last sentence of ¶ 57 in this volume he showed himself as probably the first person to recognise the speed and significance of the development of the three-masted sailing vessel in the fifteenth century.

The Last Days of Mast and Sail was illustrated with drawings from Moore's field sketches and photographs prepared by Robert Morton Nance. He was a descendant of Cornish seafaring families on both his father's and his mother's side and was much influenced towards maritime affairs by his maternal grandfather who lived at St Ives. Trained as an artist and immensely knowledgeable in the technicalities of the history of rigging he was an indefatigable field worker in the, in those days, still vast but impoverished sailing economy of the south-west of England.[4] He was especially qualified to illustrate his subjects as he does many times in this present compilation. Two books on maritime affairs by him were published: *Sailing Ship Models*, London, 1924, now another collector's

---

3 *The Mariner's Mirror*, Vol. 41, No. 3, (1955) §179

4 For a good account of how hard life was growing up in a Cornish fishing community even in the 1920s see A Smith, *Laughs and Sweet Memories*, St Austell, 1992.

piece; and *A Glossary of Cornish Sea Words*, Truro, 1963. Although he continued to contribute to *The Mariner's Mirror* from time to time (as in his article on 'The Ship of the Renaissance' in Vol 41, 1955), Nance in later life became more and more absorbed with things Cornish. He became Grand Bard and President of the Federation of Old Cornwall Societies as well as President of the Royal Institution of Cornwall.

Gregory Robinson was another distinguished marine artist who had, however, sailed round the world in the four-masted barque *Carradale*. In the words of the late George Naish, at one time Deputy Director of the National Maritime Museum and Secretary of the Society, who knew him well, 'Gregory Robinson was a much-loved stalwart in the early days of the Society, ready to write wittily and knowledgeably on a number of topics, indeed gleefully trailing his coat to trap the unwary pedant'.[5] His coat trailing should not be taken too seriously. Despite his criticisms of the maritime knowledge of the medieval artist, when the Bremen cog came out of the mud of the Weser in 1962 she showed the medieval town seals of north German coastal towns to have been remarkably accurate depictions.

There are two other figures who, though they were not so deeply involved with the Society's foundation, were contributors from the earliest issues of *The Mariner's Mirror*. Roger Charles Anderson who sometimes signed his notes in *The Mariner's Mirror* with the initials S.G. (South Goodwin) became editor of the *Mirror* as early as 1913. He remained editor until 1923 and then edited the journal in 1931 and 1932 and from 1939 to 1946. He was President of the Society from 1931 to 1960, a Trustee of the National Maritime Museum from its foundation and the second Chairman of Trustees. His publications included *The Sailing Ship*, London, 1926; *Seventeenth Century Rigging*, London, 1955; and *Oared Fighting Ships*, London, 1962. Anderson and Moore were perhaps the great figures in the history of the Society. My first encounter with Anderson was when, in 1941, then a temporary Ordinary Telegraphist RN, on leave, I bicycled from my parents' house in Somerset over to Nunney Court, where the Andersons were living, and was shown the piles of boxes in the stables which contained treasures from the National Maritime Museum, there for wartime safety, and the two fourteen-foot boats in which he and his wife Romola had cruised and camped in the Baltic. I was then given the best tea wartime could provide while we discussed things maritime and the possible future of the National Maritime Museum.

5 *The Mariner's Mirror*, Vol 53, No 3, (1967) §209

The remaining early contributor was Geoffrey Callender, Professor of History at the Royal Naval College at Greenwich and later the first Director of the National Maritime Museum. He was to be the Secretary and Treasurer of the Society for twenty-six years.

These were men of that very different world before the trauma of the First World War, which all of them survived. They lived in what Moore called 'the blaze of the old tradition'.[6] As he pointed out, '. . . in 1904 you need not be one [an antiquarian] to know what sailing vessels looked like and to recognise the different rigs. Sailing ships still carried passengers from London. Wool carriers with skysail yards could be seen in the docks. Though no merchant brig had been built in this country since 1876 there were plenty about. Scandinavian barques laden with timber or ice with a windmill pump between the main and mizen masts were so common as to be hardly worth looking at.[7] Luggers and dandy-rigged fishermen enlivened the Channel; as for Thames barges, one might as well imagine London river without them as London streets without hansom cabs'.[8]

Though their enthusiasms were diverse, the main interest these men had in common was the study of the development of the structural details, and the rigging and sails of vessels in the medieval period and the seventeenth century as revealed by iconographic and documentary evidence. This was the principal subject dealt with in the first six volumes of *The Mariner's Mirror* – 1911, 1912, 1913, 1914, 1919 and 1920 – and it continued as an important theme for a number of years. The range of the iconographic evidence they uncovered was formidable and much of it may be new to scholars of the end of the twentieth century. They were skilled draughtsmen and they reproduced much of their evidence in the pages of *The Mariner's Mirror*.

There is room for re-examination of much of this evidence in the light of late twentieth-century knowledge of the development of vessel structures in the medieval period. For example, Brindley's work on what he calls bow ropes reveals extensive iconography of a characteristic banana shaped hull structure which we now identify as the hulk – an identification that was not to be made until forty years after Brindley's work was published.

---

6 *The Last Days of Mast and Sail*, §241

7 In 1995 only one wooden merchant barque survives in the world, the *Sigyn* built at Göteborg in 1887 and now preserved in her own floating dock at Turku in Finland.

8 *The Mariner's Mirror*, Vol 41, No 4, (1955) §267

In their writings they did not make the clear distinction between history, the study of written and iconographic sources, with, nowadays, advisedly, a nod to oral traditions,[9] and archaeology, the study of the objects of the past themselves. They had, indeed, little or no archaeological evidence to use. The beginning of the development of nautical archaeology in the late twentieth-century sense with the detailed and disciplined study of vessel structures as one important part was fifty years away. Iconographic and literary evidence told them a great deal about the masts, sails and rigging, little about the ways in which the hulls were built. They hypothecated a little about the hulk and, in terms of late twentieth-century thinking, got it wrong, and they barely recognised the ubiquitous cog.

In the late twentieth-century in studying the evolution of ships and boats we are essentially concerned with the development of vessel structures as revealed by archaeology assisted by ethnography. We tend to identify four main strands in medieval shipbuilding. These are the complex traditions of round-hulled, clinker-built keeled vessels; the flat-bottomed, clinker-sided cog, the hulk with her clinker-fastened planks brought up to the near horizontal at bow and stern, and various forms of intermediate structures in which the planks were (on the whole) not edge joined, 'skeleton conceived', if you like, which preceded the fully skeleton-built vessel. For three of these four main strands we have considerable and steadily growing archaeological evidence. The hulk remains a mystery awaiting the recognition of archaeological evidence which may be revealed at any time.[10]

The founders of *The Mariner's Mirror* had little or none of the evidence on which modern ideas are based. But they made the maximum use of the evidence they had for the development of masting, sails and rigging and the details of fittings, all subjects which perhaps have attracted less attention in recent years.

Much of what was published in these first volumes of *The Mariner's Mirror* is still relevant and includes evidence which, in part at least, may well repay re-examination and re-assessment. These men, though not

9 In this connection see for instance Olof Hasslöf, 'Wrecks, Archives and Living Tradition. Topical Problems in Marine-Historical Research', *The Mariner's Mirror*, Vol 53, No. 3 (1963) §§ 162–77.

10 For the best modern, and readily accessible, studies of the development of the ship in the medieval period see Unger, ed., *Cogs, Caravels and Galleons; The Sailing Ship 1000–1650*, London, 1994, a volume in the twelve-volume Conway's *History of the Ship*, Friel, *The Good Ship, Ships, Shipbuilding and Technology in England 1200–1520*, London, 1995 and Greenhill, *The Archaeology of Boats and Ships*, London, 1995.

professionals themselves were, indisputably, laying the foundations of the modern professional study of maritime history and archaeology. Their work remains of great interest and value. At its best – as in Alan Moore's description of the rigging of the Turkish *Tchektima* on pages 39–45 of *The Last Days of Mast and Sail* – it provides a unique historical record illuminated by great knowledge and intense enthusiasm.

The use of *The Mariner's Mirror* as a forum for discussion, with notes, queries and answers, running with the main papers but often dealing with important points of detail taken up in subsequent main papers, has presented difficulties in the preparation of this volume which we have sought to overcome in our re-ordering of the material. The early editions of *The Mirror* were by no means impeccably edited; not only are the references sometimes inaccurate, inconsistent, and not easy to interpret but the pagination even is occasionally erratic. This is to be expected. *The Mirror* was not founded as a professional academic journal, but as a forum for the discussion by brilliant amateurs of a subject which for very many years was not to be accepted as academic. It was founded principally by a medical practitioner, a zoologist, two artists and a journalist. It took two generations and much hard work for the dilettante image to be shaken off from maritime history and it is only in the last decades of the twentieth century that this has been achieved. In the 1990s *The Mariner's Mirror* has become a fully refereed academic journal. The maritime aspects of history and archaeology, of which the development of the ship is an important part, are now moving into the mainstream of professional historical studies. The classical divisions are breaking down and the frequently fundamental importance of maritime dimensions are being more and more recognised. At many universities all over the world historical and archaeological subjects with a strong maritime interest are now being followed for higher degrees. The archaeology of the ship is being intensively and most productively studied at institutions in Scandinavia and in Germany. Though the process of growth has been long, the pioneering seeds sown before the First World War and represented here have flowered mightily.

BASIL GREENHILL

ARRANGEMENT OF MATERIAL

The material in this volume has been extracted from the articles, notes, queries and answers published in *The Mariner's Mirror*, volumes I–VI (1911–1920). It is arranged thematically and therefore is not presented in the order that it originally appeared. To clarify this arrangement and to facilitate cross referencing within this volume, each of the items selected has been given a distinct number. Though a new, continuous pagination has been devised for this volume, the full, original *MM* references are at the end of each item. The figures are numbered within each item. Thus Fig. 1.4 is the fourth illustration reference in ¶ 1, Fig. 18.19 is the nineteenth illustration reference in ¶ 18.

DAVID J STARKEY

MEDIAEVAL SHIPS IN PAINTED GLASS AND ON SEALS

No I

By H H Brindley

[It need scarcely be pointed out that, though seals have for long been recognised as a valuable source of information for the ships of the Middle Ages, few students have hitherto attempted to make use of the many stained glass windows in which ships are represented. – Ed.]

The lower portion of the tracery of the east window of Malvern Priory Church consists of twelve lights, each of which is occupied by the figure of an Apostle. In the fourth light from the south is St. Jude, whose right hand supports a model of a ship. The glass of this window dates from between 1440 and 1460, and the ship (Fig. 1.1) borne by St Jude represents the short one-masted vessel with high freeboard and considerable sheer which was perhaps still the commonest craft at the time the painting was executed. The artist omitted much, and not everything that he drew is accurate. The ship is so small and occupies so high a place in the window, that to make out its detail from the floor a glass must be used. With this assistance we see that the aft end of the poop is cut off by the mullion of the light, and that the planking of the stern is at the present day incomplete, a piece of yellow glass of more recent date having been inserted here, probably in repair. The mast instead of being amidships, or a little forward thereof, as in vessels of the time, is well abaft the midships line. Its position and also its unusual rake aft seem to result from a desire to show the face of the Apostle without any intervening objects. The mast is stayed by three very heavy ropes. Two of the ropes are probably shrouds, but nothing is seen of how they are made fast to the hull. The third, as thick as the others, runs to the poop, and this may be a back stay or a halyard. The only other fitting of the mast is a fighting top, which is rarely omitted in mediaeval pictures of ships. The lozenge-shaped

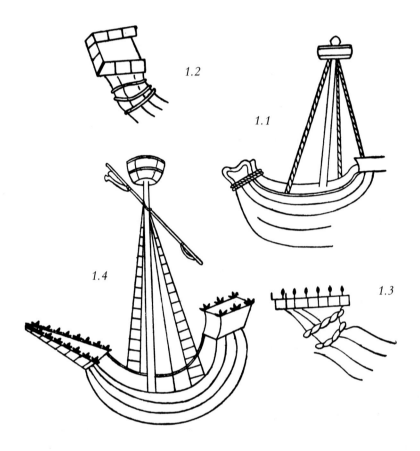

object in the top seems to be the masthead drawn in a conventional manner.

It thus appears that the ship represents very imperfectly the craft of her day and is hardly worth describing, were it not that she has one feature which is interesting, and indeed puzzling. Just under the head is a rope— there is no doubt that it is that, for the strands are painted as clearly as in the shrouds—passed twice round over the gunwales. No fall or anything else suggestive of ground tackle is shown. What is this rope? From its position it can hardly be a fender.

When I wrote my query on the subject [see 10] these ropes round the stem-head struck me as either an artist's convention, or at least a piece of gear represented imperfectly; but since then I have noticed the same arrangement in several naval and other seals of the XIVth and XVth centuries. Of these, two are in the Kettle Taylor collection of Seals in the

Museum of the Royal Naval College, Greenwich. One is 'Sigillum commune ville et hundrede de Tenterden.' This Kentish Seal is also in the British Museum [Catalogue of Seals, No. 5454]. The head of the ship thereon is sketched in Fig. 1.2. The warp is passed round the stem three times, and the turns are not close together as in the Malvern example, but are evidently rather slack. The strands of the rope are not shown. The other seal at Greenwich showing these ropes I cannot identify, as it bears no inscription, and unfortunately there is no catalogue of the valuable Taylor collection. Moreover, this seal is not in the British Museum. It may, however, be referred with some approach to certainty to the XVth century, as the one-masted ship it bears (Fig. 1.3) has the usual characteristics of the vessels on Admirals' Seals of the age, while the arms of England on the sail, *quarterly France modern and England*, fix it as later than 1405. The warp is passed twice round the stem with the turns well apart. The lower turn pinches the stem in a curious manner, and as the impression is good, this and the broken outline suggest that the engraver did not do his work very carefully. The strands of the warp are, however, shown clearly, and pains were taken to give details of the 'fore-stage'. The knobbed post of stanchions above its rail are curious, and perhaps were ornamental; they seem the same kind of thing as is depicted in the Malvern window described later.

Among the seals in the British Museum which are catalogued under 'Admiralty' there are four in which the ship has stem ropes similar to those described. The arrangement is always essentially the same, and a brief mention will be sufficient. They are, in chronological order: 1. Seal of Edward, Earl of Rutland, Admiral of England, 1391. This seal has been added since the Catalogue was published; its MS. reference is lxxxix [add. ch. 40665]. This is the only instance I can find among the seals of the warp passed four times round the stem. The turns are slightly separated and equidistant. Strands not shown.

2. Seal of Richard Cletherowe, Admiral of the West, 1406 [Cat. No. 1042]. Warp in three turns, separated and diverging slightly. Strands shown clearly.

3. Seal of Thomas Beaufort, 2nd Duke of Exeter, Earl of Dorset, Admiral of England, Aquitaine and Ireland, 1416–26 [Cat. No. 1043]. Warp in two turns, separated and divergent. Strands not shown. The turns are very faintly if at all shown in their lower part, and are *under* the planking in places. This may be due to carelessness of the engraver, and indeed in this seal of the 'fore-stage' are also shown imperfectly, a fault which does not seem to lie with the impression. Pettigrew, 'Collectanea Archaeologica,' i., 1862, pl. xv. 2, figures another seal of Thomas

Beaufort, which does not appear to be in the British Museum. Here there are three turns of the warp, separated, and their upper parts covered by a curious oval plate or board, on which the bowsprit seems to rest. It hides the rail and is an unexplained fitting which I have not found in any other case.

4. Another English Admiral's Seal of the XVth century in the British Museum. Warp in three turns, separated and equidistant. Strands not shown. The rail of the fore-stage bears knobs resembling those on the unidentified seal at Greenwich.

5. Seal of Sub-Admiralty of England [Cat. No. 1041]. This seal is ascribed to the XVth century, and the Catalogue suggests that the white hart lodged borne on the poop flag indicates the reign of King Edward IV. Warp in three turns, diverging. Strands shown on two lower turns.

The comparative frequency of these 'stem-ropes' on seals suggests that they represent a real fitting. They and an anchor seem to be mutually exclusive. The latter either catted or fished is not uncommon on seals, but if it is depicted there are no 'stem-ropes': it is curious that these ropes do not occur, or at least they are rare, in pictures of the age to which the seals belong. There is no instance of them in the very carefully drawn ships in John Rous' MS. 'Life of Richard Beauchamp, Earl of Warwick,' (Cottonian MS. Julius E. IV., Art. 6). M. de la Roncière ('Histoire de la Marine Française,' i., p. 472) reproduces a picture of ships of the XVth century, in which one has something very like the ropes, but what is shown may be strips of wood or metal. Search among early pictures is necessary before a decision can be taken as to the meaning of these ropes round the stem.

Malvern Priory Church contains another painting of a ship (Fig. 1.4) about a quarter of a century later than that which I have described. In the window of 1502 in the north transept are Adam, Noah and David, with their emblems. The ship of Noah is a model supported in his hands. The hull has such great sheer as to be almost crescent-shaped. The artist bestowed much care on the fore-stage or forecastle, which bears along its rail seven ornaments, apparently *fleurs-de-lis*. In proportion to the hull this fore-stage is as long as in any pictures of the age. Its fore-end is cut off by the leading of the glass, but in the sketch I have ventured to restore it. The short poop has similar ornaments. The mast is much too high for the length of the hull, and carries a tub-like top, but no topmast. Besides two shrouds on either side, with ratlines, the only rigging is a rope which is perhaps intended for a halyard. Shrouds were nearly always shown made fast to the mast just below the top, or else coming from its floor, but in this Malvern ship they were evidently drawn carelessly. The leading of the glass cuts short the after yard-arm, though it is a good deal longer than the other. But little of the furled sail is seen; what is shown is made fast with gaskets. The parrell is shown clearly. In this painting there is certainly more technical knowledge than in the ship of St. Jude.

We have to remember how ignorant of nautical matters nearly all early artists and real engravers were; but though we can accept no one picture as showing us what a ship was like throughout, much may be learned of the details of rig and fittings from these sources.

From Vol I, No 2, §§43–47 (*February 1911*)

2

MEDIAEVAL SHIPS IN PAINTED GLASS AND ON SEALS

No II

By H H Brindley

Villequier is a large village on the east bank of the Seine, two and a half miles below Caudebec-en-Caux. Like Vatteville opposite to it, and Jumièges several miles further up the river, in the sixteenth and seventeenth centuries ships sailed from its quays in the Newfoundland trade, and it furnished seamen for the naval wars of those times. Several of the windows of the parish church, which is dedicated to St. Martin, are beautiful examples of glass painting. Portions of the church date from the twelfth century, while most of it was completed early in the sixteenth, at which time the glass of both aisles was also put in. Remembering the maritime importance of Villequier in that age, it is not surprising to see pictures of ships in some of the windows. The window depicting scenes from the life of St. Jean Baptiste contains two vessels, and another window, an *ex voto* given by mariners of the families Busquet, Renault, and Breton, represents a naval combat.

The St. Jean Baptiste window is in the south aisle, second from the choir. The dedication bears the date 1518. The two ships are in the upper part of the window. They are painted with some care in yellow, which was the colour usually adopted for ships on glass of the time. On the poop of each stands a figure in bishop's mitre and robes, which is gigantic compared with the vessel, a not uncommon mode of representing the patron saint. One of the ships, painted ten years later, in the neighbouring church of Vatteville similarly carries a bishop, probably St. Clement, patron of Vatteville mariners, of vast stature on her poop. One of the Villequier ships lies at anchor with furled sails, (Fig. 2.1) while the other is under way (Fig. 2.2). The Abbé Cochet ('Les Eglises de l'Arrondissement d'Yvetot,' éd. 2, Paris, 1853, i.p. 118) identifies the two saints of St. Nicholas and St. Clement, patrons of seaman, the former being on board

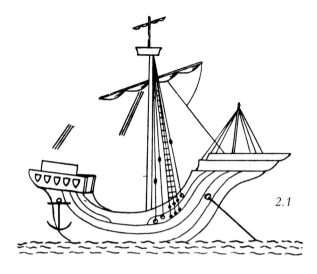

2.1

the anchored ship. The general features of the two vessels are illustrated by the sketches, in which the two saints and the members of the crews in the pictures have been omitted. In both cases the rigging is shown as in the windows, no portion of it has been extended where it might be supposed to be seen by the omission of the figures. Both vessels are three-masted, though in the anchored ship the saint regarded as St. Nicholas obscures the mizzen mast, which is suggested only by portions of three shrouds. The hulls resemble those we see in other pictures and certain seals of the period. That of the vessel under way, on whose deck St. Clement stands, is in form and general proportions probably a more truthful representation of the hull of the time than the other, in which the shortness, extreme sheer, fore-stage and poop remind us of the conventional ship of many seals. It is uncertain what such should be called. In general features, and in the relative sizes of the masts they much resemble a Flemish 'barge' reproduced by M. de la Roncière ('Histoire de la Marine Francaise,' ii. 1900, p. 244), from an engraving by the Master of unknown name who worked about 1485, and who has left us six other remarkable pictures of ships. Reproductions of these will be found in the monograph on this Master's work by Max Lehrs (Leipzig, 1895). The drawings are very valuable to the nautical archaeologist in their detail and accuracy; but the authority for calling the vessel a barge is not stated. Mr. Julian Corbett ('Drake and the Tudor Navy,' 1898, i. p. 18) considers the term 'barge' usually meant something larger than a ship's boat or tender, and mentions 60 to 80 tons as the usual size of barges in the early part of the fifteenth century. Nicolas ('History of the Royal Navy,' 1847, ii.

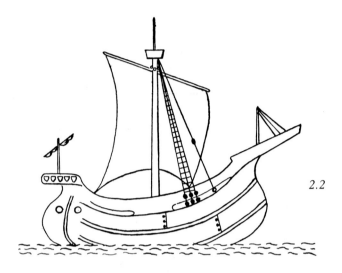

2.2

p. 159), says that barges of the later fourteenth century seem to have been smaller than cogs, which were probably the first-class vessels of the time. Jal ('Glossaire Nautique,' 1848), suggests a considerable range of tonnage for the 'barge.' What a barge really was, both as regards size and rig, is still obscure. Perhaps the shields which adorn the poops of the Villequier ships suggest that the artist had in his mind a larger vessel than what was known as a barge.

Beside St. Clement, the only figure in his ship is a man on the look-out in the top, but in the ship of St. Nicholas three small men are in a row on the poop, apparently receiving his benediction, while at the break of the poop is a much taller sailor giving orders. The chief points of interest in the ships are, I think, as follow. In both the uppermost 'waling' or 'rubbing streak' (only one waling is seen in St. Nicholas' ship) is not continued along the waist. It is usually complete in pictures of the time. The shrouds are made fast to the fore part of the waling, as they are, though without dead-eyes, in the Flemish 'barge' mentioned above. Possibly at this time a true 'chain-wale' was not employed in small craft, if, indeed, it was at all a common fitting, when the shrouds had only just come to be set up outboard. In the very detailed and careful engraving of a Flemish 'carrack,' evidently a much larger vessel than the 'barge,' reproduced by M. de la Roncière (*op. cit.* p. 220) from another picture by the Master mentioned above, the dead eyes of the ten aftermost shrouds are made fast to a wide chain-wale just above the uppermost waling, while the four shrouds forward of these have their dead eyes on the waling itself. Early methods of making the shrouds fast have been discussed briefly by Mr. Alan Moore and myself in 'Proceedings of the Cambridge Antiquarian Society,' xiv. No. 1, 1909, p. 87. In both ships a rope with a block on it, suggesting that a purchase was in the artist's mind, leads from under the top to a hole above or in the upper-most waling, and in St. Nicholas' ship two similar ropes lead down abaft the shrouds, also through holes in the waling. Perhaps the artist had halliards in his mind, and drew them outboard in some confusion with shrouds; but more probably the 'tackles,' the exact use of which is undiscovered, were intended. The blocks are but a slight guide as to what ropes were intended. It is not uncommon to find what seem to be blocks on single ropes in pictures by mediaeval artists, though now and again they evidently belong to purchase tackles drawn incompletely.

In St. Clement's ship the topmast is stepped exactly above the lower mast, but distinctly abaft it in the other. In view of the obvious imperfections of the pictures from a technical standpoint we cannot accept the stepping of the topmasts without reserve; but, as there is considerable doubt as to whether the practice of the early sixteenth century was to step the topmasts before or abaft the lower masts, the Villequier ships are of some assistance to us. A topsail is carried only in St. Nicholas' ship; topsails were common by 1518 in ships of fair size.

It is common knowledge that most of the ship pictures and seals to the close of the fifteenth century are the work of artists largely ignorant of shipping. Essential and, to an untechnical but intelligent observer, conspicuous portions of the rigging, are frequently omitted; but an examination of a series of early pictures shows that three different portions of the rigging are represented with great constancy. Two of these are the forestay and the braces. They are conspicuous ropes, whether the ship is at anchor or under way, so it is natural that they should be inserted. The forestay especially usually has full justice, being sometimes as thick as the mast, and pains are bestowed on its strands. Curiously the other fitment is a small one, the parrell. Somehow this seems to have caught the fancy of artists, and is usually drawn with care. In respect of these three portions of gear the ships of St. Clement and St. Nicholas at Villequier are exceptional, as will be seen from the sketches. We might wonder a little that these ships were allowed to stand as they are in so maritime a place as Villequier was in the fifteenth century, but when we remember other *ex votos* of mariners and the seals of admirals of the age, it is evident that, unfortunately for the nautical archaeologist, the criticisms which seaman would apply to actual vessels were remitted in the case of pictures.

From Vol I, No 3, §§71–75 (*March 1911*)

3

MEDIAEVAL SHIPS IN PAINTED GLASS AND ON SEALS

No III

By H H Brindley

Vatteville is a small village on the west side of the Seine 2½ miles below Caudebec-en-Caux. It is now a decayed port, but in the 16th and 17th centuries it shared in the Newfoundland trade with the neighbouring ports of Villequier, la Bouille and Jumièges, and furnished seamen for the naval wars. Jean Fleury, among the most distinguished of Francis I.'s commanders, one of whose victories is perhaps the subject of the admirable painting of a naval battle in a window in the church of Villequier, and Silvestre Billes, captain of *La Roumaine* in Fleury's fleet, a vessel which is represented in a window of Vatteville church, were seamen of Vatteville. (C. de la Roncière, *Histoire de la Marine Francaise*, iii, p. 251.) At the present day the bed of the Seine is half-a-mile from the village. The Church dates from the 16th century, and the Abbé Cochet (*Les Eglises de l'Arrondissement d'Yvetot*, éd. 2. Paris, 1853, i. p. 188) states 'elle présente une succession de styles en série chronologique de l'est à l'ouest.' Both the transepts are three-sided and each side has a two-light window. There is a painting of a ship in each transept. That in the south transept represents *La Roumaine* bearing on her poop St. Clement, patron of Vatteville seamen, in the attitude of benediction. The ship in the north transept windows cannot be identified, but, like *La Roumaine*, she is painted with great skill and possesses features of much interest. The Abbé A. Anthiaume, Aumônier Catholique du Lycée du Havre, informs me that no published account of the windows of Vatteville Church exists beyond the brief mention by Cochet, but that there is no doubt that they are contemporary with the fabric. The north transept was formerly the Chapel of the Virgin Mary (Cochet, *l.c.* p. 130), and some of the glass represents scenes in her life. At the base of one of the lights are a priest and two ladies kneeling, whom Cochet regarded as the donors of the window. If this surmise is correct the windows of this transept are not a seaman's *ex voto*, as are that containing *La Roumaine* and the Villequier window of 1523 mentioned above.

The north transept window at Vatteville has no dedicatory inscription. The base of the light next to that with the three kneeling figures contains a vessel under sail, with on the left a high tower and on the right a lady kneeling at a prayer desk. The Abbé Anthiaume tells me that he is inclined to regard this painting as an *ex voto* by a seaman's wife, the kneeling lady. It is not certain whether this painting was part of the

Bourges

3.1

original glass of the transept windows, some portions of which show signs of damage, as Cochet points out. Along the base of the two lights runs an inscription, 'Restaurée par les soins du conseil général, 1873.' In order to clear up the doubt thus raised as to whether the painting of the ships might not be a modern addition, the Abbé Anthiaume has examined the window since my visit to Vatteville, and has very kindly also referred to the *procès-verbaux* of the Conseil Général. He informs me that it is stated therein that nothing in the nature of extensive alterations or restoration was ordered for the Vatteville windows. Record of what was actually done in 1873 appears to be missing, but it is certain that the window with the ship has not been altered in modern times.

As will be seen from the sketch (Fig. 3.2) the Vatteville ship has the general appearance of a 'vaisseau rond' and was probably intended to represent a merchantman. No armament is visible, even the customary javelins are absent from the top. The colours of the picture are as follows: The hull is the sepia so generally employed by artists on glass in the 15th and 16th centuries. This is shaded deeply on the starboard quarter, a feature which I have not attempted to reproduce in my sketch. The sea and sail are white, the spars a gold yellow (the favourite colour for them in window paintings of the age), and the long 'gitton' (forked pennon) is white with a gold border.

Before saying anything of the other features of the vessel, reference must be made to another glass painting of a ship which has certain striking resemblances to this Vatteville ship. This is in the Musée at Bourges, which was formerly the Hôtel Cujas, erected in the latter part of the 15th century. Among the painted windows which are contemporary with the building is one which represents 'La Nef de Jacques Cœur,' silversmith, merchant adventurer, naval financier, constructor and commander to Charles VII. This very beautiful painting is reproduced by F. de Lasteyrie (*Histoire de la peinture sur verre d'après ses monuments en France*, (Paris, 1853. II.pl.53). The whole painting is in different shades of sepia save for the following in gold; the mast and yard, the three small cannon (the objects are more like cannon than the usual bundles of 'dardons') in the top, the short crane projecting aft between the cannon, the discs and half-discs on the poop bulwark bearing flamboyant carvings, the jacket of the man in the port after corner of the poop, the hulls of the small boat and of the anchored vessel in the background. The shield of arms of Jacques Coeur on the poop bulwark is *ar. a fesse or with three escallops sa. between three hearts of the second two and one.* The forked armorial pennon or 'gitton' has the same blazon. This account of the painting is made from de Lasteyrie's coloured plate.

3.2

Vatteville

I am indebted to M.A. Auxenfans, of Bourges, for permission to reproduce the photograph of Jacques Cœur's ship published by him (Fig. 3.1). A comparison with the Vatteville ship reveals the remarkable similarity between them, and certainly suggests, in spite of the great distance between Bourges and Vatteville in the 15th century, either that the artist of one had the other in his mind, or that both the paintings were by the same hand. It is unnecessary to mention many of the features in which the two vessels agree, they are seen in the illustrations. The painting at Vatteville gives less detail in many respects. There are no small boats, no ship at anchor, no cliff with trees, no ship's company or passengers (there are two female figures in Jacques Coeur's ship), nothing in the top, fewer cloths in the sail, and fewer flamboyant ornaments on the poop-bulwark, and the artist has omitted the port hand jaw of the tiller on the rudder-head.

Also the shrouds are different in being all led from the curved base of the top in one case, while in the other they are made fast to the mast under a top which has a flat bottom. In both vessels only some of the shrouds are fitted with ratlines, which is in agreement with certain other pictures of the age which go into details, and we may venture to conclude that this was a common practice. (It may be remarked here that in spite of the great care bestowed on details in the Bourges painting, the artist drew one shroud less on the port side, and the ratlines on different shrouds from the starboard ones so fitted.) The most important point about the shrouds is that they are led outboard in the Vatteville ship, while in the ship of Jacques Cœur they are led inboard. In the former the round objects on the hull seem to be dead-eyes, but no means of setting up the shrouds is shown. In Jacques Coeur's ship six dead-eyes on the starboard side can be made out, though not the lanyards which should lead down from them. Above the dead-eyes, as also above the three blocks of the running rigging there are turns of rope. These long turns round a standing part appear in other drawings of ships of the 15th century and seem to have been the recognised practice.

The Bourges ship has no bowsprit, for though this spar would be hidden by the sail, there is no fore-stay leading from the mast-head. On the other hand, the Vatteville ship carries a very long bowsprit, and as she is depicted more on the broadside, we see the whole spar. It has two fore-stays, which is an unusual feature for the age. Of greater interest are the two ropes below the bowsprit, which look like slack bobstays. But the great bulk of evidence is that bobstays were not fitted for nearly two centuries after the time of this painting. From the way in which the two ropes are drawn, it is tempting to regard them as bobstays, but is more likely they were intended for something else, possibly for sprit sail gear. Again it is not uncommon in fifteenth century pictures of ships to see lines hanging from the bowsprit end which bear grapnels and sometimes heavy objects of doubtful nature, and in certain examples these ropes are shown made fast to the hull, as in Mr. Nance's illustration, (see 44) and in two drawings by the fifteenth century master of unknown name reproduced by M. de la Roncière (*l.c.*, ii., pp. 220 and 244) as 'Carraque' and 'Barge.' In the running rigging no halyards are shown in either ship. More unusual is the omission of the parrell, a piece of gear which, from the care with which it is very often depicted, seems to have taken the fancy of mediaeval painters. The braces are drawn quite similarly in the two ships. The lifts are very curious, and unless we suppose that one picture is a copy of the other, and that thereby a conventional idea of lifts was reproduced, it seems probable that the two paintings record for us a method of rigging the lifts which has been forgotten. The very definite manner in which a tackle on the port and a single rope on the starboard side are drawn in both cases, suggests strongly that we are looking at an imperfect representation of an accepted form of gear. These lifts cannot be represented completely, for as they are they could not be worked. Perhaps we ought to see the fall of the tackle brought down to the deck through a sheave in the yard arm; and, if this was the actual arrangement, then the pennant would lead through a sheave in the mast head to make fast at the starboard yard arm, one purchase being used for getting up the yard. This suggestion is offered with reserve towards the solution of the puzzle. It is possible that readers may come across other instances of such lifts as these painted ships possess, if so it is to be hoped that they will record them. I know of no others.

It is by no means safe to conclude that because a mediaeval artist without technical knowledge drew gear which could not be worked he was wholly inventing; it is very likely that he was representing something which existed in his day. In the absence of contemporary written seamanship, such pieces of gear passed away without record of how they were used.

From Vol I, No 5, §§129–34 (May 1911)

May I venture to suggest that Mr. Parker's use of the term 'formations' is somewhat ambiguous? I take it that what he wished to imply is that Vroom's disposition of the ships represented was injudicious in that it adversely affected the 'composition' of his pictures.

¶ 4   MEDIAEVAL SHIPS

In his article on mediaeval ships in the May number, (see 3) Mr. Brindley says that the Bourges painting shows the ratlines on different shrouds port and starboard. At first sight this seems clearly to be the case; but I think that the true explanation of the irregular appearance of the standing rigging is thus—that the artist has shown the *tackles* as well as the shrouds. Later, in the 16th century, the tackles were certainly brought down inboard of the shrouds, and it might have been inferred that they were so fitted from their first introduction, but in this Bourges ship we have a proof that that was the arrangement in favour in the latter part of the 15th century. It seems to me that the artist has intended to represent four shrouds, two swifters, and two tackles a side. Owing to the quartering view, the tackles on one side naturally appear abaft the shrouds, and on the other side before them. The swifters on the starboard side can be clearly made out, brought down outboard, and set up to deadeyes;

whence it is obvious that the artist has accidentally omitted the after swifter on the port side. In the Vatteville ship (Fig. 3.2) the arrangement of shrouds and swifters is the same, but the tackles are entirely omitted.

The turns of the shrouds, and of the pennants of the braces and lift, about their own part are interesting evidence, for they serve to demolish the belief, which is perhaps fairly widely held, that till well into the Tudor period the method in favour for turning in a deadeye or for stopping a block was to timber hitch it in. These turns are quite incompatible with the timber hitch theory.

As for the ropes under the bowsprit of the Vatteville ship, it seems most probable that the inner one is either a spritsail halliard, or "the horse whereon the spritsail rideth,' if indeed it did ride on a horse at so early a date; while the outer, as Mr Brindley suggests, may perhaps fairly be referred to the grapnel. The lifts are so peculiar that they need more discussion than can be put into the tail end of a short note.

By 'S.G.', from *Notes* Vol I, No 6, §184 (*June 1911*)

¶ 5   THE BOURGES LIFT

As there seems to be no name for the fashion of rigging lifts depicted in the Bourges and Vatteville ships accompanying Mr. Brindley's article in the May issue, (see 3) the first step necessary towards a discussion of this obscure fitment is to give it a name by which it may conveniently be known. I would submit that 'The Bourges Lift' will serve the purpose.

The first point to notice is that in neither ship are any of the ropes which we know must have come down by the mast shown, not even the halliards. If, therefore, the fall of the lift purchase came down by the mast, it is only in order that it should have been omitted by the artist. If it had led down to the deck from the yardarm, it would certainly have been much more obvious, and quite probably would have been represented.

Now, what are the functions of lifts? They are:-

(1) To support the yardarms, especially when the men are on the yard to furl the sail.

(2) To square the yard, or to cockbill it, at need.

(3) They must be so long as to permit the yard to be lowered down on to the gunwale, a-portlast.

The question is whether the Bourges lift as depicted would serve these purposes.

In order to try to answer the question I have rigged a model mast and yard. All the running rigging that seems really necessary towards a solution of the problem is a halliard, a truss-parrell, braces, and the lifts. Everything, of course, can be singled, except the lifts. The result of a certain amount of experimenting is as follows:-

If the lift pennant be rove through a sheave hole in the mast, it is perfectly easy to cockbill the yard to a very acute angle by hauling on the fall of the purchase, without letting go the truss; but when the purchase is slacked off again, the yard does not square itself. To square it a pull down on the upper yardarm is needed. This can be obtained either by rigging a martingale for the purpose, or by hauling down on the slack of the brace. The yardarms are supported, as long as the downward strain on each is approximately equal; and, if the fall of the purchase be led to the mast-head, and thence down on deck, the purchase (shown as the larboard) yardarm will be found to be supported against any unequal downward strain. But with the yardarm rigged with the pennant (shown as the starboard) the reverse is the case, for any extra strain on it will top the yard up at once, unless (what is unlikely) the brace be used to martingale the other yardarm down. It would therefore, with this arrangement, have been exceedingly inconvenient, if not impossible, to haul up the clue on the purchase (larboard) side, without raising the other clue at the same time. It would thus have been practically impossible to set the goosewing on the pendant (starboard) yardarm. But we know that not long after the date of this picture ships lay to in a gale under one goosewing of a course, even when they had a mizzen; so that a ship without a mizzen would be still more likely to lie to in that manner.

It is also an important consideration that with one yardarm unsupported, the men could not safely be sent on to the yard to loose or furl the sail. If any extra number got on to the pendant (starboard) yardarm, the yard would certainly cockbill itself, and they would stand a very fair chance of being shot off into the sea.

Again, even when the pendant is made as long as possible, it is impossible to lower the yard on to the gunwale; but this we know was habitually done. If it is attempted, the upper purchase block goes up to the sheave hole, and acts as a stop. The yard comes little more than half way down the mast. Also, it may be added, the turn of the end of the pennant about its own part above the upper purchase block, as shown in the Bourges ship, proves that that block can never have gone chock up to the sheave hole.

It seems, then, fairly clear that the suggestion of a pendant rove through a sheave hole in the mast head will not stand.

Probably the explanation is this: The starboard lift was single, rove through a block under the top, and so down on deck. The larboard lift may conceivably have also had a block under the top for its 'tie,' but more probably the part from under the top was merely a pennant, all the hauling being done on the purchase. As to the lead of the fall of the purchase, it is only necessary to remember the duties of a lift to make it seem most probable that the hauling part was rove through a block at the masthead, and thence down on deck. Any other arrangement would result in great loss of power, to say nothing of having the fall in the way if it led from the yard.

It should be remembered that it was long the custom in harbour to cockbill the lower yards up to a very acute angle, in order to keep them from fouling other ships, etc. Carpaccio's 'Departure of the Bride and Bridegroom' shows this very well. Now, this yardarm purchase would come in very handy for this extreme and constant topping up, and I would suggest that that was what it was there for. It will be interesting to hear whether the usage was distinctively French.

By 'S.G.', from *Notes*, Vol I, No 6, §§184–85 (*June 1911*)

⸆ 6 MEDIAEVAL SHIPS

In connection with S.G.'s note (see 5)on the turns of the shrouds and of the pennants of the braces and lift about their own part in the Bourges ship (see 3) I give a sketch of how the shrouds are brought down in the two ships in action in one of the windows of Villequier Church, near Candebec-en-Caux. (Fig. 6.1.) The date on the glass is 1523. The sketch shows all the details given, except another shroud forward of the four here reproduced, which is painted incorrectly, for the mouth of a brass cannon and its port-hole take the place of a dead-eye; this cannon is the aft one of a row of three, and the shroud is led down to its muzzle. It will, therefore, be seen that no chain-wale or manner of making the dead-eyes fast to the hull is shown. The line between the dead-eyes is merely that of a seam between two planks. The 'knots' on the shrouds are difficult to interpret, but it seems possible that they are intended to represent turns of the rope end as in the Bourges ship. There are ten on each of the two after-most shrouds, fewer on the others. Below the rail they are round, above it oval, with short 'tags,' as in the sketch. Do these tags represent a seizing with small stuff? Similar 'knots' are seen above the dead-eyes of two masts of the other ship in the painting, but I find I have no note of their exact forms. My rough sketches of a year ago, made at Villequier, suggest that the 'knots' of the other ship's shrouds are all oval. The suggestion that these 'knots' are an imperfect method of representing

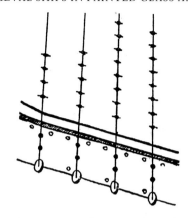

6.1

turns of a rope end receives confirmation from the prints of the unknown Flemish Master at the end of the fifteenth century, one of whose ships has been reproduced in the Mariner's Mirror, by Mr. Morton Nance (see 44). In this, and in one of the eight ships by this master, reproduced in the monograph by Max Lehrs (Leipzig, 1895) on his work, the shrouds bear oval 'knots,' another has similar 'knots' on the chains, two other have turns round the shrouds just as in the Bourges ship, and another has either the 'knots' or the turns, it is difficult to say which is intended. The general impression given by this series of pictures is that very possibly the same method of setting up is intended in all cases, and perhaps the variations are the result of slight differences in the actual practice. Certainly in no instance among these is there anything which suggests a timber hitch. Another of the Flemish master's vessels has her shrouds set up in quite a different manner, which merits a special description, which must be reserved for a future note. I may say that the Vatteville ship (see 3) has neither turns nor 'knots' on her shrouds, another instance of the omission in this painting of details given in the Bourges ship, which that of Vatteville so much resembles in general details.

By 'H.H.B.', from *Notes*, Vol I, No 7, §§184–85 (*July 1911*)

¶ 7   MEDIAEVAL SHIPS

In my note (see 6) on methods of setting up the shrouds in the XVth century, I referred to the variation seen in this respect in the eight vessels drawn by the unknown master, probably Flemish, who worked at the end of the fifteenth century, and signed his engravings with the device reproduced in the sketch I append. I mentioned that one of the vessels has her shrouds set up in a peculiar manner quite unlike the two, or

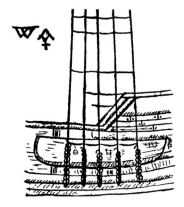

7.1

perhaps three, other devices seen in the rest of the craft. This is illustrated
in my present sketch (Fig. 7.1). The main shrouds lead down opposite the
break of the poop (the vessel has a small foremast almost at the extreme
end of the 'fore-stage') over a deep oblong piece. This piece is drawn
similarly in four of the other ships in the master's prints. It looks at the
first glance like a chain-wale, but it is apparently not placed at right angles
to the hull, for in one of the ships seen from the stern, the shrouds lead
down straight as they come below it, not turning inwards to meet the
waling piece beneath, where they are made fast. The oblong piece of
wood which seems to act as a chain-wale, (see 8) considered throughout
the series of five prints showing it, gives the impression of being nailed
flat to the hull, but at the same time thicker below than above, so that its
triangular section serves to spread the shrouds a little. If this interpretation
of it is correct, the drawing of the vessel seen from the stern must be
faulty as regards the shrouds (this particular vessel has been reproduced
over the title 'Barge' by Mons. C. de la Roncière, *Hist. de la Marine Franc.*
ii. p. 244). Of the remaining three vessels drawn by the master, two are
without the supposed chain-wale, while in the remaining one, which is
known as 'the Flemish Carrack,' and is the vessel of greatest size in the
series, there is a true chain-wale, with two rows of dead-eyes above it. In
many other respects than the shrouds the vessels by this unkown master
repay study. Seven of them have been reproduced from the scattered and
scarce impressions of them by Max Lehrs in his monograph on the
master's work (Leipzig, 1895), and an eighth by Mr. Morton Nance (see
44) and I shall be very glad if other members of the S.N.R. will examine
the possible chain-wale, and record their opinions on it, and also if they
will tell me of any other instances they know of shrouds set up as shown

in the present sketch. The shroud itself is encircled with what appears to be a series of turns, one row on either side. There is evidence that the series is worked from below upwards in the rope end, which is seen very clearly projecting forwards at the top of the rows of turns on the second to the fifth shrouds. Are these an ornamental kind of turn round the standing part? A difficulty is introduced by our not being able to see how the standing part ends below the rounded strake, for here the shading is deep, and nothing like an eye-bolt is visible, any more than in other vessels of the master. Just above the series of turns the shrouds are joined up by a thick piece of line, which is perhaps only the lowest ratline. Above this what are clearly the ratlines come as shown in my sketch, which reproduces the deficiencies in the drawing. The great care as to small details shown in 'The Flemish Carrack' is not always found in the master's other sketches as noticed by Mr. Morton Nance (see 44). My sketch also reproduces the unequal length of the rows of turns seen in the print.

By 'H.H.B.', from *Notes*, Vol I, No 9, §§250–51 (*September 1911*)

¶ 8   EARLY CHAINWALES

The 'Nuremburg Chronicle,' of 1493 contains many ships that adorn its views of maritime cities. These, designed by the same artist, although varying considerably in detail, all show common features. The figure-subjects of the book are, however, by another hand, that of Michael Wohlgemuth; and in one instance, where he wished to draw the ship of Ulysses, this artist seems to have gone to W.A. for his model, for every detail of this vessel shows the mannerisms of that engraver. From this picture the chainwale in Fig. 8.1 is copied, with its adjacent parts. This it will be seen is strikingly like that illustrated by Mr. H. H. Brindley (see 7), with the exception that the end of each shroud seems to twine round its standing part with fewer and slacker turns. The chainwale itself is drawn much as it is in that copied by Mr Brindley from W. A.'s ship; but it seems here to suggest less that it is actually fixed flat to the vessel's side, like that of a Dutch galliot; but rather that defective drawing is the cause of this apparent flatness.

The ship engraved by Joannes a Doetecum on his fine title-page to Waghenaer's *Spieghel der Zeevaerdt* of 1583 (familiar in its slightly altered form as the cover of the MARINER'S MIRROR), well as it is designed, has a chainwale that is drawn in exactly the same false perspective, the double line that marks its edge being continued all round; while the dead eyes

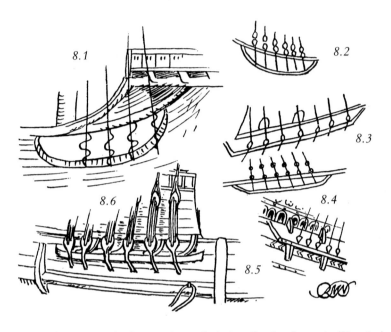

seem as though made fast to the wale immediately above it (Fig. 8.2). Exactly the same fault is to be seen in the chainwales of the small ships that enliven the *Civitates Orbis Terrarum* (Fig. 8.4), while the ship on the title-page of *The Primrose of London*, 1585 (representing not the little *Primrose*, but an Admiral Ship of England), has similar chainwales with a single row of dead eyes, correctly placed (Fig. 8.3). The picture of Henry VIII embarking at Dover, (Fig. 8.5) formerly attributed to Holbein, shows chainwales of the same sort; but here we have, also, the knees that from the early sixteenth century onward to the nineteenth continued to support the chainwales. These knees, with dead eyes, lanyards, chainplates, etc., are very well shown on the chainwales of a ship actually drawn by Holbein, at the Städel Institute, Frankfort-on the Maine. (Fig. 8.6) This drawing was made between 1520 and 1530 and shows, as drawn by a skilled artist, the actual chainwales of that time, which differ but slightly from those of a century later; although they are rounded off fore and aft in the earlier style of Figs. 8.1 and 8.2.

With these examples of ill and well drawn chainwales of the sixteenth-century before us, it is easy to reconcile the apparent shapes given to them in the cruder prints of W.A., already quoted by Mr. Brindley, with the more correctly drawn chainwale of his *Kraeck*, obviously drawn by another artist (see 46).

By 'R.M.N.', from *Notes*, Vol. II, No 9, §§283–84 (*September 1912*)

MEDIAEVAL SHIPS

No IV

By H H Brindley

One of the most beautifully executed manuscripts in the Bibliothèque Nationale, Paris, is 'MS. français 5594.' It consists of 285 folios of vellum, and among them we find 66 miniatures, most of which fill their folios. All are painted very delicately, and the colours are in excellent preservation. A description of the work will be found in 'Catalogue des Manuscrits français (Bib. Nat.), tome V., Ancien fonds,' 1902, p. 34, which gives the authorship thus—'Composé par Sebastien Mamerot de Soissons, chantre de chanoine de l'église Saint Etienne de Troyes, par l'ordre de Louys de Laval, seigneur de Chastillon, lieutenant-général du Roy Louys l'onzième et gouverneur de Champagne. Rédigé à Troyes, jeudi xiii. jour de janvier, 1473.' The MS. itself begins 'Les passages faiz oultremer par les Roys de France et autres princes et seigneurs françois contre les turcqs et autres sarazins et mores et oultremarins.' The 'passages' occupy FF. 5 to 277, the latter bearing the words, 'Cy furent les passages d'oultre mer faiz par les nobles françois.' The remaining eight folios, possibly not all from the hand of Canon Mamerot, present us with a curious variety of subjects, including some poetry and an argument between Alexander, Pompey and Charlemagne, in which each sets forth his claims to the title 'great.'

As the bulk of the work is concerned with operations 'oultre mer,' Mamerot drew many vessels, and to turn over his folios is a delight to the nautical archaeologist. The miniatures which contain ships are disposed thus: F. 33, two one-masted vessels and a row boat; F. 34, three one-masters with long pointed 'fore stage; and a poop or more accurately an 'aft stage' of similar shape; F. 109, a one-master with a small boat astern of her in a kind of dock surrounded by cloisters; F. 112, three one-masters alongside a quay (reproduced by M. Charles de la Roncière, to whom I am indebted for calling my attention to Mamerot's work on a recent visit to the Bibliothèque, in his *Histoire de la Marine Française*) F. 157, several small craft; F. 205, many vessels similar to those of FF. 35, 157; F 211, several three-masters; FF. 217, 232, 269, 274, fleets of one-masters; FF. 248, 251, vessels at a distance; F. 267, many flat barge-like craft, probably 'péniches' or 'gabares.' These miniatures contain abundant evidence that Canon Mamerot, or if he did not himself execute the paintings for his history, the artist he employed, was without the technical knowledge necessary to be an authority on the ships of his time. On the other hand, the painter of the miniatures was an able artist in the fashion of his day, and on his numerous ships he bestowed the same care as on the other subjects in his pictures. Thus, though his proportions often seem incorrect, though much of his rigging is without meaning, and though he certainly had a type of vessel which he repeated again and again regardless

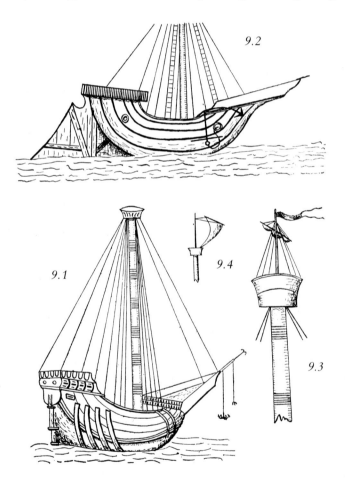

of the date of the events she helps to illustrate, the craft he drew are by no means valueless to us in our endeavour to reconstruct the shipping of the XVth century, in respect both of the types employed and of details of hull and rigging.

Mamerot's favourite vessel is sketched in Fig. 9.1; he gives us whole fleets of such craft in several of his miniatures. They are usually crowded with men in armour, and probably we are right in looking on them as 'vaisseaux ronds' employed as transports. The shortness of the hull, the great sheer and the long 'fore stage' coming to a sharp point are familiar features in miniatures of the XIVth and XVth centuries: there is no need to enter into details about them. The massive outside 'timbers' near the stern are found in most of Mamerot's craft, and these, too, occur in certain other mediaeval paintings. The vessel has a kind of aft-castle, for there are evidently four long narrow windows under the shields carved or painted on the bulwark of the poop. The hull below this is pierced with an oblong port or window. The step-like build of the rudder is curious, but perhaps what we see is partly stern post and partly rudder. In any case the rudder terminates at its upper end in an unconvincing manner. The only war-like suggestion borne by this vessel is the double hook at the bowsprit end, unless the forward of the two objects suspended from the bowsprit is something aggressive; its exact nature cannot be made out. Aft of this there is the grapnel, which is often seen slung thus in pictures of the age. The mast has six equidistant wooldings, and is very taunt, more so, indeed, than the sketch shows it. There is no topmast in any of the one-masted craft, and we do not see the usual bundles of spears in the top. The rigging appears to be all shrouds (without ratlines) and fore and back stays. No yard or running rigging obviously for hoisting one occurs in any of the vessels with one mast. Such is the vessel which Mamerot repeats many times where he wishes to show us a fleet of transports in a roadstead or river. The three one-masted craft in F. 34 differ from the above in carrying a yard with furled sail and long pointed fore and aft stages. In addition to a forestay, five ropes come down on either side the mast, but their identifications are uncertain. The vessel on F. 109 differs from all the others in having an enormous rudder (Fig 9.2), the details of which are painted so carefully that one is inclined to think it was done from the real. It reminds us of the rudder of a modern canal or dumb barge, and to some extent that of a sailing barge. The two vessels in Memlinc's painting of St. Ursula landing at Bale (Musée de Bruges), have somewhat similar rudders.

The hull of this vessel is not unlike that of the ship carrying St. Nicholas in one of the windows of Villequier Church in Normandy [see

2]. The anchor and its cable are drawn with care. It is uncertain if the mast carries a hoisted yard, as its upper part is cut off by the border of the miniature, as shown in the sketch. The leading of the starboard shrouds is obviously incorrect.

The only three-masted vessels are on F. 211, and their mainmasts are illustrated by Fig. 9.3. Perhaps these were the 'nefs' or great ships. Save for the lifts of the very small topsails the meaning of the topmast rigging is doubtful, though it is probable that such topsails were hoisted and often sheeted from the top. I know an engraving from a work of the XVIth century, the exact reference to which I have not at hand at this moment, in which topsail is shown set 'flying' as in Fig. 9.4. The sheets lead into the top, and I think that this fashion existed is now well established. The four ropes below the top in Fig. 9.3 are probably the lifts. The small fore and mizzen masts carry no topmasts, the top contains either a banner staff or nothing.

Mamerot's drawings are at fault technically in the proportions of the lifts to the shrouds; the former (painted in gold) are thick ropes, showing the strands, while the latter are smaller and shown merely as black lines. His few small boats have no features worth particular mention, and not much can be learnt from the barge-like mastless craft on F. 267. These are probably 'gabares' or 'péniches.' The time at my disposal for examining MS. 5594 was insufficient for ascertaining if the author names these vessels. I hope to learn something on this point in the future. Mamerot omits the bundles of javelins or 'dardons' so generally shown in the tops of vessels of his age. His shrouds always end at the rail, and perhaps he intended them to be led inboard, as they often were at the time he wrote, though from his inaccuracies in depicting rigging in general it seems very possible he knew little about dead-eyes and their lanyards. Except in one or two cases he omits the ratlines.

In the Victoria and Albert Museum is an oil painting by a German master of the XVth century. It is one of a series of which the others are in St. Severin's Church at Cologne. The subject is the Martyrdom of St. Ursula and her Virgins. Two or three vessels lie alongside a quay, and, as the painting is a large one, we see a good many details of such portions of them as are not hidden by the quay. The nearest vessel is probably three-masted, and most of what we can see of her is shown in Fig. 9.5. The deck is in rather deep shadow, and I have not attempted to reproduce what is doubtfully visible in it. It is of interest that what we can see of this vessel calls to mind at once the eight remarkable engravings of craft by the unknown master, of the close of the XVth century, usually supposed to be a Fleming, whose works bear the signature

Seven of his nautical engravings are reproduced by Max Lehrs in his monograph on the artist's works (Leipzig, 1895), and Mr. Morton Nance has sketched another [see 44] from a print in the nautical collection at South Kensington. In three of these the pointed and projecting forecastle, with side panels, is almost identical with that of the German painting. This structure has the special interest of being not a fully developed forecastle in the modern sense; it seems to be really a coalescence of the beak-like forestage of the previous century with the 'forecastle,' the latter no longer a temporary structure set up only for battle, but one permanently fixed to the deck. This is thrown out merely as a suggestion as to what seems to have been the course of evolution of what may be called the forecastle in the craft noticed by this paper. The subject in general has received treatment at the hands of the late R. C. Leslie in his delightful 'Old Sea Wings, Ways and Words,' Mr. M. Oppenheim in the chapter on Shipping in Barnard's 'Companion to English History,' and Messrs. Speight and Morton Nance in their little work on the history of our Navy. There is still much which remains doubtful about the development of the forecastle, and possibly it has arisen by more than one line of descent in craft of different types and nationalities. Two of the 'Flemish Master's' drawings have a dragon's or serpent's head 'langued' as a decoration for the beak-head, and one of them [see 44] has a bowsprit ornament, much like that in the Cologne painting, on what Mr. Nance regards as a foreshadowing of the spritsail topmast. The short crane in the main top, with its crane line to the deck, are seen in very similar form in three of the ships by the 'Flemish Master.' On the other hand, he never represents a single row of dead-eyes or a 'crow-foot' on the forestay, such as we see in the German painting. Fig. 9.6 shows the masthead of a large vessel, most of which is hidden by that sketched in Fig. 9.5. The rigging is painted with care, but where the ropes lead to below cannot be seen. At some distance from the quay is a vessel beached on the river bank, and, as shown in Fig.9.7, she is partially a wreck. She is worth recording, for, contrasted with the large vessels in the foreground, she seems intended for a coaster or river craft.

Like Canon Mamerot, the artist of the Cologne painting was not faultless in drawing ships, but comparison of their works with each other and with those of the 'Flemish Master,' bearing in mind that the three were contemporaries, provides a suggestion of some of the differences between French craft and those of the Low Countries and Germany in

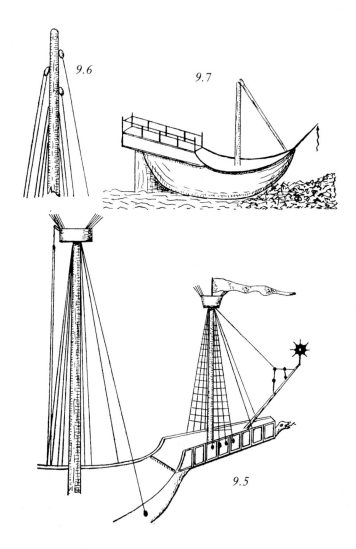

the latter part of the 15th century. Just possibly, in view of the expeditions related by Mamerot being against 'Turcqs et Sarazins,' he had Mediterranean craft in his mind, but in our ignorance of his ever having resided in the south, it is reasonable to think that a Canon of Soissons would know more of shipping of northern waters. I have referred above to Hans Memlinc's paintings of St. Ursula's history on her shrine in the Musée de Bruges. It is believed that these were completed by 1480. The craft represented are small and there is much that is unconvincing about the sails and rigging. It is worthy of record, however, that the shrouds are set up outboard, in one of the vessels with one row, and in two others with two rows of dead-eyes. Little is yet known as to the time when outside dead-eyes came into general usage and of the nationality and kind of craft which took the lead in this practice; in fact, much remains to be ascertained as to the setting up of the shrouds in the distant past. Thus any drawing illustrating one method or another deserves recording.

Of the artists whose craft have been considered in this paper, the 'Flemish Master' undoubtedly had the greatest technical knowledge, and he is the only one whose ships were portraits and not merely incidental to the picture. It should be remembered, however, that we do not know if all the eight engravings of ships ascribed to him were certainly from the same hand. The German artist of the Cologne picture painted carefully what he understood of a ship's rigging and the dainty and finished execution of Mamerot's miniatures is a delight. Even Memlinc's rather conventional craft have something to tell us. Certainly all help us towards knowledge of the shipping of their age.

From Vol I, No 8, §§193–200 (*August 1911*)

(*Editor's Note*: a paper published in the *MM* Vol. 76, §§345–61 written by AW Sleeswyk suggests that Master W was a Flemish engraver named William a Cruce.)

¶ 10   ROPE PASSED ROUND STEM-HEAD

In the east window of Malvern Priory Church, the glass of which is c. 1480, St. Jude is holding a model of a one-masted ship (see 1, 1.1). Round her stem-head, below a small 'fore-stage,' a thick warp is passed twice. There is no fall or anything else like a connection with ground tackle, and no knot is to be seen. I know of no other instance of a fitting of this kind, and shall be glad to hear if anyone else does, and a suggestion as to its meaning.

By H. H. BRINDLEY, from *Queries*, Vol 1, No 1, §32 (*January 1911*)

¶ 11   ROPES PASSED ROUND STEM

In Mr. M. Oppenheim's chapter on Shipping in Barnard's 'Companion to English History' (Middle Ages), pl. lxii., fig. 2, shows the 'forestage' or 'forecastle' of a ship with its forward support made fast to the stem head by ropes passed round the latter. It is just possible that the ropes round the stems of mediaeval ships of later date (i.e., when the forestage was no longer a temporary structure), which I described in the February *Mariner's Mirror*, (see 1) may be related to the ropes shown in Mr. Oppenheim's sketch. The original of the picture is, I think, in a 13th century MS. at Corpus Christi Coll., Cambridge.

By 'H.H.B., from *Answers*, Vol I, No 3, §92 (*March 1911*)

¶ 12   ROPES PASSED ROUND STEM

There seems to be no direct evidence as to the purpose of these stem ropes. Several suggestions have been received:—

C.A.G.B. asks:—'Could this be the anchoring cable, the stem head being used like the bollard in a whale boat or the bitts in later vessels, as the object round which the cable was taken to secure it when the anchor was down? The rope and the anchor [see 1] "seem to be mutually exclusive" which seems to mean that when the anchor was down the rope round the stem would appear, but when the anchor was up, the turns of the rope round the stem would necessarily have been cast off.'

A difficulty in the way of this theory is that none of the drawings showing these ropes seem to show the cable leading (or perhaps one should say 'growing') down to the water. As some at least of the ships illustrated have a forestage, under which the turns are taken, it would certainly have been a long job to bitt the cable in this way; but as we do not know how mediaeval ships bitted their cables, it is impossible to be sure that this explanation is not right.

By 'C.A.G.B.', from *Answers*, Vol I, No 3, §92 (*March 1911*)

¶ 13   ROPES PASSED ROUND STEM

R.M.N. says:—'My suggestion would be that this may have been a conventional survival of what once meant something. Nothing like it is found in reasonable attempts at shipping as late as the glass painting of circa 1480. There is, however, a drawing of the time of Henry III where an arrangement like this seems to be used for setting up the stay.'

Another suggestion is that these turns may have been a girdling, used in ships which proved too weak to carry the weight of a 'forestage' without straining.

By 'R.M.N.', from *Answers*, Vol I, No 3, §§92–93 (*March 1911*)

¶ 14   ROPES PASSED ROUND STEM

It is quite probable that these stem ropes are the unexplained fitting which occurs in early Tudor inventories as 'Bow seizures' variously spelt.

By 'A.H.M.', from Answers, Vol I, No 4, §120 (April 1911)

¶ 15   ROPES PASSED ROUND STEM

It seems to have escaped notice that these ropes occur in the ship on the noble of Edward III, (Fig. 34.2) which was issued in July, 1344. In the reproduction of it given on the cover and title page of the volumes of the Navy Records Society, the stem ropes are not shown, but in a larger reproduction at p. 37 of Mr. T. W. Fulton's 'The Sovereignty of the Seas' they appear very distinctly.

By 'Ed', from Answers, Vol I, No 4, §120 (April 1911)

¶ 16   ROPES PASSED ROUND STEM

Among the answers printed I see no suggestion that these ropes may have been a gammoning. It may be possible that the artists forgot the bowsprit and remembered the gammoning. On page 20 of Lever's 'Seamanship,' 1808, is a drawing (Fig. 152), reminding one very much of these stem-ropes. It shows an outer gammoning passed right round the stem close abaft the figure-head, the inner gammoning being rove through a hole in the stem. The mere fact, however, that a fitting appears in many drawings should not, I think, be taken as conclusive evidence of its existence. The art of cribbing was practised in very early times, and one drawing was probably the father of many, as it may be even unto this day.

By 'G.R.', from Answers, Vol I, No 4, §120 (April 1911)

¶ 17   ROPES PASSED ROUND STEM

The gammoning theory will probably not stand, for there is no evidence that gammoning existed at so early a date. In Edward III's noble (Fig. 34.2) the ship has a bowsprit, and has these stem ropes; but the heel of the bowsprit is not confined by the ropes. Of course, large allowance must be made for 'cribbing,' but the representation of these ropes is so widespread that it cannot be altogether explained thus.

By 'Ed.', from Answers, Vol I, No 4, §120 (April 1911)

18

MEDIAEVAL SHIPS

No V, Part I

By H H Brindley

In The Mariner's Mirror, Vol I, No 2, pp. 45–46, (see 1) I described certain XIVth and XVth Century representations of craft having two or more turns of rope passed round the stem. These were from two different seals of Edward, Earl of Rutland, Admiral of England, 1391; seal of Richard Cletherowe, Admiral of the West, 1406; two different seals of Thomas Beaufort, Duke of Exeter, Admiral of England, Aquitaine and Ireland, 1416–26; east window of Malvern Priory Church (glass of 1440–60) in which the stem ropes are seen in the ship borne by St. Jude; seal of Sub-Admiralty of England, XVth century (probably of reign of King Edward IV); seal of Tenterden, Kent, XVth century; and an unidentified seal, almost certainly of the XVth century, in the R.N. College Museum, Greenwich. Since the account of these curious stem ropes appeared several suggestions having been made (see 11–17) as to their meaning, and therefore it may be of interest to readers of THE MARINER'S MIRROR to mention some examples of this unexplained fitting which have been noticed since my article appeared, and also to attempt a summary of the speculations which have been made as to their meaning. It may be said that there is no reasonable doubt that the stem ropes were a real fitting, their representation is too widespread for them to have been merely a fancy of artists and seal engravers. Moreover they are depicted in a manner so uniform that they give the impression of a fitting represented accurately in all main respects, though more or less conventionally.

The examples of stem ropes quoted above occur between 1391 and 1500. An examination of the other English seals bearing ships in the British Museum to the close of the XVIth century has not furnished any others. With the kind assistance of M. Auguste Coulon, Keeper of the Seals, I have recently examined all that bear ships at Les Archives Nationales, Paris. Of seals with ships engraved up to 1600 the collection has 28 French and 11 of other countries besides Great Britain. None of the ships on these have stem ropes. There are at least 60 British seals

Reign	Coin	When issued	Number of turns of rope round stem
Edward III	Noble	1344	3 (probably)
,,	,,	1346–1351	3
,,	Half noble	1346–1351	1, 2 or 3
,,	Noble	1351–1360	3, or 2 (occasionally), or 0 (rarely)
,,	,,	1360–1363 (approximately)	4, 5, 6 or 7
,,	,,	1363–1369	2, or 3
,,	,,	1369–1377	3
Richard II	,,	1377–1399	3
,,	Half noble	1377–1399	2
Henry IV	Noble	1399–1413	3
,,	,,	c. 1412	4
Henry V	,,	1413–1422	
		1st issue	4
		2nd ,,	4
		3rd ,,	3, or 4
		4th ,,	3
,,	Half noble	1413–1422	2, or 3
Henry VI	Noble	1422–1461	3
,,	,,	c. 1460	4
,,	Half noble	1422–1461	2, or 3
,,	Angel	1470–1471	2
Edward IV	Noble	1461–1483	2, 1, or 0, or (rarely) 3
,,	Half noble	1461–1483	2, or 3
,,	Angel	1461–1483	2, or 0, or (rarely) 1
,,	Half angel	1461–1483	1, or 0
Edward V	Angel	1483	2
,,	Half angel	1483	0
Richard III	Angel	1483–1485	2
,,	Half angel	1483–1485	0
Henry VII	Angel	1485–1509	
		Early issues	2, or 0
		Later ,,	0
,,	Ryal	1485–1509	0
Henry VIII	,,	1509–1547	1 (?)
,,	Angel	1509–1547	0
Mary Elizabeth	Angel and Ryal	1553–1603	0

bearing ships up to the close of the XVIth century (the total number is probably much greater, but I have found no more at present), and only 7 have the stern ropes. The great majority of the seals up to 1600 belong to the XIVth and XVth centuries, in which were engraved all the examples with stem ropes, so their representation on seals is not common.

I am indebted to the Editor of THE MARINER'S MIRROR for his note [see 15] that stem ropes are represented on the ship of the gold noble of

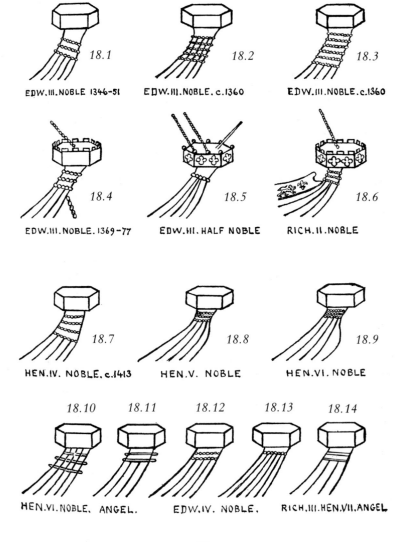

18.1   EDW.III.NOBLE 1346-51

18.2   EDW.III.NOBLE. c.1360

18.3   EDW.III.NOBLE.c.1360

18.4   EDW.III.NOBLE. 1369-77

18.5   EDW.III. HALF NOBLE

18.6   RICH.II.NOBLE

18.7   HEN.IV. NOBLE. c.1413

18.8   HEN.V. NOBLE

18.9   HEN.VI. NOBLE

18.10   18.11   18.12   18.13   18.14

HEN.VI.NOBLE. ANGEL.   EDW.IV. NOBLE.   RICH.III.HEN.VII.ANGEL.

King Edward III, [Fig. 34.2] for I had overlooked their presence on this well-known coin. Since his note appeared I have examined the nobles and other mediaeval coins bearing ships in the British Museum and in the Fitzwilliam Museum at Cambridge, with the results tabulated below. I have to thank Mr. G. C. Brooke, of the Coins and Medals Department of the British Museum, for much kind assistance in this enquiry.

From this table it will be seen that the stem ropes on the gold coinage cover a longer period (1344 to *c.* 1490) than the recorded examples from seals and painted glass (1496 to *c.* 1460). Fig. 18.15 (Richard II), Fig. 18.16 (Henry V), and Fig. 18.17 (Henry VI) are photographs of nobles in the Fitzwilliam Museum, Cambridge, and illustrate the ship (in whose form there is little variation throughout the series) and the stem ropes. Figs. 18.1 to 18.14 are sketches of the stems of the ships to show the variation of the ropes. As Figs. 18.15–17 illustrate the general features of the ship, in Figs. 18.5 and 18.6 alone are the details of the forestage given. It is six-sided always, or nearly always, throughout the series. The fore-stay and bowsprit (if present) are also omitted in most of the sketches.

On the other hand, the number of planks shown is that on the coins. It will be noticed that Figs. 18.4 and 18.6 and 18.15 show an embattled forestage; this is characteristic of the last issue of King Edward III, and disappeared with the end of the heavy coinage of King Henry IV. The presence or absence of an anchor cable (Fig. 18.4) will be referred to later on.

Taking the whole series, we find the number of turns of the stem ropes is greatest in the coinage of King Edward III. (The lower numbers on coins of half-values, as, *e.g.*, Fig. 18.5 are probably due to the difficulty of inserting details on small pieces, and may be disregarded.) The turns are often four in nobles of the House of Lancaster and after that decline, to disappear entirely in the reign of King Henry VII, though the ryal of King Henry VIII has perhaps one stem rope. Not only this, but they show a kind of decadence in their latter days; thus in the Lancastrian period we see them begin to be confined within the outline of the stem and thereby lose the appearance of being really passed round it. I am not sure that this feature does not exist in some of the earlier coins, but it is conspicuous in the later ones (Figs. 18.8, 18.9, etc.). Fig. 18.10 is from one example in the British Museum, the stern ropes and planking are badly confused, and it looks as though the engraver did not understand what he was representing.

A similar confusion appears in a seal of Thomas Beaufort, 2nd Duke of Exeter, Admiral of England, Aquitaine and Ireland, 1416–1426 (Brit. Mus. Seal xliii. 138), which I have described in THE MARINER'S MIR-ROR (see 1).

18.15

18.17

18.16

18.18

18.19

In the Angel of King Henry VI the stem ropes appear as flat bands (Fig. 18.11), and from King Richard III's time onward they are always thus. Also one of the ropes is often distinctly bigger than the other, as shown in Fig. 18.14. With regard to the possibility that the ropes appearing without strands might be the result of wearing of the coins, I was assured by Mr. G. C. Brooke that the examples quoted here must have borne plain bands when issued for circulation. The general impression given by the whole series is that in the earlier coins the artist was representing, though perhaps imperfectly, something which ships really carried, and this something persisted in a conventional form on the coins after the fitment had ceased to exist in real ships.

From Vol II, No 1, §§1–6 (January 1912)

19

MEDIAEVAL SHIPS

By H H Brindley

As to the use of the stem-ropes, the presence of which in mediaeval representations of ships I have summarised [see 18], the following suggestions have been made in THE MARINER'S MIRROR by members of the Society:-

(i) They represent a gammoning (see 16). The Editor has remarked on this (see 17) that there is no evidence of gammoning so early as King Edward III's time. Now it is in his coinage that stem-ropes are especially prominent, at least in the number of turns, yet the heel of the bowsprit is never confined by them. The same is true of all the seals in which stem-ropes occur, whether the ship has a bowsprit or not: the turns are always passed round the stem only. A good example of the ropes in a vessel with a bowsprit is one of the two seals of Edward Earl of Rutland, Admiral of England, 1391 (Brit. Mus. Seal lxxxix. 49), reproduced in Fig. 18.18. The heel of the bowsprit comes down aft of the fore-stage, and the stem-ropes are evidently not concerned with it.

A ship with bowsprit, and no stem-ropes, is illustrated by the seals of John Holland, 2nd Earl of Huntingdon, Admiral of England, Ireland and Aquitaine in 1435, which have claims to be regarded as among the most beautifully executed naval seals we know. The British Museum has three seals of John Holland, none of which show stem-ropes, and that illustrated by Fig. 18.19, is one of the two seals made for him between 1435 and 1442. The care exhibited in the engraving of the three seals suggests that if the stem-ropes were a part of the standing rigging, such as gammoning, they would not have been omitted. In this connection it is of interest to note that though in seals the heel of the bowsprit is sometimes shown coming down aft of the forestage, as in Fig. 18.18, in the nobles and other coins, the bowsprit, if represented, has no heel, or rather, its heel is all within the forestage, *e.g.* Fig. 18.5, and also the noble of King Edward IV. This absence of the heel may have been an artist's omission, or, perhaps, the real bowsprit was sometimes so small that it could be

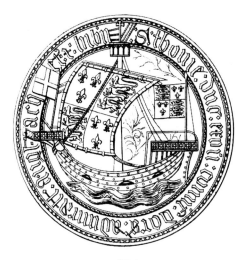

19.1

19.2

secured sufficiently within the forestage. The example of a true gammoning resembling the mediaeval stem-ropes, quoted by 'G.R.' from
D'Arcy Lever (see 16), seems too late to be evidence in the matter.
Making all allowance for errors by seal engravers, the examples of stem-
ropes without any suggestion of being connected with the bowsprit are
too numerous to permit acceptance of the gammoning theory.

(ii). The stem-ropes have to do with the forestay, and may be a device
for setting it up, a suggestion by 'R.M.N.' (see 13), This correspondent
quotes a drawing of King Henry III's time in support. I shall be very glad
if 'R.M.N.' will kindly give the reference to this drawing in the 'M.M.' I
have come across several instances of the forestay made fast round the
stem in a manner which resembles the stem-ropes. In Torr's 'Ancient
Ships' (Cambridge University Press, 1894), Fig. 32, on pl. 6, reproduces a
Roman merchantman from a relief of about 200 A.D. in the Lateran
Museum. The stem and forestay are sketched from this drawing in Fig.
19.3. The forestay seems to be passed twice round the stem. The same
kind of device is seen in a ship on a cross at St. Oran's Chapel, Iona. The
age of this cross is uncertain; it is not earlier than 1250, and the style was
carried down to 1500. The rudder suggests that this ship was carved
considerably later than 1250. The sketch (Fig. 19.5) is a tracing made
from pl. 100 of Brindley and Weatherley's 'Ancient Sepulchral Monuments' (London, 1887), with the permission of the authors.

Harl. Roll Y6, in the British Museum, illustrates the life of St. Guthlac,
and is described by Birch and Jenner ('Early Drawings and Illuminations
in the British Museum,' p. xiv) as in the style of early in the XIIth
century. This roll has eighteen medallion drawings illustrating the life of
St. Guthlac, and Fig. 19.4 is a sketch of the stem of the boat, a one-
masted vessel of the size of a dinghy relatively to those of the Saint and his
companions, in which he is sailing to Crowland. The forestay is brought
once round the stem, and is apparently intended to be jammed. The
backstay is similarly made fast to the high stern piece. In two ships in 'La
Vie de St. Thomas,' which was written in England 1230–1260, there are
two 'ships' with fore and back-stays made fast to the hull by five turns
round the stem and stern-pieces respectively. These craft are reproduced
photographically in Meyer's monograph on the MS. (Soc. des Anciens
Textes Français, Paris, 1885).

Moreover, in both coins and seals, the forestays (there are often two)
almost always lead into the forestage, and so are well forward of the stem-
ropes (see Figs 18.4–6, 18.15–17). An exception is furnished by the two
seals of Thomas Beaufort, Admiral of England, Aquitaine and Ireland,
1416–26, viz., that mentioned earlier in this paper, and another which is

not in the British Museum. The latter is illustrated by Pettigrew in his paper 'On the Seals of Richard, Duke of Gloucester, and other Admirals of England' (*Collectanea Archæologica*, I. 1862, pl. xv., Fig. 2). I am indebted to the British Archaeological Association, the publishers of the *Collectanea*, for permission to reproduce the drawing (Fig. 19.1). In the British Museum seal the forestay is led down just aft of the forestage, and almost meets the foremost stem-rope, but in the seal in the *Collectanea* it is led in a line with the stem-ropes. At the same time, it will be noticed that in the latter the forestay is large and shows its strands, as is usually the case in mediaeval drawings, while the stem-ropes are of small size. Though it is possible that stem-ropes are in some way connected with the forestay the bulk of evidence is against this explanation. It may be pointed out that the seal of Thomas Beaufort reproduced by Pettigrew has a kind of plate partly hiding the stem-ropes and extending above the rail to the bowsprit (see Fig. 19.1). It looks like a real fitting, but what it is for remains a puzzle. I have not seen anything similar in other representations of mediaeval ships, whether stem-ropes are or are not fitted. It is, of course, possible that the feature is merely an artist's error.

(iii) Stem-ropes are the anchor cable, 'the stem head being used like the bollard in a whale boat or the bitts in later vessels.' This suggestion was made tentatively by 'C.A.G.B.' (see 12), and he added (in connection with my statement (see 1) that the ropes and the anchor seem to be mutually exclusive) the surmise that when the anchor was down the ropes would appear (supposing they are part of the cable), while with the anchor up the turns would necessarily have been cast off. This suggestion is, of course, a reasonable one, but if the stem-ropes are the cable made fast we should expect to see the latter growing into the water, for it seems hardly likely that the making fast of a rope should be shown and not its continuation.

The seals with stem-ropes fail us in this matter, for in all the ships are under way. In the Malvern painted glass (see 1, Fig. 1.1) the sail is not set, but though we see the stem-ropes no cable comes down from them. Turning to the gold coinage, throughout which the ship's sail is furled, the cable is seen rarely; it occurs only in some of the later nobles of King Edward III (see 18, Fig. 18.4), and also in some of King Richard II. If the stem-ropes are part of the cable we should expect to see the latter in the early issues of the former reign, in which the stem-ropes are so emphasised. The evidence of the coinage is decidedly against the cable suggestion for the stem-ropes. From the practical point of view the difficulty and lengthiness of bitting the cable, especially in ships with a forestage, by passing it round the stem is obvious, and has been pointed out already (see 12).

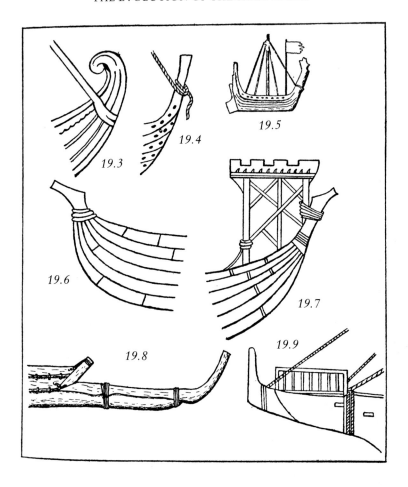

A naval friend offers the suggestion that the stem-ropes represent a spare cable laid out round the ship's head to dry, and that artists may have been attracted to perpetuate it not only as a characteristic of ship life, but as its introduction helps to break up the stiff lines of the stem from a pictorial standpoint. In this case we should not see a warp growing to the water, and the rarity of the warp in ships with stem-ropes has been noticed above.

I am indebted to the Editor for telling me that a practical seaman without any antiquarian tendencies has suggested to him that stem-ropes may have been fitted to take the chafe of the cable on the bow when the ship rode up over her anchor or sheered about, much as nowadays a wooden fender is sometimes put under the hawse hole for the same purpose. The Editor comments on this suggestion that it does not seem to hold good, because no such practice is recorded in later times, though the need for it may be supposed to have increased, and because experience shows that hemp cables chafe wood very little.

I am indebted to Mr. Morton Nance for calling my attention to the ship in one of the reliefs on the shrine of St. Peter Martyr, in the Church of St. Eustorgio, Milan. This ship has been described by Mr. Nance (see 35). There is a full-size reproduction of the shrine in the Victoria and Albert Museum. The original was the work of the Pisan sculptor, Giovanni di Balduccio, who finished it in 1339. The ship is executed with much care and gives valuable information on XIVth century practice in the Mediterranean. It is reproduced in Fig. 19.2. The anchor, which has no stock, is seen fished by a line round one fluke over the gunwale. From a knot outside the ring a rope, certainly small for a cable, is rove through the ring and apparently passes into the hawse hole, but this rope is nearly hidden by the stout warp which leaves the hawse hole and passes round the stem.

This warp is curious in being split into two as it leaves the hawse hole. Whether the warp leads up to the hawse hole on the portside is uncertain, as the relief is not high enough to decide this point. What is the warp for? From what has been said above of the anchor, it does not, in spite of its coming from the hawse hole and its slack condition, look like the cable, and it is not easy to see why a cable should be led round the stem. On the other hand, it differs from typical 'stem-ropes' in its slackness and in not passing right round the stem. It has the look of a fender, but then the forestage projects well forward of it. I hope that other members of the S.N.R. will examine this warp and record their impressions of it. At present it seems hardly related to the stem-ropes of the coins and seals.

(iv) I have ventured the suggestion (see 11) that stem-ropes may have some connection with the ropes by which the fore and aft stages were lashed to the hull when these stages were temporary structures set up in the ship only when about to sail on warlike purposes. We know that a special grade of ships' carpenters existed for building the fighting stages. A good example of the fighting stage lashed to the hull occurs in the *Chronica Majora II* of Matthew Paris, which is preserved in the Library of Corpus Christi College, Cambridge, to the Master and Fellows of which Society I am indebted for permission to make sketches from this MS. It was executed *circa* 1260. The miniature on folio 55b depicts the siege of Damietta.

In Fig. 19.7 I have sketched the stern of the ship, whose aft stage is seen secured to the hull by at least four turns of rope. In the miniature two of the turns are white and two green, while below them is a black line which is perhaps a fifth turn. It will be seen that the front part of the stage is also made fast to the hull, apparently somewhere inboard. The ship has no forestage, but there was very little difference between the early fore and aft stages. In the latter part of the XIVth century, when we first meet with stem-ropes on seals and coins, the fighting stages appear to be no longer temporary structures, but built into the hull as fore and aft castles. Is it possible that the stem-ropes are 'survivals' of the old stage lashings with perhaps no function other than an ornamental one? This is thrown out only as a guess, but it is well known that the innate conservatism of man has begotten many 'useless' survivals in his handiwork. It will be noticed in Fig. 19.7 that below the stem lashing are four bands looking rather like ropes, but in the original drawing they are merely white strips or bands with red outlines, and as they do not project they look quite different from the coloured ropes above them. The stem of the ship has similar bands, and nearly all the craft drawn by Matthew Paris have this fitting at both bow and stem. Usually the fitting is one or more flat-looking bands which do not project beyond the outline of the vessel, as the miniature shewing King Henry III sailing to Brittany (Brit. Mus. MS., Roy. 14, c. vii). In the shipwreck of Hugo de Boues (folio 42b of the Corpus MS.) we see two whole mastless boats and two ends of two other boats. Seven of the boat ends have from two to six bands, while the remaining one has three turns of what seems a rope (Fig. 19.6), and quite similar 'ropes' appear round both stem and stern in the ship carrying King Henry III home from Gascony (MS. Roy. 14, c. vii). It should be mentioned that Matthew Paris never shows strands in his ropes, but from their close resemblance to the lashing of the stage of the Damietta miniature there is no reasonable doubt that what is reproduced in Fig. 19.6 should be looked on as turns of rope.

What do these turns of rope and 'bands' mean? It is clear that in the majority of the drawings made by Matthew Paris they have nothing to do with the fighting stages, especially as in the Damietta miniature we see the bands as well as the stage lashing. This brings us to suggestion

(v) The stem-ropes are a girdling, perhaps adopted in particular in ships which could not carry the fighting stages without straining (see 13). This suggestion by the Editor appears to have been followed up by 'A.H.M.' in his note (see 14) that stem-ropes are possibly the 'bow seizings' of early Tudor inventories. Now something resembling stem-ropes and very like the 'bands' of Matthew Paris is to be seen in many early drawings of ships. They occur, for instance, at both bow and stern in the ship about to anchor, in the Bayeux tapestry, and on the stem piece in a small craft of the XIIth century, in the Egerton MS. It is, however, difficult in some of the drawings to decide whether the bands are really gear or whether they are a kind of ornament for the base of the stem and stern-'head'. Save that he sometimes shows us what seem to be ropes instead of bands, the fittings drawn by Matthew Paris might well be described as merely ornaments. It is of much interest to recognise something very like stem-ropes in ships before the Christian era. Torr illustrates (*op. cit.*, pl. 1, figs. 4 and 5) two Egyptian ships of about 1250 B.C. from reliefs in the temple at Dêr-el-Bahari. A sketch of the stem is reproduced in Fig. 19.9. Round the rise of both stem and stern are passed taut two or three turns of large rope, whose strands are shown distinctly. Quite near the stem head are lines which look like bands bound round it, but these may be only ornaments. Torr (f.n. 101, p. 41) regards the turns of rope as a device for strengthening the hull and refers to similar turns round the stern of a Greek warship of about 200 B.C. in a frieze from Pergamos. He thinks that the girdling ropes were not the making fast of the long cable stretched from stem to stern over posts amidships (of which the fore end is the stout aftermost rope seen in Fig. 19.9), the purpose of which was to save the ship from hogging in the absence of a deck. The pictures certainly do not suggest that the girdlings and the long cable are the same rope.

I have to thank Mr. Cecil Torr for permitting me to reproduce his drawings in Figs. 19.3 and 19.9.

We see a fitment resembling girdling ropes at the present day in certain craft of primitive peoples; Fig. 19.8 is a sketch of the stem of a model canoe, from the Entebbe district of Uganda, in the Museum of Ethnography at Cambridge.

It is hoped that the future will bring to light drawings or MSS. which will satisfactorily explain the mediaeval stem-ropes, for the evidence we have at present is not conclusive. On the whole it may be said to support the suggestion that they are girdlings or 'bow seizings' for strengthening the stem under the weight of the forestage. This view has the advantage of regarding the ropes as something complete in themselves, and the evidence that they are connected with the fore stay, bowsprit, mooring gear, or fighting stages is very slender. It may be noted that the gold coinage gives some degree of support to the girdling view, at least indirectly. The nobles of King Edward III and the next one or two reigns bear a ship which is more or less a portrait of the sailing vessel of the times, and this ship is reproduced on the nobles and other coins of succeeding reigns, down to that of King Henry VII, with little or no modification. Thus in his reign and several of the preceding ones the ship of the coins is a ship of the past, for actual vessels had become longer and less crescent shaped, while the fore and aft stages had ceased to be platform-like and were becoming incorporated into the hull. We have a kind of parallel in the persistence of the full-rigged ship in the copper coinage late in Queen Victoria's reign. Now it is from the reign of King Henry VI onward that we see what I have ventured to call the degeneration of stem-ropes. Is it possible that the artist reduced and altered the stem ropes because he was depicting something which had passed away, or at least was becoming rare in real ships? It is just possible that in the latter girdling ropes, when no longer necessary, continued to be represented by some kind of band with little more than an ornamental use. Comparatively clumsy though the device is, there is no doubt that girdling ropes were employed in the far past, and exist at the present day in certain kinds of small craft, so if they were employed in English ships of the Middle Ages that instance would not be unique.

From Vol II, No 2, §§44–52 (*February 1912*)

¶ 20   STEM ROPES

Mr Brindley is, I think, quite right when he suggests that D'Arcy Lever (1819) is too late to quote as evidence on mediaeval matters, but perhaps I may be permitted to say that an Egyptian ship of 1250 B.C. is a little early (see 19). My reason for giving the instance in Lever was that it so closely resembled the 'stem ropes' of an earlier date, in that they passed round under the stem and not through it, as they appeared to do for about 150 years. As a matter of fact the gammoning remained constant in position; the cut-water enclosed it. Through the kindness of Mr. R. C. Anderson, I am able to show an example of gammoning of the early seventeenth century, before the introduction of the cut-water (Fig. 20.1).

GAMMONING.
Early XVII cent.

Late XVII cent.

20.1

The sketch is from a photograph of a picture belonging to the Earl of Sandwich, a contemporary painting representing the *Royal Prince* which was built in 1610. It is obvious that here is a fitting of no young growth. In my own mind I have never doubted that long before the seventeenth century, the bowsprit must have had a stout gammoning, but had no reliable evidence as to how it was fitted until I saw this photograph. Big bowsprits were in use (I suppose) at the end of the fifteenth century—I seem to remember in the Rous MS. at the British Museum a ship with a pretty healthy spar. Before that date, the marine artist perhaps found a big bowsprit an awkward thing to deal with on a seal or a coin. A big bowsprit must have had some sort of seizing to something substantial, and the most natural thing would be the stem and the knee which supported the head or forestage, for you would hardly put the strain on to the staging itself. I'm afraid we shall never know what the designer of the Golden Noble of Edward III had in mind when he drew those stem ropes (see 17 and 34)—not with any certainty, but perhaps it will be admitted that this note brings the gammoning theory 'into the picture.' R.M.N.'s suggestion of the forestay (should it not be the mainstay?) seems sound enough. The mainstay must have had a fine holding somewhere, but I should think it would have found it more conveniently at the stemhead. That the addition of the fore and after staging assisted the natural tendency of a ship to hog there is no doubt, though it is difficult to see how the stem ropes of the mediaeval artist could correct it. Hogging is caused by the upward pressure of the water at the centre of the ship being greater than at the ends, so that the centre of the ship is forced upwards, and the ends fall. The true remedy then would seem to be the strengthening of the ship longitudinally.

In a previous communication on this subject I apologised for the introduction of the word 'gammoning' into the discussion, as being somewhat suggestive of the word 'gammon.' The editor, in a laudable effort to preserve the high standard of humour which the Journal has always maintained, omitted the sentence. Perhaps it will now be admitted when advanced seriously and without apology: for I find that *gammon* is a good Anglo-Saxon word meaning false, and that the French for the outer gammoning is, *la fausse liure*. The Italians use the word *legatura*, meaning, I believe, a tie, a binding—not very far removed from seizing. Is it not possible that the 'bow seizings' of early Tudor days were the gammonings? It seems to me, at any rate, preferable to their identification with a fitting, the existence of which depends only on a doubtful interpretation, the evidence of the seal makers and coin-makers of the Middle Ages.

By GREGORY ROBINSON, from *Notes*, Vol II, No 12, §§379–80 (*December 1912*)

21

MEDIAEVAL SHIPS

No VIII STEM ROPES—Pt III

By H H Brindley

In my second article on the unexplained 'stem-ropes' or 'bow-warps' of many mediaeval representations of ships (see 19) I summarised the various suggestions which had been made as to their use. Since the article appeared the subject has received attention at the hands of several members, so I venture on an attempt to set forth our progress towards an understanding of the puzzle.

Mr. Gregory Robinson (see 16 and 20) has followed up Mr. Alan Moore's suggestion (see 14) the stem-ropes may be the unexplained 'bowe sesynges' of early Tudor ships, and he has made a suggestion that the latter were gammonings. This is possible, but we appear to have no undoubted representation of gammonings before the first decade of the XVII century. Mr. Robinson (Vol. II, p. 380) reproduces the gammonings of the *Royal Prince* of 1610 as an early example and makes the apposite comment that 'here is a fitting of no young growth.' In my own remarks on the gammoning theory of stem-ropes (see 19) I was inclined to reject it, having in mind the smallness of the bowsprit in the XIV and early XV centuries, the period of stem-ropes, and also because in seals and coins of this period the stem-ropes are sometimes present when no bowsprit is shown. But Mr. Robinson (see 34) seems inclined to throw overboard what has come down to us from coin and seal designers, setting forth his reasons in an article which I am sure has delighted many other readers of THE MARINER'S MIRROR, as well as myself. At the same time I wonder if some of them agree with my conviction that Mr. Robinson has been too drastic in his treatment of the mediaeval artist. For instance, he speaks of the difficulty the designer of the gold noble of King Edward III must have had to get the King, the ship and the sea into his coin, hence 'the ship was cut in where there was room for her, and so the ship of the middle ages came by her wondrous sheer,' and he asks, 'did the oak planking take that wonderful turn upwards' (*i.e.*, in real ships)? But it may be pointed out that the 'crescent shape' of hull is not confined to seals and coins, it is the regular form seen in the miniatures of the same period, and this being so, it can hardly be conceded that, however ignorant mediaeval artists were of things nautical, they invariably drew ships as they were not. The crescent shape hulls, with their immense freeboard, suggest a very crank craft, which it is difficult to imagine ever sailing well under any conditions of wind and weather, but is it really likely that the artists of those days departed so outrageously from fact as Mr. Robinson would have us suppose, even when we make much allowance for ignorance of technical matters and for the exaggeration of certain features and the distortion of others for the sake of art? If we think of hulls of the present day we have in a familiar type of small coasting steamer—the 'puffers' of the North of Ireland are a good example—or in an ordinary steam trawler a very crescentic looking hull, especially if we contrast it with that of a battleship or passenger liner. The small coaster or steam trawler is certainly more like a half crescent than a whole one, while the ship of the mediaeval artist is a whole crescent, but there is no doubt that the craft of the middle ages, like their successors to late in the XVII century were given much more freeboard aft than forward. The latter were half crescents, the opposite way to the steam trawler. In the XIIIth century the high stem and stern pieces gave the appearance of greater shear, and this was increased when fore- and aft-castles began to be fitted. As these became more and more built into the hull, as they were about the same size, the ship came to have a crescent shape which artists made the most of for their own purposes, no doubt, but I venture to think that if they had had to represent a 'puffer' or steam trawler and had treated her in the same way she would have been quite recognisable for what she is, though appearing somewhat fanciful to a seaman. No doubt, as Mr. Robinson suggests, 'the sailors didn't worry much about the ship' (of the artists); but I imagine that some of their commanders did. It does not seem at all likely such men as the Earl of Rutland or Thomas Beaufort would have allowed imaginary and purposeless ropes to be bowsed round the stems in their Admiral's seals. They may have been at sea when their seals were cut and so had to take what was offered, but I think that some officer in the Sub-Admiralty of Cornwall or some burgess of Tenterden would have vetoed the stem ropes on their seals if they represented nothing real. I cannot follow Mr. Robinson in his surmise that stem ropes first saw the light on the drawing board of an artist who had before him 'an awkward junction of lines' which he wished to conceal. There seems to be no question of any 'awkward junction' in the seals which show stem ropes or in the ship of St. Jude in the glass of Malvern Priory Church. And we must take Mr.

Robinson as making only a playful suggestion when he tells us that 'the designers far inland must have found it' (*i.e.*, the ship of the gold noble) 'very useful.' Perhaps now and then they looked at it 'when making their stained glass windows' but Mr. Robinson knows very well that crescent-shaped hulls were drawn before the days of gold nobles.

Many readers of THE MARINER'S MIRROR, I am sure, feel indebted to him for his delightful article, but I think that Mr. Robinson in writing his strictures on those who have put faith in the mediaeval artist has forgotten how frequently they have placed a *caveat* on their statements by the admission that the seal engravers and other artists of the Middle Ages were for the most part very obviously without technical knowledge of ships, and so it is only by a comparative examination of many representations of ships that we can hope to separate the true from the false, and to arrive at some conception of what the mediaeval ship really was. In some form or other this has been said again and again in these columns, and I do not think that the influence of symbolism on mediaeval work has been forgotten by members who have written on mediaeval ships. I am inclined to think that one first approaches the artist of the Middle Ages with much scepticism, and expects to find the grotesquely untrue when nautical subjects are represented, while greater familiarity modifies this attitude, and the conclusion is reached that he was much more worthy of credence than appeared at the outset, for many of his impossibilities resolve themselves into distortions or imperfect representations of actual things, and that after all much is to be learnt from him. Mr Robinson's article is a timely warning not to carry this increasing respect for the mediaeval artist too far, which is an easy thing to do. But I do not think that Mr. Robinson himself remains in the field of hostile criticism so entirely as he makes out, or that he wishes his readers to do so either, for after all in the same number of the 'M.M.' which contains his doubts as to whether there ever were such things as stem-ropes, he has a note treating them as real and advocating with much cogency that they were gammonings. So I will continue in my belief that the ship of the gold nobles was 'more or less a portrait of the ship of the times.'

That stem-ropes were connected with the setting up of the fore-stay, (see 19) has received mention more than once since the article was printed. Mr. Morton Nance holds that we have evidence in favour of the view from W. A.'s *Kraeck* (see 46), though he admits that gammoning is an alternate explanation. He has also pointed out (see 36) that the ships in the Bodleian miniature 'Venice' (see 27) have stem-ropes, and these he is inclined to think are the fore-stay lanyard set up round the stem instead of to a lower deadeye. These stem-ropes occupy one side of a huge semi-circular hawse-hole, and this reminds us of the rope which passes through a hawse hole and round the stem in the ship carved on the shrine of St. Peter Martyr at Milan (see 35), though it must be remembered that the latter was a work of 1339, while the Bodleian miniature is English work, and dates from 1410–20. In describing the stem-ropes in the seal of Thomas Beaufort, Admiral of England. 1416–20, (see Fig. 19.1) I referred to 'a kind of plate' which partly hides the stem-ropes. Mr. Nance tells me that he thinks it possible that this 'plate' is really a space and represents a stage in the evolution of the hawse hole, viz., a very large fairlead which in later ships became closed in above. If this view is accepted we have another instance of stem-ropes connected with the hawse-hole. In describing the Beaufort seal I said that the stem-ropes in this case do not seem to be the fore-stay because the latter is a stout rope and the stem-ropes are much smaller stuff, but if as Mr. Nance suggests, the stem-ropes in the 'Venice' miniature are the lanyards of the stay it may be this is also the case in the Beaufort seal, which dates from almost the same year. In the seal of Edward Plantagenet, Earl of Rutland, Admiral of the North and West in 1391 (see 26.3) we see an earlier phase of the connection of stem-ropes with the anchor cable fairlead, for here they are not actually in but a little forward of it. The fore-stay theory of stem-ropes has certainly gained strength at Mr. Nance's hands since he first advanced it (see 13). Possibly the stem-ropes of the Middle Ages are the lineal descendants of the earlier simple make fast of the fore-stay to the high and slender stem, as it were to a bollard, instances of which are furnished by St. Guthlac's ship (early XII century) and St. Thomas a Becket's ship (1230–60), and by a Roman vessel of c. 200, A.D. (for sketches see 19) Mr. Geoffrey Callender has recently given another instance from the Jerusalem Chamber glass of the XIIIth century (see 22).

From Vol III, No 11, §§337–40 (*November 1913*)

THE SHIP IN THE JERUSALEM WINDOW

By Geoffrey Callender

There is one scrap of evidence on the Stem Rope Mystery which has not until now been brought forward. This is contained in a panel of Gothic glass in the Jerusalem Chamber, Westminster Abbey.

The Jerusalem Chamber abuts at a right angle on the southernmost of the two towers which adjoin the western entrance of the Abbey. In size it is thirty-six feet long and eighteen feet wide. It was built by Abbot Nicholas Litlyngton, whose term of office lasted from 1362 to 1386. It was probably begun about 1376 and finished some ten years later. The Chamber was built as a withdrawing room or parlour to the Abbot's Hall which now serves as a dining-room for Westminster School. The Chamber itself to-day is used for sittings of Convocation and meetings of the Dean and Chapter.

'Jerusalem' is first mentioned in history in connection with the death of King Henry IV. This monarch's fatal sickness, whether leprosy as the chroniclers affirm or a complication of ailments induced by an injury to his leg, was in any case of long standing. In the autumn of 1412 however the sickness took a turn for the worse, and the King formed a resolve to visit the Holy Sepulchre of Christ, there to ask forgiveness of his sins and lay down the burden of his life: for it was foretold him that he should die in Jerusalem. On 20th November, so Fabyan tells us, a council met at Whitefriars, and the building of Galleys to convey the King and his retinue was immediately put in hand. The utmost speed was enjoined, and the shipbuilders made such good progress that by Christmas the vessels were almost complete. King Henry accordingly visited Westminster in order to do obeisance before his departure at the shrine of the Confessor. His prayers were interrupted by a recurrence of most painful symptoms, and so overcome was the King that fears were entertained that he would die there and then. He was, however, safely conveyed to the Abbot of Westminster's Warming Room, and a bed was made up for him before the fire. On coming to himself and being informed of his

whereabouts the King realized that the prophecy which he was endeav-
ouring to fulfil would be fulfilled without his aid.

The fireplace in 'Jerusalem' to-day dates from the time of James I.
Together with the overmantel it was fitted by the order of Lord Keeper
Williams, then Dean of Westminster. A visitor standing with his back to
the fireplace would have the large north window on his right hand side.
Into this window at one time or another have been inserted eight panels
of antique glass. The Rev. Thomas Hugo, F.S.A., read a paper on the
Jerusalem Chamber before a meeting of the London and Middlesex
Archaeological Society on 25th October, 1860. In this he attempted to
describe the glass and designated the subjects of the medallions as follows:
(1) The Slaughter of the Innocents; (2) The Stoning of St. Stephen; (3)
The Last Judgment; (4) The Descent of the Holy Ghost; (5) The Ascen-
sion; (6) St. Peter walking on the Sea; (7) The Beheading of St. John the
Baptist; and (8) An heraldic shield (much mutilated).

A closer examination, however, will show that the sixth medallion
cannot possibly represent 'St. Peter walking on the Sea.' The artist shows
us a ship containing four passengers. One of them, the steersman, is well
preserved. The remaining three are somewhat injured but, so far as one
can judge, they are intended to be dramatically posed. Their gesticula-
tions obviously refer to some kind of incident which has just taken place.
The nature of this can only be guessed at, for the glass below the starboard bow of the ship is more injured than anywhere else in this particular medallion. A somewhat shapeless mass is seen as plunging into the
water. This may perhaps be cargo, though I think it unlikely because the
attitudes of the mariners suggest helplessness and resignation rather than
exertion of any kind. For the same reason one may dismiss the theory
that they are deliberately drowning some Jonah or Captain Glen. The
most natural conclusion to draw is that someone or other has by accident
fallen overboard.

The most interesting figure in the group is placed on the extreme right
of the picture. He is standing in the water which rises above his waist. He
is youthful in appearance, wears a mitre on his head, and carries a crozier
in his left hand. In his left hand also he appears to be holding the slack of a
rope. His entire attention is riveted upon the falling figure to whose
assistance he is evidently pushing his way. It is not quite certain what he is
doing with his right hand. It almost looks as if he were fending off the
on-coming bows of the ship.

Most probably the picture is intended to illustrate one of the innu-
merable legends of the great St. Nicholas of Bari, the patron saint of boys,
of travellers, of sailors, and of seaports engaged in commerce. This

22

hypothesis is supported by the mitre and crozier and the beardless face of the Saint.

There is a pretty story of St. Nicholas, which runs as follows. A certain man possessed of great wealth and estates was deeply grieved to think that he had no son to succeed him in the enjoyment of his revenues. He, therefore, made a vow that if a son were born to him he would present to St. Nicholas the richest chalice that ever goldsmith modelled. In due time the child was born, and some time afterwards the father recalling his vow ordered the cup to be made. The goldsmith set to work, and made a Chalice so exquisite that the father's senses were ravished. He turned a deaf ear to the prickings of conscience, and reserved the offering for himself, drinking wine from the goblet daily. The goldsmith made a silver cup to be offered at the shrine of St. Nicholas, and when this was ready the father and his son set out to the sea-coast. They took ship, and journeyed toward Bari.

On the way the father allowed his son to play with the golden goblet, and the child, as he tried to fill it with water, fell overboard. Thus a double punishment descended upon the sinner who lost in one moment the two of all his possessions which he valued most. Still intent upon the letter of his vow he completed his journey, and placed the silver cup upon the altar of St. Nicholas. Of its own accord the cup fell from its place. Three times the father restored it, but always with the same result. Then at last he realized his sin and, as remorse came to him, he bent his head. Earnestly he prayed for forgiveness and, when his shame passed from him and he dared to raise his eyes, he beheld his son in the flesh come down the alter steps with the golden chalice in his hands.

It seems likely enough that from this story the artist selected his episode for the Jerusalem Chamber glass. Or again the picture may represent another St. Nicholas story. For there is a legend that certain mariners, losing one of their company in a storm, cried aloud to their patron saint for assistance, and he drew them safely into harbour.

It would be quite in keeping with the principles of mediaeval art to represent St. Nicholas beginning to tow the frightened ship before the body of the man overboard had reached the water and, if this were the scene depicted in the Jerusalem glass, the rope in the left hand of St. Nicholas would be at any rate accounted for. But to all appearances the figure of the Saint is not concerned with the safety of the vessel, but with that of the victim plunging to his death.

Apparently there are no records to show where this glass came from. All authorities are agreed that it is very much older than the Chamber in which at present it is enshrined, and it seems more or less certain that it belongs to the very earliest period of English Gothic glass, that is to say, to the thirteenth century.

Mr. W. R. Lethaby's *Westminster Abbey and the King's Craftsman A Study of Mediaeval Building* (1906) contains a multitude of new facts gathered from a close study of the Fabric Rolls. 'Glazing was going forward at the Church,' he writes 'as early as 1253. In this year's ac-counts* we find that white and coloured glass was issued from the stores for certain windows which were to be done by task work. White work was to be done at fourpence a foot, coloured at eight pence. . . . The completion of the glazing for the work of Henry III is probably recorded

---

* The Fabric Roll of 1253 has been printed and explained by Professor Willis in Sir Gilbert Scott's *Gleanings from Westminster Abbey* (1863), pp. 231–51.

in 1290 when £64 (say £1,200) was paid to 'John of Bristol, king's glazier, for making glass windows in the Church of Westminster.' . . . We must suppose that the East windows and roses of the transepts, at least, would have had pictured glass of the highest scale of colour— sapphire, ruby and emerald. The fine early panels in Jerusalem Chamber may come from the Church.'

If the Jerusalem ship is really intended to illustrate some scene from the life of St. Nicholas, then with some probability it may be urged that the glass came in the original instance from this Chapel of St. Nicholas in the South Ambulatory. The Abbey archives prove conclusively that a certain amount of old glass was moved from the East Window of the Chapel of St. Nicholas, but there does not appear to be any record as to the nature of the glass or its destination when disturbed.

The ship of the Jerusalem window is in some respects peculiar. It is not the sharp-ended craft of the thirteenth century which the seals of Sandwich, Hastings, and Winchelsea have taught us to expect. In the shape of the hull it is more nearly akin to the ships of the Bayeux Tapestry. For the stem is surmounted by the head of a basilisk, and the stern by the head of some other creature, 'Very accurate deductions respecting the size, rig, and appearance of vessels in the reign of Henry III,' writes Sir Harris Nicolas, 'cannot be drawn from the notices of ships in English records; and it is doubtful if they differed materially from those of the preceding century.' The Jerusalem ship may perhaps be a belated *Esnecca*: for this type survived, it is known, until 1299 when more than one took part in Edward I's war against Scotland.

But if the carven terminals take us backwards in date, the presence of the 'Top' carries us forward. The 'Top' appears to have been very generally accepted by the beginning of the fourteenth century as we may gather from Guiart's *Chronique Métrique*, describing Philippe de Bel's naval expedition against the Count of Flanders. The first 'Top' was doubtless introduced many years antecedent to 1300. But the last vessel in which one would expect to find it would be a ship that adhered, so closely to the old dragon type as the vessel in the Jerusalem window.

In this presentment the top is not quite complete, but what there is of it is carefully drawn especially the ornamental tracery upon it. It appears to be fastened to the fore side of the mast, as we should expect, but is very much flatter in shape than the barrel-like fixture shown by Nicolas (I. 365) in his drawings from an early fourteenth century manuscript.

The sail appears to be fastened to the yard somewhat differently on either side of the mast. On the port side it would seem to be shaped along the head into shoulder-straps to slip over the yard-arm. The sail itself is of diminutive size and short in the hoist.

The rigging shown is very slight. One cannot be sure on account of the injury to the glass whether or no there is a starboard brace. There is almost enough to suggest one. There are two back stays very clearly shown in respect of their rope-strands though the artist does not reveal how they are fixed to the mast or whither they lead. The most interesting feature by far is the mainstay. And this is clearly shown almost throughout its length, and is *lashed to the stem-head*. By itself the evidence afforded by this single example as to the meaning and use of a stem-rope does not perhaps amount to much. It may be explained away by saying that the artist was lacking in skill or drew from his imagination. Yet for all that it is not without interest, and it is certainly very direct and definite in its assertiveness.

Hardly less interesting is the object immediately above the head of the Saint. What this can be I am quite unable to conjecture. It cannot be a bowsprit-trophy, because there isn't a bowsprit. It cannot be a nimbus for the Saint, because it is too far removed from his head and the mask of the basilisk intervenes. If it really be part of the vessel's furniture, if (for example) it be a talisman or mascot of some kind, then perhaps the stem-rope may serve to pay a double debt by keeping it in position.

From Vol III, No 4, §§97–103 (*April 1913*)

23

MEDIAEVAL SHIPS

No VIII STEM ROPES—Part IV

By H H Brindley

In his remarks on the gammoning theory of stem ropes (see 20), Mr. Gregory Robinson says: 'big bowsprits (I suppose) were in use at the end of the XVth century.' But by 'big' does he mean a heavy spar, or only a long light one? It is only the former, and then only if it were fairly long, that would require gammoning. Now the bowsprits seen in mediaeval representations are not of this kind. Roughly they fall into two categories. In one the bowsprit is a long and comparatively light spar with its inboard portion, below and abaft the fore-stage, usually shown. Examples are: The Second Town Seal of Southampton (see 31) and several other XIIIth century seals, the XVth century seal of Thomas Beaufort, second Duke of Exeter (see 19), and the glass of the same century in Vatteville church (see 3). The bowsprits of the *Warwick Roll* ship and of the Ashmolean painting (see 43) are of the same kind, though in their case we do not see so much of the inboard portion. Mr. Robinson mentions the *Warwick Roll* ship as having a bowsprit which might require gammoning (see 20), but if he will compare its small section with that of later bowsprits, he will recognise its family relation to the other examples mentioned above. The other kind of mediaeval representation of the bowsprit is a comparatively heavy and short spar which does not visibly come down below or abaft the fore-stage, and appears therefore to be stepped further forward than is the long thin spar. Among examples which have been illustrated in THE MARINER'S MIRROR are the gold nobles of Edward III (see Fig. 18.5) and Henry V (see Fig. 18.16), the two XIVth century seals of Edward Duke of Rutland (see Fig. 18.18), the seal of John Holland, Earl of Huntingdon (see 18.19), a miniature in the Bibliotèque Nationale (Fig. 37.1), the Bodleian 'Venice' miniature (see 27 and 36), the 'Florentines' (see 49), Hans Burgkmair's *Navicula penitentie* (see 56), and some of W.A.'s ships (see 44).

It is not suggested by the distinction drawn above that there were two distinct types of bowsprit in the Middle Ages; it is merely a statement of

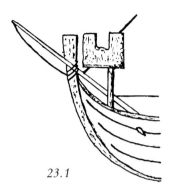

23.1

the way in which most of the representations so far examined group themselves, though among these there are intermediates besides other fittings which may be called 'bowsprits' provisionally and do not concern us here. What is urged is that the mediaeval bowsprit was a small or light spar, one of whose early uses was to carry grapnels, and which later on had the fore-stay made fast to it. A bowsprit fitted only for such purposes as these would hardly want such a heavy make-fast as gammoning. The only instance I have found of anything like gammoning for the typical medi-aeval bowsprit is in the XIIIth century seal of Great Yarmouth (Fig. 23.1). We see a light lashing passed several times round stem and bowsprit. This may be a permanent make-fast to hold the bowsprit to the stem and to maintain its steeve, but it be the fall of the grapnel line given several turns round stem and bowsprit; on the other hand the fall of the grapnel line is perhaps the rope indicated by the horizontal line in the sketch (further aft is a sailor handling this rope), though the seal shows no continuity between the grapnel line and this horizontal rope. On the whole the turns round the stem have the look of a lashing for the bowsprit, but they have little likeness to the heavy warp passed tautly round the planking as it rises into the stem, which is the typical stem-rope. It seems reasonable to suppose that true gammoning did not come in till after the bowsprit had developed into a heavy spar for carrying sail, and this stage of its evolution was reached long after the first appearance of stem ropes.

On the suggestion that the stem-ropes of mediaeval artists represent a girdling, Mr. Gregory Robinson remarks (see 20) that it is difficult to see how such ropes could correct a tendency to hog, and he goes on to say, 'the true remedy would seem to be the strengthening of the ship long-itudinally.' This latter remark is, of course, true; I do not think, however, that any writer in THE MARINER'S MIRROR has suggested that the mediaeval stem-ropes were a safeguard against hogging. In my reference

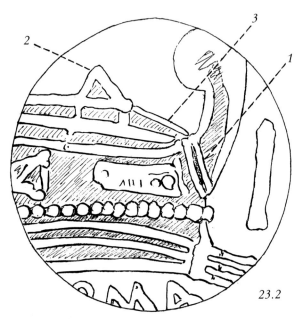

23.2

(see 19) to a fitting resembling these stem-ropes in an Egyptian warship of
c. 1250 B.C. (see Fig. 19.9) it was pointed out that the ship had also a
longitudinal cable to resist hogging, and that Mr. Cecil Torr, from whose
Ancient Ships the example was taken, considered that this cable had
nothing to do with the ropes passed round the stem. His drawing certainly supports this conclusion.

I am indebted to Dr. Jules Sottas for a drawing, which is here reproduced (Fig. 23.2), of the stem of a galley on a Roman Republican AS, in
which there are two bands[1] round the rising stem which certainly remind
us of mediaeval stem-ropes. Dr. Sottas informs me that he is inclined
to think that these are connected with the small shelter, or 'chateau
d'avant',[2] by a stay.[3] The same fitting, if fitting it be, for perhaps it is
really only a decoration, is found in many other issues of the AS. It does
not appear to have anything to do with a fore-stay, and therefore seems
to be distinct from the make-fast of the fore-stay as seen in a Roman
masted ship (see Fig. 19.3).

Mr. L. G. Carr Laughton has recently called my attention to Jal's
discussion of *Catena* in the *Archéologie Navale* and *Glossaire Nautique*, in

(1) Arch. Nav. II, pp. 41, 42.
(2) The text is in *Pardessus, Collection des Lois maritimes antérieurs au xviii siecle,*
Paris, 1828–45.
(3) *The Black Book of the Admiralty*, II, p. lix.

76

view of the possibility that there may be a relation between one form of *catena* and stem-ropes. I am indebted to Mr. Laughton for kindly handing over to me his notes on the subject. *Catena* in Italian, as in Latin, seamanship means 'chain,' and Jal concludes (1) that in the Middle Ages it was sometimes the custom to fit a girdling chain round the hull, because the construction of those times, though heavy, was not always very strong. He also regards this chain as the successor of earlier 'espèces de sangles', warps which he seems to infer were of rope, hide, or other flexible material and probably in vogue from the far past. He bases his view on the use of *cathena* (Low Latin, Genoese, Venetian) and *cadena* (Venetian, Catalan, Old Spanish) in two books of Sea Law, *Capitulare nauticum pro emporio Veneto*, 1255 (2), and the Catalan *Consulat de la Mer*, which, according to Twiss (3), dates from at least as far back as 1435, and may be more than a century earlier. In a footnote on p. 42 of the *Archéologie*, Jal states that subsequent references to other works has led him to give up the belief that *cathena* and *cadena* were a chain, and in the *Glossaire*, published eight years later, he refers to this change of opinion and says that: 'La *Cadena* . . . était un des barreaux de l'avant; ce devait être une pièce principale, et dont las place était marquée ou bien connue, puisque l'endroit auquel elle correspondait sur le pont, dont elle était un des soutiens transversaux, en même temps qu'elle servait de liaison ou de chaine aux deux côtes du navire, . . . était une limite,' &c. This makes *cadena* or *cathena* a specially stout deck-beam in the fore part of the ship. In support of this new view Jal seems to rely on the sense in which *catena* is apparently employed in *Ordinamenta et consuetudo maris . . . civitatis Trani* (1063)[4]. Moreover he finds another passage in the *Consulat de la Mer*, from which it appears that in Catalan any of the deck-beams was called a *cadena*. Jal considers that the passage in the '*Customs of Trani*' is 'très-clair sur la Catena,' but it is in no sense a definition of the term, it is merely one of the articles (No. XXV) of the sea-law, viz., 'Nisumo patrone non possà bactere nisumo marinaro; ma lo marinaro deve scampare et gire de prode a la cadena del rêmigio . . . Et se lo patrone passasse la catena pe bacterlo, la marinaro se deve defendere. . . .' (No master may beat any mariner, but the mariner ought to escape and make for the bow at the chain of the rowers. . . . And if the master does pass the chain to strike him, the mariner may defend himself. . . .). It is difficult to understand why Jal decides on the strength of this quotation, as he seems to do, that *catena* was never a *chain* in mediaeval shipbuilding. His many references to the term and the full quotations he prints in the *Glossaire* demand

(4) Text in Twiss, *Black Book*, iv., p. 522.

an article to themselves; at the same time I think that members of the Society, on reading these, will agree with me that there is nothing which precludes *catena* in the Middle Ages from being in some cases a chain passed across the hull with a strengthening purpose.

(*To be continued.*)

From Vol IV, No 4, §§110–14 (*April 1914*)

24

MEDIAEVAL SHIPS

No VIII STEM ROPES—Part IV

By H H Brindley

Whether the *Catena* was a chain or a specially stout deck-beam, there seems little doubt that it marked a definite point in the vessel. The Catalans had a rule similar to that of Trani with regard to a mariner's guiding himself by the *cadena* when avoiding punishment; possibly this was borrowed from the rules of Trani. It appears also that the *catena* was well forward. This has been suggested already, and Jal[1] gives a quotation from the *Convention pour le nolis de douze navires pour la première croisade de St. Louis; Génes, 13 septembre,* 1246[2], which runs, 'Et in cathena ante artimonem (alta) palmis octo,' on which Jal comments, 'Le barreau devant le mât d'artimon (qui alors était le mat de l'avant, était ce qu'on appelle aujourd'hui de Bau de Cottis.' The words of the *Convention* place the *cathena* well forward; we do not know where the foremast was stepped in the Mediterranean craft in which St. Louis embarked his army at Aigues-Mortes and other ports in the Gulf of Lyons, but in the above quotation we have the suggestion that some of his transports were two-masted.

Whatever meaning, in addition to its *general* one of 'chain,' *cadena* had in the shipbuilding of the Middle Ages, it seems clear that in later times it came to denote something in wood-work, for Jal[3] says that Venetian shipbuilders of the XIXth century employed *catena* as an equivalent of 'barrotins,' a diminutive of 'barrots,' which he defines[4] as 'lighter pieces than "baux," which they assist in supporting the deck.' Mr. Carr Laughton points out to me that they have their nearest equivalent in 'deck carlings,' for some of them ran fore and aft from beam to beam. Jal quotes Röding's *Allgemeines Wörterbuch der Marine* (late XVIIIth century), 'Catene (Venet.): die Ribben zwischen den Deckbalken.' Thus we find

(1) Glossaire, art. *Catena*.
(2) Documents in édits publiés par M. Champollion-Figeac, II, p. 53 (1843).
(3) Arch. Nav. loc. cit.
(4) Glossaire.

the term used for a longitudinal piece of wood-work, whereas the medi-aeval *catena* was transverse. In the *Glossaire* Jal also gives two uses of *cadena* in Spanish seamanship of recent times for wooden fittings of quite dif-ferent kinds from those discussed in this article.

The above very partial account of Jal's remarks on *Catena* may serve to show that it must not be disregarded in any enquiry into the nature and purpose of stem-ropes; though the possible relation between them can-not be dealt with satisfactorily within the limits of the present article.

Mr. Gregory Robinson, in support of his expression of doubt as to whether stem-ropes had any existence at all (see 34), mentions that no instances of them have so far been found in France, which is curious in view of the general similarity between French and English ships of the Middle Ages. I have mentioned (see 18) that I found no representation of stem-ropes in the 37 non-British seals bearing ships at Les Archives Nationales, Paris; and it may be pointed out also that to the present no examples from the Low Countries or Germany have been described. I have looked for stem-ropes without success in many Flemish and French XVth century MSS. I have, however, recently come across a suggestion that stem-ropes may be found in mediaeval painted glass in France. The windows of the apsidal chapels of the Abbaye-aux-Hommes at Caen are XIXth century work. In the medallion representing Our Lord and St. Thomas the boat has a bow as shown in my sketch (Fig. 24.1). The two bands round the stem are evidently ropes from the careful painting of the stranding which they show: save in this feature they are very like the bands round the stern and stem of the boat in the *Chronica Majora II* of Matthew Paris of *c.* 1260 (see Fig 19.6). The modern glass in the Abbaye-aux-Hommes was made from designs by Steinheil. I am indebted to

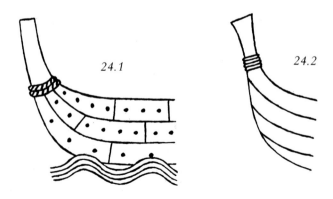

24.1   24.2

Dr. Jules Sottas for very kindly making enquiries for me as to this artist's work; it appears that he did much designing for reproduction in painted glass, and that he was in the habit of copying from early sources. Thus it seems very likely that there exists in some church in France the original of the boat at Caen, and it is hoped that it may be traced.

In view of the present want of examples of stem-ropes in any medi-aeval work other than English it may be suggested that they represent a peculiarly English fitting, and that if they were a girdling to strengthen the hull in the face of weakness of construction at the stem—a view to which I have already expressed a provisional adherence and to which I am still inclined—it is possible that on the other side of the Channel the problem was solved by some other and less clumsy means. Against this conclusion, that stem-ropes were some real and important fitting, it may be urged that the most striking examples are almost confined to seals and a particular series of coins. Does it not appear from this that they were a convention of engravers in metal, and that they caught the fancy now and then of the painters of miniatures and glass? An answer to this may be that a large number of seals bear ships, and that seals are brought together in collections: pictures on glass and illustrated MSS. involve more ex-tended search. Then it may be asked—'Why are most of the ships on seals without stem-ropes?' As suggested above, stem-ropes may have been only one way of effecting a certain purpose and the artist may have followed fact in not always representing them. To their absence from most of the ships on seals and their careful representation when they are shown we have a kind of parallel in 'Queen Mary's Psalter,' preserved in the British Museum. This is an English work of the earlier part of the XIVth century. It has among its many miniatures 19 which contain 'ships,' of which there are 21 altogether. Of these 11 have no mast or sail, 3 have a mast only and 7 have mast and sail, the latter being set in 4 and furled in 3 cases. The hulls are much of a pattern, as is usual in miniatures of a series. Only one of these craft has stem-ropes[5], and this one has similar ropes round the stern. The stem is sketched in Fig. 24.2. No stranding is shown, the 'ropes' are like those in the boat of Matthew Paris mentioned above. They are thus an instance of the kind of stem-rope which has less the appearance of being a girdling than those shown on the seals or the gold nobles. But whatever it was, the impression given is that the artist depicted something real.

In the discussion of stem-ropes in THE MARINER'S MIRROR certain examples of ropes whose function is quite clear have been quoted as

---

(5) Min. 150a. in S.C. Cockerell's facsimile edition.

possibly throwing light on the nature of the unexplained fitting: such are the setting-up of the fore-stay and the lashing which attaches the fore or after stage to stem or stern, as in the drawing of Matthew Paris (see Fig. 19.7). Setting such examples aside and confining the term 'stem-ropes' to those ropes or bands which are only passed round the stem and do not lead away therefrom, such 'ropes' fall into two classes. There are those which encircle the planking and consequently look like a girdling (the seals, the gold coinage and St. Jude's ship in the east window of Malvern Priory Church are typical examples); and there are the collar-like ropes which are passed round the stem only (of these we have examples in the drawings of Matthew Paris and in Queen Mary's Psalter). I have pointed out (see 19) that the latter kind of 'stem-ropes' much resemble certain bands round stem or stern which do not project from the outlines thereof and so seem to be stripes of paint or something else purely ornamental. Such 'stripes' are seen in some of the Bayeux Stitchwork ships and in some of the ships of Matthew Paris, who, as has been said, also depicts the collar-like 'stem-rope.' Thus an additional difficulty arises; but if the collar kind of stem-rope is a real fitting, it seems just possible that it has no relation to the more massive ropes which are lower down the stem and so encircle the planking. The suggestion may be offered that the collars were a kind of fender, much the same as we see to-day on the stems of dumb barges and ships's boats.

Whether the other kind of stem rope was a girdling to give additional strength to the stem or something else altogether, mediaeval representations at present unknown to us may decide. The matter is not yet ripe for dogmatic statement; as the Editor has recently reminded us, our Society has hardly got as far as marking out the ground for excavation.

From Vol IV, No 5, §§129–33 (*May 1914*)

¶ 25   REEF AND REEF POINT

There seems much obscurity as to when these terms came into use, and as to what the term 'reef' really meant at first. The N.E.D. art. 'Reef,' quotes Gower, *Confessio Amantis* (1393), Book VIII, line 1983, in Pauli's edition, 1857. Here 'ref' or 'rif' is clearly something that could be 'slaked.' Is there an earlier reference? Was the term 'reef,' used for a bonnet as well as in our modern sense, which, after all, is dual? That is to say it seems to mean both that part of a sail that can be gathered up, and also the appliance by means of which this can be done. Skeat, 'Etym. Dict.,' Edition 1910, gives Pom. raff = bonnet. A confusion between the two devices—a permament piece of sail, which can be gathered up and a detachable piece—seems not unlikely. 'Bonetz' were fitted in 1338 (Naval Accounts quoted by Nicolas, *Hist.*, II, p. 475), and we find 'bonnet' in the anonymous 'Tale of Beryn,' I., 871 (Circa 1430).

In XVI century, 'refe' or 'ryft' is spoken of as something that could be taken in (*vide* the fragment, 'Cocke Lorell's Boat,' 1515, p. 12, Roxburghe Club, 1817, and Earl of Surrey, 1557, in Tottel's 'Miscellany,' 1870, p. 27). But where are the reef points in pictures of this time? We see what look very like reef points in the thirteenth century seal of Hastings, fourteenth century seal of La Rochelle (in both cases at foot of the sail), and in the seal of the Earl of Huntingdon (either John Holland, 1352–1400, or his son, John Holland, 1395–1447). Can anyone tell me which of them had this seal with reef points, as Jal held them to be? These 'garcettes' are near the head of the sail. Were reef points fitted at all from 1500 to the second Dutch war? A portion of a sail may be taken up and made fast by a lacing, by beckets, or by fixed reef points; what was the common device in the fourteenth to sixteenth centuries? Or were several in vogue? Jal gives 'garcette de ris' as reef points, and suggests that 'garcette' and 'gasket' may be related. The galley *La Philipe* of 1336 (accounts printed by Nicolas, I, p. 472), had eight 'rifropes,' but the meaning is obscure. Mr. Alan Moore suggests to me that these may have been reef tackles.

By H H Brindley, from *Notes*, Vol I, No 1, §29 (*January 1911*)

26

MEDIAEVAL SHIPS

No VI—REEFING GEAR

By H H Brindley

In a paper, read before the Cambridge Antiquarian Society, last year, and published in the *Proceedings*, Vol. XV, 1910, p. 26, I called attention to the slight knowledge which we possess, and the great uncertainty which exists as to how the reefing of sails was done previously to the sixteenth century. The main points advanced were:–

(i) That in the absence of works on seamanship (for Wagenhaer's *Speculum Nauticum*, the earliest known book which can be called a work on seamanship, did not appear till 1584), our information is derived only from pictorial representations of ships on painted glass, seals and miniatures, scattered allusions in poems, and certain inventories preserved at the Record Office. Thus difficulties arise in more than one direction; where pictures are available, we have small means of judging how far they are conventional, certainly very many artists and seal engravers of the middle ages had little knowledge of the craft they illustrated; and when we have documents referring to ships, the information conveyed does not seem to allow of the reconstruction of the vessels.

(ii) From the information at our disposal, it seems certain that two methods of reducing or adding sail were in use in the middle ages, viz.:—

(a) The 'bonnet,' a strip of canvas which could be laced to the foot of a sail; in Tudor times it was common to have two bonnets, the lower one being know as a 'drabbler.' The earliest mention of a bonnet I know is in the inventories of certain ships of the Navy of King Edward III, preserved at the Record Office. These are dated 1338. Bonnets were in use in the Royal Navy as late as 1720, and they survive still in certain local small craft.

(b) Reefing by means of reef points, *i.e.*, short pieces of rope sewn into the sail on either side, by means of which a portion of the sail could be furled and secured. According to the position of the reef-points, this reduction of canvas was effected either at the foot of the sail or at its head; in the latter case the reef points of the two sides of the sail were tied

26.1

26.2

26.3

26.4

together over the yard. For the use of reef points in the Middle Ages, we have to rely entirely on pictorial representations, the earliest of which that I have been able to find is the twelfth century seal of La Rochelle (Fig. 26.1).

(iii) It is not possible to decide, at least in the majority of cases, whether a mediaeval writer is speaking of bonnets or reef points when he describes the proceedings of shortening or increasing sail: the word 'reef' on etymological grounds seems to have borne both meanings and this conclusion is fortified by the context.

(iv) No original representation of reef points later than 1528 has been found, and there is no statement by Wagenhaer, Raleigh, Smith, Boteler, or other writers of the late sixteenth and early seventeenth centuries which warrant a belief that sails were reduced by reef points in their time. On the other hand it is quite clear that bonnets were then in use.

(v) Reef points reappear in pictures at the time of the Second Dutch War, and continue to the present day.

(vi) It is unquestionably a puzzle that so convenient a method of shortening sail as reefing by reef points should have lapsed for more than a century, and yet it seems impossible that if reef points were fitted to sails from 1530 to 1665 we should not find them in pictures of the time, especially as engraving was by then an everyday art and the number of pictures of all kinds was so much greater than those of the preceding age. Thus it is desirable to place on record the early instances in which reef points are represented.

At the time of writing my first paper, I had been able to find only six cases of what may fairly be regarded as reef points, with one doubtful case. These were in the seals of La Rochelle (Fig. 26.1), Hastings (Fig. 26.2), Rye (Fig. 26.4), and painted glass in Thaxted Church, Essex (Fig. 26.5), and the churches of Villequier and Vatteville [see 2 and 3] on the lower Seine. The doubtful instance is some of the drawings of ships in the Life of Richard Beauchamp, Earl of Warwick (Brit. Mus., Cottonian MS., Julius E., iv., Art. 6), in which it is possible that reef points may be represented in one or two cases, but what is depicted is perhaps really the lacing of a bonnet. All the above cases, of which a tabular summary is given later on, fall between the twelfth century and the first quarter of the sixteenth century. Since publishing the article in which these cases were described, I have been able to find five or six more representations of ships with reef points, all of which are works dating from the century 1391 to 1493. In chronological order these are:—

(i) Seal of Edward Plantagenet, Earl of Rutland, Admiral of the North and West in 1391. The British Museum preserves two different seals of this Admiral, both of which bear ships. In one seal (No. lxxxix, 49), the ship's sail bears his coat of arms, but in the other, which is attached to a document (Additional Charters, No. 40665), the sail has reef points. These are distributed throughout the sail, as in the three examples mentioned above. This seal is illustrated in Fig. 26.3. The impression is a fragment, and it appears to be the only one extant, but fortunately the whole of the ship is preserved, though there are some cracks in the sail. These do not, however, obscure the reef-points, which stand out distinctly. They are in three rows, and do not all hang alike. They are the earliest instance I have found of what may be called for convenience double reef-points. It will be seen that some of them, most clearly those on the port side nearest the head of the sail, are in two pieces, as though they were sewn in on the bight. This feature will be seen again in later representations.

Incidentally, it is worth noting that the document to which this seal is appended has reference to Dunwich in the days when it possessed a harbour: for it is an exemplification in Latin of a suit before John Aslah and John, his brother, Attorneys General for Edward, Earl of Rutland, Admiral of the North and West, in the Court of Admiralty against Peter Elmoth and others of Dunwich for trespass at the entrance of Dunwich Port. The accused were acquitted. The document is dated December 3rd, 1392 (Brit. Mus., Cat. of Additional Charters, Vol. XVI).

(ii) Harleian MS., No. 1319, is French and is ascribed to the year 1399. The latest description of it is by Sir E. Maunde Thompson (*Burlington Magazine*, V, 1904, pp. 160–172 and 267–270), under the title, 'A Contemporary Account of the Fall of Richard II.' He states that the authorship is shown by a copy in the Bibliothèque Nationale at Paris (No 275 Fonds St. Victor); it was the work of Jehan Creton, *varlet de chambre* to Charles VI. Three of the beautifully executed miniatures show ships, and in two of them the sails have reef points. In the other the ships are much the same in general features, but they lie at anchor with their sails furled: they are the ships which brought stores from Dublin to the harassed English Army in Ireland. The miniature on fol. 14 shows John de Montacute, Earl of Salisbury, bringing his ships into Conway. He had Jehan Creton on board with him ('pour rire et chanter'), so perhaps we may regard the drawings of ships in this MS. as having more than usual authority. Fig. 26.6 is a photograph of the miniature, and it will be seen that the reef-points, which in the original are carefully sketched in brown pigment on the white sails, are double, as in the Earl of Rutland's seal of the same decade. The lines across the sail from which the reef-points depend suggest that the artist had reef-bands in mind. Each double reef-

Fig. 26.5 Ship in the St Christopher Window, Thaxted Church, from a tracing.

point is attached to the sail by what seems to be a knot, an arrangement to be considered later on.

The miniature on fol. 18 is reproduced in Fig. 26.7. The subject is King Richard II, sailing from Ireland to Milford. Here we see four ships running before a strong breeze: that bearing the King is distinguished by a heraldic sun-in-splendour on her sail, the reef-points which the sails of the other ships carry being omitted. These reef-points are just like those in the other miniature but nothing suggesting reef-bands is seen. In King Richard's voyage we are shown the fore sides of the sails, while in the Conway scene the sails are seen from aft; we have thus some evidence that the reef-points of the time were sewn in on both sides, as at the present day. It is difficult to believe that they were ever in the Middle Ages fitted to one side of a sail only, but I think the suggestion has been made. From a technical standpoint the sails are the best part of the ships in the two miniatures of Harl. MS., 1319, for what rigging is shown is unconvincing and certainly important ropes are omitted or drawn incorrectly. An apparent confusion between fore-stays and shrouds is revealed by comparing the ships of King Richard's fleet. Jehan Creton, or the artist who drew his miniatures, seems to have sought to express 'the way of a ship in the sea' well: in this he succeeded, for in both miniatures the

26.6

26.7

ships and sea have much life; perhaps more care was bestowed on the sails and the broken sea than on hulls and rigging. Such inconsistency for art's sake is quite possible: in these miniatures, as in so many others of the Middle Ages, we find extreme neglect of proportion between the sizes of the vessels and their passengers.

From Vol II, No 5, §§129–34 (*May* 1912)

27

MEDIAEVAL SHIPS

No VI—REEFING GEAR (Pt ii)

By H H Brindley

(iii) Bodleian MS. misc. 264, contains the well-known miniature representing Marco Polo embarking at Venice (fol. 218), which is English work, and was executed probably between 1410 and 1420. I am indebted to the late Mr. E. W. B. Nicholson, Bodley's Librarian, for permission to have the photograph made which is reproduced on Fig. 27.1, which shows the portion of the miniature containing ships. Both those at anchor and those under way have several features of interest besides the reef-points on the sails of the latter, and it is hoped to say something more of these vessels in a future article. Mr. Morton Nance, to whom I am indebted for calling my attention to this miniature as an instance of mediaeval reef-points and for kind assistance in the reproduction of the photograph, has pointed out to me that the lowest ship under way is evidently intended for a galley, and the representation suggests that the artist has never seen one. As the artist was an Englishman this seems very likely. All three ships have reef-points, the sails of the upper right-hand one having two rows, the left-hand one three, and the 'galley' perhaps four. I am indebted to Mr. Falconer Madan, Bodley's Librarian, for the information that the faded appearance of the right-hand portion of the miniature is the result of fingering in the days when MSS. were less jealously guarded than now, so that it is possible that the marks in the lower part of the 'galley's' sail do represent a row of reef-points.

(iv) The next instance in chronological order is the ship in the 'Compost et Kalendrier des Bergiers.' The oldest known edition of this work is that published by Guiot Marchant at Paris on April 18th, 1493, and reprinted by him on July 18th of the same year. The first translation into English was published in Paris in 1503 as 'The Kalendayr of Shyppars,' without printer's or publisher's name. A perfect copy at Chatsworth, an imperfect one at Althorp Park, and two leaves at the Bodleian are all that are known to survive of this edition. The Chatsworth example has been reproduced in *facsimile* by Dr. H. O. Sommer in 'The Kalender of

parole de la grande Ermenie se perde.
ille qui ple monde font.

27.1

Shepherdes,' London, 1892, the latest work on the Compost. The first edition printed in England is that of Pynson, 1506. The work was very popular in both France and England, and many editions were published, the last known English one being that of 1656. The photograph reproduced in Fig. 27.2 was taken from the woodcut on sig. f. 8b of No. 6770 in the Cambridge University library, which is an English edition of *c.* 1580, perhaps printed by Wally. This cut of a man in a ship is in the first French edition (1493) of the Compost. The British Museum possesses an example of the July or second impression of the French edition of 1493.

The ship illustrated in Fig. 27.2 differs from that of the first French edition in having one reef-point less, for in the cut of 1493 there is one in the upper starboard corner of the sail. There are also many minor differences, but in all chief respects the ship is the same in the two cuts. A comparison of the 'ship cut' in the various editions of the Compost is therefore a matter of bibliographical rather than nautical interest.

Fig. 27.2 Ship in the 'Shepardes Kalendar', Edition of *c*1580, from a photograph reduced.

Is this drawing of a ship older than 1493? Sommer (*op. cit.* pp. 61–63) states that the first blocks were all by French artists, but in many cases the designs were copied from German works. The 'ship cut' is not specially mentioned by Sommer in this connection, but from the context he seems to regard it as French. So for the present the drawing must be ascribed to 1493.

The introduction of the ship in the Compost is, like so much of the work, by way of allegory. The B.M. example of 1493 has below the woodcut, 'L'homme mortel vivant au monde bien est comparé au navire sur mer ou rivière perilleuse,' etc., and in the Pynson edition of 1506 there is 'Here after foloweth of the man i the shyppe that sheweth of the unstableness of the worlde,' while the legend under the cut runs, 'The world is unstable and may be lykened to a shype being in the se that is tossyd & whorlyd with the waues of adversyte,' etc. In the English edition of *c.* 1580, and I believe in earlier ones, we read

Nos sumus in hoc mundo sicut navis super mare.

I have to thank Mr. Charles Sayle of the Cambridge University Library for kind assistance in tracing the 'ship cut' through the early editions of the Compost. It has been said that some of the cuts were copied from German drawings, and though Sommer seems to regard the 'ship' as of French origin, it has certain features, for instance the fore-stage, the fighting top and the flag-staffs, treated in a manner which reminds me of some of the ships in the Nuremberg Chronicle and of the vessels drawn by the supposed Flemish artist with signature which were contemporary with the 'Compost'.

In spite of the technical errors of the artist, such as sheeting the sail wholly on one side of the mast, it is difficult to imagine that the knotted rope ends on the sail can be anything but reef-points drawn in a conventional manner. In their scattered arrangement on the sail they resemble the reef-points of the ship in the window of 1465 in Thaxted Church, the drawing of which, from my previous paper, is reproduced in Fig. 26.5 by permission of the Council of the Cambridge Antiquarian Society. To quote from that paper—'The impression which the Thaxted example gives is that the artist began with rows, and that in the lower part of the sail he put the reef-points in irregularly, so that none of them might be hidden by the mast or other gear.' This remark applies also to the ship in the 'Compost'.

In being 'double' the reef-points of the latter resemble those of Harl. MS., 1319, and of the windows of Villequier and Vatteville churches. The description of some of the reef-points in the Earl of Rutland's seal (1391) as 'double' (see 26), and therefore resembling the examples just mentioned, is misleading. It should have been pointed out that the reef-points of the Rutland seal are double only where they leave the sail, a feature which is unique; in all the other cases of 'double' points the rope is in two pieces down to its end. Reference to the table given later shows that 'single' and 'double' reef-points are intermingled through the centuries it covers, and that the instances of either are about equal. There seems to be sufficient evidence that double reef-points were employed in the Middle Ages. The knots of the reef-points in the 'Compost' ship seem to explain the spots of paint in the Harl. MS. 1319 ships, where the reef-points are made fast to the sail. The same spots are seen in *La Roumaine*, one of Jean Fleury's ships under Francis I., in the glass of Vatteville Church. These spots seemed at first to be very likely only an artist's convention, but the 'Compost' ship suggests that they indicate knots. Moreover, the spots of white paint with which the shrouds of the vessels in Harl. 1319 are led into the hull, certainly suggest knots. We have thus some evidence that early reef points were sometimes made fast to the canvas by knots, instead of by sewing.

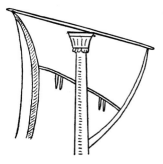

Fig. 27.3 Sail of a ship in 'Le Kalendrier des Bergiers', Rouen ?1505

As has been said above, there were many editions of the Compost. In those already mentioned the woodcuts are either from the same blocks or else are fairly faithful copies of those of the 1493 work, but in certain cases the book was reproduced imperfectly on smaller paper, and in these examples there is sometimes no attempt to follow the lines of the original artists exactly. Thus the ship in the Lyons edition (or rather, imitation) of 1551 (Brit. Mus., C47, h 13), has only three reef-points in her sail, while an imitation of the Compost, issued at Rouen, by Raulin Gaultier, perhaps in 1505 (Brit. Mus., 532, f 34), shows the ship (fol. 41) sailing to right, instead of left, and without the stern anchor or *dardons* in the top. The reef-points in this case are shown in Fig. 27.3. There appears to be a reef-band, and the reef-points are double without the knots of the origi-nal design. The only other case of early reef-points sketched thus that I know is in one of the ships (the only one under canvas) in the beautifully painted window of 1523, in Villequier Church. This example is therefore also from Normandy, and, though it is a mere speculation, the thought arises that a Norman artist may have endeavoured to make the reef-points of his ship like those he had seen on actual craft. There is nothing to go on besides these two instances that the craft of Norman waters had reef-points of this kind, and the Rouen Compost ship's in being hauled to the upper edge of the top discredits the artist's knowledge of rigging. The whole cut, like the others in the book, is executed roughly.

The representations of reef-points in the Middle Ages, or what at least have claims to be regarded as such, which have come to my knowledge so far, may be summarised as shown in the table on page 96.

In addition to these instances may be mentioned provisionally a minia-ture representing the arrival of Isabella of France, Queen of King Richard II, at Dover, in 1307, which is at present known to me only by a woodcut published in 1884, without exact reference to its source. Since

Date	Example	Side of sail seen	Position on sail	No. of rows	Single or double	Reef-bands
XII century	La Rochelle seal	aft	lower half	three	single	present
XIII century	Hastings seal	aft	lower two-thirds	three	single	present
1391	Earl of Rutland's seal	fore	all over	three	mostly single	none
	Harleian MS. 1319, fol. 14, miniature	aft	all over	three	double	perhaps present in one ship
1399–1400	Harleian MS. 1319, fol. 18, miniature	fore	near head and near foot	two	double	none
1410–1420	Bodleian MS. Misc. 264, fol. 218, miniature	fore	upper two-thirds of all over	two, three and ? four	single	none
XV century	Rye seal	fore	all over	three	single	none
1465	Thaxted Church window	aft	all over	roughly, six	single	none
1485–1493 (very possibly)	Cottonian MS. Julius E. iv. Art. 6, drawings		doubtful, if reef-points are present			
1493	'Compost et Kalendrier des Bergiers' (Paris), woodcut	aft	all over	roughly, four	double	none
1505 (?)	'Kalendrier des Bergiers' (Rouen), woodcut	aft	middle	one	double	present
1523	Villequier Church windows	aft	middle	one	double	none
1528	Vatteville Church window	aft	upper half	two	double	present (probably)

the above lines were written Mr. P. B. M. Allan and Dr. Jules Sottas have kindly ascertained for me that the original is in the Bibliothèque Nationale at Paris (MS. franç. 2643, f 7) [see 28]. Though it is impossible to trust to a reproduction which is not photographic and which may be a copy of another woodcut, I venture to quote it here as very probably another instance of reef-points by a mediaeval artist, because the points are placed on the spread sail of Queen Isabella's ship with care and do not look at all like an addition by a modern artist. They are disposed in four rows which occupy the upper two-thirds of the sail; in the lowest third none are shown, but this part of the sail is somewhat hidden by the shrouds and other rigging. Apparently the whole of the sail is not set, for a portion of it seems to be made fast to the yard by lashings of some kind, and the way things are depicted suggests that one reef has been taken in the sail, *i.e.*, the lashings shown are really the uppermost row of reef-points keeping their part of the sail to the yard. Should the original be found to confirm this view the picture is the only one known to me in which the reef-points are shown in use.

It is hoped that further representations of early reef-points will be found and that they will help to throw light on the difficulties mentioned in this article. It will be seen that the examples quoted are all from northern waters or at least that they are probably from the hands of northern artists. It is quite possible that much is to be learnt from miniatures and other works from countries bordering on the Mediterranean. Evidence from this source would be important in assisting to solve part of the vexed question as to how far northern practice borrowed from the South.

The reef-points in the Lübeck painting of *Der Adler*, described and illustrated by Messrs. R. Morton Nance and R. C. Anderson (see 60) can hardly be considered serious evidence of the use of reef-points between 1530 and the second Dutch War. As the authors point out, there is far too little certainty about dates and as to what happened on the several occasions when the painting was renovated. Was this painted ship kept up-to-date by the insertion of new devices without abolishing those they replaced in actual ships? I imagine that her reef-points were added either late in the seventeenth century, or possibly later still.

In my previous paper (Camb. Ant. Soc. *Proc., loc. cit.*) among the references to bonnets in mediaeval literature I quoted *Morte Arthur, c.* A.D. 1400, line 3657.

> 'They . . . trussene up sailes,
> Bet bonnettez one brede,'

concerning which I was indebted to Professor Skeat for the meaning of the second line, which is that they 'made good the bonnets on broad,' *i.e.*, set them to advantage. I pointed out that as 'trussene' clearly implies that they shortened canvas, the setting of bonnets at the same time is an inconsistent manoeuvre. Since then my friend Capt. Boyle Somerville, R.N., has suggested to me that what is meant is that they trussed up the *yards* by hauling the trusses taut, so that the yards would stand well home to the masts and thus carry the strain of the increased canvas better. This appears a quite possible solution of the puzzle.

From Vol II, No 6, §§166–73 (*June* 1912)

28

MEDIAEVAL SHIPS

No VI—REEFING GEAR (Pt iii)

By H H Brindley

In The Mariner's Mirror for June, 1912, (see 27), I referred to a miniature in MS. possessed by the Bibliothèque Nationale at Paris, known to me at the time only by a woodcut reproduction published in 1884, as probably giving a representation of reef-points by a mediaeval artist. Through the kindness of Dr. Jules Sottas I have lately obtained a photograph of this miniature, and it will be seen from the reproduction illustrating this article that the sail bears what I think may be fairly regarded as reef-points. The miniature, for the tracing of which I am indebted to Mr. P. B. M. Allan of Clare College, Cambridge, is on f. 7 of MS. Français 2643, which appears in the 'Catalogue des manuscrits français,' tome I., ancien fonds, 1868, p. 438, as 'Chroniques sire Jehan Froissart: commençant par "Afin que nobles faitz d'armes et honnourables advennues par les guerres de France et d'Angleterre," et finissant par, "ne retourne pour telz choses sous la paine d'estre noyez, car autant de menaiges qui vendront pour ceste chose, nous les getterons en Mouse" ' (vélin, XV siècle). The miniature represents the arrival at Dover of King Edward II and his Queen, Isabel of France, in 1307 (Fig. 28.1).

The reef-points are in four rows, which are evenly arranged in the upper half of the sail, which resembles the disposition of the reef-points in the seal of Rye (see Fig. 26.4) and in the miniature in Bodl. MS. Misc. 264 (see Fig. 27.1), both of which are also works of the XVth century. The reef-points in the French MS. agree also with those of the two examples just referred to in being single, and like them too, the sail carries no suggestion of reef-bands. This is of interest, as in representations of the previous century we find several instances of what seem to be reef-bands, and they appear again in the early part of the XVth century (see table in 27). The photograph shows that the whole of the sail is set, and not with its upper part furled to the yard, as I thought possibly the case from an examination of the woodcut reproduction. The surmise in 'M.M.' for June (see 27) should therefore be disregarded.

28.1

The hull of the Royal ship and those of the others in the miniature are much like those of other representations of the XVth century, but there are one or two features which deserve notice. The spar of square-section looking rather like a bowsprit under the fore-stage of the Royal ship is, I think, unusual. The fore-stay in the form of a crowfoot, with part of it let into the hull like a kind of forward shroud, is an arrangement of standing rigging I do not recollect having seen in any other picture. One is inclined to think that this 'shroud' is really a shroud shifted forward so as to allow an uninterrupted view of the tapestry hanging over the gunwale. The duplication of the forward hawse-holes, their diminutive size, the omission of lifts and braces, the placing of the starboard yard arm on the wrong side of the mast, the obvious faults in the shrouds which bear ratlines, and the absence of a rudder, are features which do not inspire us with confidence in the artist's knowledge of a ship, or at least convince us that his first thought was to give us a clear view of the personages she carries. The grappling hooks on the yard, and the fitting of stays to what seems only a flag topmast are of interest, as is also the fore-mast, a spar which none of the other ships seem to carry. It is unfortunate that the date of the MS. seems not to have been identified more closely than to its century. On the whole the miniature suggests the first half of the XVth century. Save for its marked forward rake, the small foremast reminds us of a Venetian *bragozzi*. Did the foremast come into use in northern waters in this form? One of the puzzles offered by XVth century craft is how the one-masted ship so characteristic of the Middle Ages, at least in Northern Europe, passed into the three-master of the last decades of the XVth century. Were two-masted vessels ever common in the Middle Ages outside the Mediterranean, and for how long? It is beyond the scope of this article to attempt a discussion of the subject, but I venture to suggest the importance of noting all representations of two-masters executed in the XIVth and XVth centuries. They appear not to be numerous.

The seaman standing on the fore-stage of the Royal ship is apparently getting in the foresail, perhaps he is intended to be brailing it up. He is hauling with both hands, and it is of interest that he has taken a couple of turns about his wrists with the fall of the rope.

The ship we see just to the left of the sail of the Royal ship carries an ornamental wind vane above her pennon. This is, I think, a very unusual fitting in pictures of mediaeval craft.

In the trader sketched by Mr. Morton Nance from a miniature in MS. Français 2810 (Bibliothèque Nationale, Paris), executed in the later part of the XIVth century (see 37), we have, I think another representation of early reef-points. Mr. Nance leaves it an open question as to whether reef-points or the lacings of a bonnet are included. They seem too high upon the sail to be the latter, though in this conclusion one has to suppose the artist put them in the right place. May not the line across the sail lower down be intended for the division between 'corps' and bonnet? If the fittings are reef-points, they are of the 'double' type with a 'knot' where they are made fast to the sail, which I described in the 'M.M.' for

28.2

May (see 26) and June (see 27). As the miniature is of the XIVth century it is earlier than any of the examples I quoted, though Harl. MS. 1319, was written perhaps as early as 1399. As in the ships in one of the miniatures therein, a reef-band seems to be shown in the ship in MS. Français 2810. It may be noted that the Harl. MS. is also French work. No great stress can, however, be laid on this, as in the other Harleian miniature (see Fig. 26.7), we see no sign of reef-bands.

The following table (p. 103) summarises the mediaeval and early XVIth century representations of what I am inclined to believe are reef-points rather than anything else. The seal of Dublin will be referred to in a future article.

Date	Example	Side of sail seen	Position on sail	Number of rows	Single or double	Reef-bands
XII century	La Rochelle seal	aft	lower half	three	single	present
1297	Dublin City seal	fore	all over	three	single	present
XIII century	Hastings seal	aft	lower two-thirds	three	single	present
XIV century (late)	MS. français 2810, in Bibliothèque Nationale	fore	upper half	one	double	present (probably)
1391	Earl of Rutland's seal	fore	all over	three	mostly single	none
⎫ 1399–1400 ⎬	Harleian MS. 1319, fol. 14, miniature	aft	all over	three	double	present in one ship
⎭	Harleian MS. 1319, fol. 18, miniature	fore	near head and near foot	two	double	none
1410–1420	Bodleian MS. Misc. 264, fol. 218, miniature	fore	upper two-thirds or all over	two, three and ? four	single	none
XV century	Rye seal	fore	all over	three	single	none
XV century	MS. français 2643 fol. 7, in Bibliothèque Nationale	aft	upper half	three, or perhaps four	single	none
1465	Thaxted Church window	aft	all over	roughly, six	single	none
1485–1493 (very possibly)	Cottonian MS. Julius E. iv. Art. 6, drawings	aft	doubtful, if reef-points are present		single	none
1493	'Compost et Kalendrier des Bergiers' (Paris), woodcut	aft	all over	roughly, four	double	none
1505 (?)	'Kalendrier des Bergiers (Rouen), woodcut	aft	middle	one	double	present
1523	Villequier Church window	aft	middle	one	double	none
1528	Vatteville Church window	aft	upper half	two	double	present (probably)

The accompanying reproduction of 'the man in the ship' cut from the 'Compost et Kalendrier des Bergiers,' Paris, 1493 (see Fig. 28.2), may interest readers of the 'M.M.' as a comparison with an English copy of *c.* 1580 reproduced in the June number (see Fig. 27.2). As mentioned there, the 1493 edition is the earliest known (the illustration is a photograph of the cut from the July reprint by Guiot Marchant of his first issue of the 'Compost,' in May, 1493, and was made from the copy in the British Museum). It will be seen that the English cut lacks the starboard upper reef-point and the *dardons* in the top are treated more conventionally, so that they resemble the rays of a crown. Beyond these the differences are minor ones. In the English cut the waves are treated with much less detail and here and there shading which we see in the original is omitted.

From Vol II, No 8, §239–43 (*August* 1912)

¶ 29   SHIPS IN A XV CENTURY FROISSART MS.

I remember to have seen, I believe in a popular edition of Froissart, two woodcuts after miniatures in an unnamed fifteenth century Froissart MS.; of these I have kept pencil sketches, and it seems to me clear that the original pictures were the work of the same hand that designed the picture of a ship with a foremast (see Fig. 28.1) that illustrates Mr. H. H. Brindley's sixth article on 'Mediaeval Ships.'

The two ship-pictures of the wood-cuts show in nearly all cases a vane above the masthead streamer; but this is of woven fabric, not of wood or metal, and perhaps the most marked likeness of these vessels to Mr. Brindley's ship is seen in the deep tops with trestle trees below and around their top-armings that in some cases show the heraldic bearings of their respective countries and in others have lettering of the same charac-ter as that upon the top-arming of the fore-masted ship. In two of these top-armings I read NOR—for Normandy, and ANGLETE—for Eng-land. Does JED HAY, for Jehan de Haynault, come out in Mr. Brindley's photograph? In the reproduction it is not at all certain. The peculiarly shaped sail, drawn as though it were triangular, is repeated in each ship, and in some cases the reef-points and yardarm sheer-hooks have not been neglected by the engraver. Three rattled shrouds and a tackle on either side again compose the rigging. The ship's hulls, too, are quite of the same type as that of the foremasted ship, carvel built with wales, but far better drawn; as will be seen by the specimens (Figs. 29.1 and 29.3) which I have chosen as giving the most true seeming idea of the ships them-selves. The 'skids' of Fig. 29.1 are so much like those of the 'hulks' of

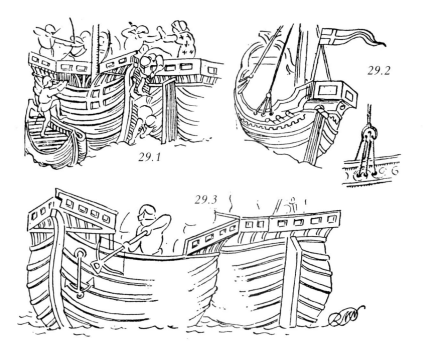

29.2

29.1

29.3

Flanders a century later that it would be interesting to know if a Flemish artist is credited with this work, and the samson-post with timbers that curve away from its foot, all supporting the fore part of the sterncastle, show a very reasonable and probable bit of construction, for, although an arch like that of the forecastle is sometimes shown here, to repeat this would be a mistake easily made, and the drawings that show it are not perhaps of the most reliable. The curious beak-like timbers of the miniature are repeated in these engravings and no bowsprits are shown; but the 'foremast' is not seen on any of their ships, and, although the painter has certainly in that given by Mr. Brindley, made a foremast of it, unless others like it turn up in this MS., this spar will not be quite beyond the suspicion of belonging to the small boat behind from which two lines seem to lead up to it. Judging from these other pictures the crowfoot stay or shroud mentioned by Mr. Brindley is really a conventional tackle; but the 'foremast' has a sort of crowfoot at the foot of its shroud or stay which suggests that this ship may, like the Scheveningen pink or the fifteenth century ship (Fig. 29.2) copied from a MS. Bocaccio by La Croix, have had shrouds set up with a dead-eye above and holes drilled in the gunwale below in which to apply the power of the lanyard; nothing to corroborate this is seen in the engravings quoted above, however.

The artist responsible for these pictures was evidently no sailor, and it would be too much to expect that even in fifty pictures by him we could find material from which to reconstruct a ship of the type drawn by him from keel to truck. I would suggest, however, that the Bibliothèque Nationale Ms., Français, 2643 (see 28) and any other work by the same artist, would be well worth following up for the sake of the other ships which may occur there.

By 'R.M.N.', from *Notes* Vol III, No 6, §§182–84 (*June 1913*)

℈ 30   SHIPS IN XV CENTURY FROISSART MS.

In Vol. III (see 29) Mr. Nance calls attention to the similarity between the ships in 'two woodcuts after miniatures in an unnamed fifteenth century Froissart MS.' and the photograph of the miniature showing the ship of Isabel of France in MS. Français 2643, Bibliothèque Nationale reproduced in 'M.M.' Vol. III (see Fig. 28.1). Mr. Nance is right in his supposition that the ships in his sketches (see Figs. 29.1, 29.3) are in MS, Fr. 2643. I have this week gone through the MS. and found the originals in two of the larger miniatures. Each of these represents a sea fight with four vessels alongside in the foreground. Mr. Nance's sketch (Fig. 29.1) is the left hand and next ship in the miniature of the Battle of Sluys, 1340. The left hand ship is English, as shown by a banner and the arms painted

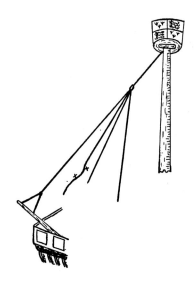

Fig. 30

on her top, while the top of the next alongside bears the letters NORME and the two leopards, or gules, of Normandy fly from a banner staff. The English ship is the only one having anything like a bowsprit. I reproduce part of her in the accompanying sketch, from which it will be seen that the woodcut Mr. Nance copied is not accurate: where I have ended the mast and rigging they vanish in the crowd of soldiers occupying the deck. The short bowsprit projects at the back of the bowman in Mr. Nance's sketch. Where the two crosses are placed are the hands of two soldiers hauling on one of the ropes, which is shown *pushed* from the straight by their efforts. The top bears France and England modern quarterly. The trestle tree under the deep top is repeated in all the larger ships in the MS. Mr. Nance's sketch (Fig. 29.3) is the right hand and next ship in the miniature depicting the Battle of Guernsey in August, 1342, between the English Squadron and the Spaniards and Genoese (Nicolas, *Hist.*, II., p. 75 and de la Roncière, *Hist. Mar. Franç.*, I. p. 467, where the miniature is reproduced.) The right hand ship carries the Spanish flag and the soldier with the cross-bow fires from another of the enemy's vessels.

The anchor in this ship in Mr. Nance's sketch is in the original supported by a long peg (painted gold) passed through the hawse-hole and the anchor ring. The two sea-fights are represented in very nearly the same way; four large ships in close action in the foreground and two or three others far away are the main feature of both. The two left hand ships in the Guernsey fight are English and their long pennants bear 'Saint George' in gold on red. In this MS. eight of the miniatures contain ships, and Mr. Nance has rightly distinguished the conventions of the artist in his mention of the curious triangular form of the sails, the scattered reef-points, the sheer hooks, the three rattled shrouds, and the tackles led to the rail. These features and the carvel hulls with wales and other details occur throughout; the artist drew one type and all the details of it are well shown in Queen Isabel's ship as reproduced in Vol. II (see Fig. 28.1). Concerning Mr. Nances' comments on this miniature:— (1) He asks if JED HAY (for Jehan de Haynault) appears on the top of the Queen's ship. There are in the original gold letters which *may* be JEDHAY on the red-painted top which do not appear in the photograph. In several other cases what seem to be letters may be only ornaments; though painted delicately in gold they are very small. (2) An examination of the miniature of Queen Isabel's ship reveals that the photograph shows the rigging accurately, but I am quite willing to join Mr. Nance in his suspicion that the supposed foremast is really the mast of the small boat partly behind the bow of the Queen's ship, and in his conclusion that 'the artist responsible for these pictures was evidently no sailor': of this everyone of his miniatures is evidence. The man handling a rope in the bow of the Queen's ship is not of much assistance to us in deciding whether the rope comes from a mast on his own craft, for the artist seems to have reproduced this man to give a flavour of seamanship to the proceedings; he occurs, armoured or in a hat, in four of the miniatures and altogether five times; in one other case besides Queen Isabel's ship the fall of the rope is crossed over his wrists. (3) The apparent crowfoot on the forestay may well be the conventional tackle of the artist rather elaborated. In the originals all the 'blocks' of his tackles are ovals in gold. (4) The only certain bowsprit is that in the accompanying sketch. (5) The wind vanes, alluded to by Mr. Nance as shown of 'woven fabric, not of wood or metal' in the woodcuts indicate faulty copying by the woodcutter, for where they occur in the original miniatures they are painted 'hard' in sepia or black. (6) So many miniatures of the XVth century now in France came from Flanders, and the resulting Flemish influence on French work seems to render it very likely that the skids characteristic of Flemish 'hulks' should appear in miniatures of both French and Flemish artists of the time. (7) The tendency to confusion between the details of bow and stern construction alluded to by Mr. Nance must, I fear, be regarded as possible to the artist of MS. 2643. In conclusion, it may be said that with all his obvious faults the latter has usefully given us one of the few records of true reef-points and his wind-vanes have the look of reality and are another fitting apparently rare in the day when these pictures were made.

By 'H.H.B.,' from *Notes*, Vol IV, No 7, §§215–16 (*July 1914*)

31

MEDIAEVAL SHIPS

No VII

By H H Brindley

One of the earliest representations of reef-points is in the ancient seal of the City of Dublin (see Fig. 31.1, *left*), which Birch (Brit. Mus. Cat. of Seals, IV., p. 178) gives as dating from 1297. Reference to the table already given (see 28) of the representations of early reef points so far collected will show that only the XIIth century seal of La Rochelle (see Fig. 26.1) and perhaps the XIIIth century seal of Hastings (see Fig. 26.2) are older than the Dublin Seal. The cast reproduced in the upper part of the accompanying plate is a copy of the British Museum impression of this seal. Its most projecting part, the side of the hull, is so worn that the lines of the planking save in the bow and stern have vanished, thus it cannot be seen whether the ship was fitted with the pointed fenders or short rubbing wales which are so characteristic of ships by mediaeval artists and which are seen typically in the lower seal in the plate, which is also one of the XIIIth century. This will be referred to later. The sail of the Dublin ship is of eight somewhat unequal cloths (the flat appearance of those most bellied out in the middle of the sail is the result of wear), and these cloths are divided up into four oblongs each by three equidistant bands which look like ropes sewn into the sail. From these bands, which perhaps we may call reef-bands, depend regularly between the cloths short pieces of rope which are exceedingly like reef-points. They are all about the same length, but they are not all straight. Most of them are more or less bent or curved and not all in the same way, so that they suggest very clearly loose ends lying against the canvas. The foot of the sail is finished off with a strong rope-like band, and the thickness of this and the deep roach suggest for a moment that a reef has been taken in. But more likely the artist wished to show the crew plainly; we should be sorry to miss the man who is taking refreshment. The man just behind him may be holding out his hand for the wine cup, or he may be shouting an order as the seaman in the bow of the lower ship appears to be doing. The seal of Dublin is the earliest instance known to me of a sail

Fig. 31.1 *Left*. Dublin, city seal. AD 1297. *Right*. Southampton, Second town seal, thirteenth century.

apparently made by sewing together a series of oblong or square pieces of canvas. There are a good many instances of this in the Flemish or Franco-Flemish miniatures illustrating volumes of 'Chroniques' of Froissart and other historians in the British Museum, but these are mostly mid XVth century work: the Duke of Bourbon's ship in Harl. MS. 4379, fol. 115, is a good example. In none of these that I have seen are anything like reef-points depicted. In the way in which the reef-points are represented the three earliest instances so far collected, viz., the seals of La Rochelle, Dublin and Hastings have certain features in common:—reef-bands, three rows of points, the points are single, and they do not all hang in the same way. Dublin differs from the other two in having the uppermost row quite near the head of the sail. The main respects in which the reef-points and bands of these three seals differ from later examples are indicated sufficiently in the table (see 28) and need not be repeated here. It may be suggested that we now possess fairly satisfactory information as to the usual arrangement of reefing gear in northern ships during the latter part of the XIIth and in the XIIIth century.

Besides the reef-points the Dublin ship has one or two other points of interest. The series of short vertical lines—*striæ* as it were—from the yard are curious. They are evidently intentional and perhaps represent the lacing. The port sheet and port brace are shown clearly, the latter is double and rove through a block at the yard arm. It seems unlikely that the apparent rope coming down behind the cap of the man blowing a horn in the aft stage is the brace continued, it is not in line with the latter. This seal is evidently the work of an engraver who was careful about details, for what is left of the smaller features, such as the roping and reef-points, the three-pointed pennon and the lettering, are executed admir-ably. Possibly the line behind the hornblower's cap is part of the cap itself. As in the La Rochelle ship the mast is surmounted by a cross. The seal (see Fig. 31.1, *right*) is the second town seal of Southampton, and dates from the XIIIth century. The photograph is from a copy of the British Museum impression. The hull is of a later type than that of the Dublin ship, which is early in several features, *e.g.*, its sharp sheer into quite narrow stem and stern pieces, the small fore and aft stages, and the absence of a top. The beast's head carved on the *stem* piece is certainly an early feature; whether the stem piece carries a similar ornament cannot be made out. The hull of the Southampton ship has much less sheer and the larger fore and aft stages look more like permanent structures. The latter is supported by what seems to be a V-shaped skid. The mast has a top which is fitted only on its fore side, possibly an early arrangement. In this seal we have one of the earliest representations of a bowsprit. It is shown with great steeve and stepped well abaft the fore stage. Exactly the same arrangement is seen in the much later seals of Edward Earl of Rutland, 1391 (see Fig. 26.3), of Richard Cletherowe, Admiral of the West, 1406, of Thomas Beaufort, second Duke of Exeter, 1416–26 (see Fig. 19.1), in another of his seals not figured in the 'M.M.,' and in the XVth century seal of the Sub-Admiralty of England. In the series of gold nobles and angels of King Edward III onward where a bowsprit is represented it comes through the floor of the forestage and so is stepped much more forward than in the cases noted above (see 18). The seal of S. Sebastian gives another example of a bowsprit in the XIIIth century. This seal is figured in the British Museum Catalogue of Seals, VI, pl. xxii. The vessel has a high stem piece and no fore-stage, but the large bowsprit has considerable steeve and is stepped as in the Southampton seal. From its head leads a slack double rope to the stem piece. What was this rope and what was the use of the bowsprit itself in these mediaeval vessels? It is important that we should put on record all the early representations of this spar and of the rigging it carries. Was it fitted first only to carry the grapnel as in such examples as that figured in the 'M.M.' for August, 1911, (see Fig. 9.1). With the introduction of a foremast it became a useful spar to make forestays fast, as in XVth century ships, for instance, that illustrated in the 'M.M.,' May, 1911, (see 3), and in those of the Rous Roll, discussed by Mr. L. G. Carr Laughton in the 'United Service Magazine,' February, 1908, p. 459. As the foremast increased in size and importance it became still more necessary for the lead of various parts of the fore rigging, as pointed out by Mr. Norton Nance in the 'M.M.,' August, 1912, (see 46). The earliest mention of the bowsprit in MSS. I have seen is 'bowsprete' in Exch. K.R. bund. 19, No. 31 (expenses of building the 'galley,' *La Philipe* at Lynn, in 1336), and the N. E. D. quotes 'bouspret' from R. Brunne, *Chron.* (K. O.), *c.* 1330. The evolution of the bowsprit must be considered with that of the foremast, and as yet we know but little of the advance from the one-masted to the two- and three-masted craft in Northern waters.

From Vol III, No 1, §§14–17 (*January 1913*)

32

EARLY REEFS

By H H Brindley

In a paper on the St. Christopher window (1465) in Thaxted Church (see Fig. 26.5), published in the *Cambridge Antiquarian Society's Communications*, xv, 1910, p. 26, I pointed out that though bonnets were in use in the Navy from at least 1338 (inventories of certain ships of King Edward III preserved at the Record Office) continuously to 1720, and still survive in certain local small craft, reef-points (of which the earliest known representation is the twelfth century seal of La Rochelle) fell into disuse during the first half of the sixteenth century and reappeared at the time of the Second Dutch War (1665). The puzzling disappearance for more than a century of so convenient a method of shortening sail has been further discussed by myself in THE MARINER'S MIRROR for May, June and August, 1912 (see 26, 27, 28) and a considerable amount of search has taken place for contemporary representations of or references to reefing by reef-points between 1500 and 1660. As a result a number of notes on the subject have been published in THE MARINER'S MIRROR by several contributors, and these all tend to the conclusion that reef-points did fall into disuse during the period mentioned; for it seems most unlikely that if reef-points were fitted from 1530 to 1665 we should not see them in pictures of the time or not find them referred to in works dealing with seamanship. So the subject still remains a puzzle.

A considerable number of early instances of reef-points have been brought to light since attention was first called to the subject, and most of these are embodied in a paper published in the *Cambridge Antiquarian Society's Communications*, xxi., 1919, pp. 83–99. I am much indebted to the Council of that Society for kindly giving me permission to reproduce much of the above paper in the present article and to borrow the blocks illustrating it. The latter are indicated by C.A.S. following the legend. Since the paper was published two additional representations of early reefs, both of the XV, century, have come to my knowledge, viz., one in the brasses on the tomb of St. Henry of Finland in Nousis [Nousiainen, Finland] Church, and the other in a window in Gresford Church. These are included in the following table, which summarises the mediaeval

Date	Example	Side of sail seen	Position on sail	Number of rows	Single or double	Reef-bands
II century	La Rochelle Seal	after	lower half	three	single	present
XIII century	MS. français 403, Bibliothèque Nationale	after	all over	four	single	none
XIII century	Bodleian MS. Auct. iv. 17	after	all over	four	single	none
XIII century	Hastings Seal	after	lower two-thirds	three	single	present
1270	Marlay Add. MS., Fitzwilliam Museum, Cambridge	after	lowest third	two	single	none
1278	Bergen Seal	after	all over	four	single	none
1297	Dublin City Seal	fore	all over	three	single	present
1375	Richard Stewart's Seal	fore	all over	three	single	none
XIV century (late)	MS. français, 2810, Bibliothèque Nationale	fore	upper half	one	double	present (probably)
1391	Earl of Rutland's Seal	fore	all over	three	mostly single	none
1399–1400	Harleian MS. 1319, fol. 14	after	all over	three	double	present in one ship
1399–1400	Harleian MS. 1319, fol. 18	fore	highest and lowest thirds	two	double	none
1410–1420	Bodleian MS. Misc. 264, fol. 218	fore	upper two-thirds or all over	two, three and ? four	single	none
1425–1430	Cottonian MS. Domit. A, xvii	after	upper half	two	double	present
1412–1450	Nousis [Nousiainen] Church, Finland, brass	after	upper half	one	single	none

Date	Example	Side of sail seen	Position on sail	Number of rows	Single or double	Reef-bands
XV century	MS. français, 2643, fol. 7, Bibliothèque Nationale	after	upper half	three, or perhaps four	single	none
	The same, fol. 118	after	all over	five and six	single	none
XV century	Rye Sale	fore	all over	three	single	none
1465	Thaxted Church glass	after	all over	roughly, six	single	none
c. 1470	Breslau Froissart, 11. fol. 48v	both	all over	five	double	none
late XV century	Hillesden Church glass	fore?	all over	three	double	none
c. 1480	Gresford Church glass	fore	upper and lower halves	two	single	none
1493	'Compost et Kalendrier des Bergiers' (Paris), woodcut	after	all over	roughly, four	double	none
c. 1505	'Kalendrier des Bergiers' (Rouen), woodcut	after	middle	one	double	present
1523	Villequier Church glass	after	middle	one	double	none
1528	Vatteville Church glass	after	upper half	two	double	present (probably)
c. 1550	'Orbis Civitates Terrarum', woodcut	fore	lower half	one and two	single	present

representations of reefs so far known. Where the nature of the representation is not stated it is a miniature.

The following notes are on the instances which have not been published in THE MARINER'S MIRROR.

The miniature in the Bodleian Apocalypse (MS. Auct. iv. 17) represents the voyage of St. John to Patmos. I am indebted to Mr. Falconer, Bodley's Librarian, for permission to have a photograph made of this and of the miniatures of the embarcation of St. John and his arrival at Patmos. No reef-points are shown in the former and in the latter only the bow of his ship is seen.

The Apocalypse in the Bibliothèque Nationale whose press mark is MS. français 403 I have been enabled to examine by the kindness of M. Léon Dorez, Conservateur des Manuscrits. It is contemporary with the Bodleian MS., and like it is English work of the latter half of the thirteenth century. The miniatures of the two represent the same subjects and resemble each other so closely that they may be regarded as copies, though it is not possible to say which is the earlier work.

The manuscript of Vegetius's *De re militari* recently acquired by the Fitzwilliam Museum (Marlay Add. i) is a translation into Norman French followed by the Latin original written on 149 pages of vellum. It dates from 1270 and seems to have been written at Acre by an English or Anglo-Norman scribe for Queen Eleanor of Castile. It contains two miniatures, one of King Edward I as Prince of Wales and the sea fight here reproduced (see Fig. 36.6).

The seal of Bergen of 1278 (see Fig. 32.4) bears a ship which was probably somewhat out of date in having its stem and stern pieces carved as beasts' heads. This subject and also other features of this ship and of those in the Bodleian and Paris Apocalypses I have discussed in 'The Ships in the "Cambridge Life of the Confessor" ' and in 'The Ship of the Seal of Paris' (*Camb. Ant. Soc. Communications*, xvii. 1916, p. 310 and xviii 1917, p. 155).

For the seal of Richard Stewart (*c.* 1375) (see Fig. 32.1) I am indebted to Mr. W. R. Macdonald, of Edinburgh, who has kindly given to me a copy of the cast in his collection of Scottish seals.

All the above examples resemble one another in the reef-points being single and in being sewn in over most of the sail, thus agreeing with the Dublin seal (1297) (see Fig. 31.1), the Earl of Rutland's seal (1391) (see Fig. 26.3), the miniature of Marco Polo sailing from Venice in Bodleian MS. Misc. 214 (1410–1420) (see Fig. 27.1) and the fifteenth century seal of Rye (see Fig. 26.4)

We now come to the earliest representation known to me of double reef-points. The text figure is a sketch (see Fig. 32.2) from a drawing by

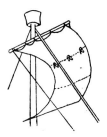

Fig. 32.1 Seal of Richard Stewart, *c*1375.

Fig. 32.2 Livres des Merveilles. Late fourteenth century.

Mr. Morton Nance (see 37) of a miniature representing two ships under way in a 'Livre des Merveilles' in the Bibliothèque Nationale (MS. français 2810) of late in the fourteenth century. The points seem to be sewn into a reef-band, as in one of the ships in Jehan Creton's miniature of King Richard II's voyage from Ireland (Harleian 1319, fol. 14) of 1399–1400 and as in the La Rochelle, Dublin and Hastings seals of the twelfth and thirteenth centuries (see Figs. 26.1–7, 31.1).

Fig. 32.4 Bergen, 1278.

The brasses representing St. Henry of Finland and scenes in his life were placed on his cenotaph in the church of Nousis [Nousiainen] in Finland between 1412 and 1450. St. Henry, by birth an Englishman, was Bishop of Upsala about 1150. One of the brasses represents the arrival of St. Henry and St. Eric in Finland, each in his own ship. Both have one mast and square-sail set, the King's ship has a round top, but this fitting is not carried by the mast of St. Henry's ship. The yards have lifts and at least one brace can be made out. Both vessels have an embattled fore-stage and a short bowsprit without any fittings. The margin of the brass cuts off both their sterns. The forward halves of two similar ships under way are shown in the brass which probably represents St. Henry saying farewell to St. Eric. None of the sails are fitted with reef-points, but a

Fig. 32.5 King Henry VI's psalter, 1425–30.

row of single points are seen in the upper part of the sail of one of the two ships on the brass which represents St. Henry appearing in the clouds to succour the crew of the other vessel, which is foundering. The photograph of this scene (see Fig. 32.3) is made from the set of rubbings of the St. Henry brasses possessed by the Society of Antiquaries, to whose Council I am indebted for permission to reproduce it. Dr. M. R. James has described these brasses in the *Cambridge Antiquarian Society's Communications*, X pp. 215—21, and they have been illustrated in the *Portfolio of the Monumental Brass Society*, part for June 1903. In the brass representing the finding of St. Henry's finger after his murder there is a small boat rowed by two men. Like the sailing ships, she has wide planking and an uprising stem, but this is without the fore-stage. This boat, however, is of some interest as two thole pins are shown for each oar. The oar out of water has a rather narrow blade ending in a blunt angle.

The Cottonian MS. Domitian A xvii in the British Museum is a Psalter written for King Henry VI when about ten years old (see Fig. 32.5). In the miniature of Our Lord stilling the Storm double reef-points

Fig. 32.6 Fitzwilliam Museum, 1270.

in two rows and apparently sewn into reef-bands are represented in the upper half of the sail. The ship is interesting also in the details of its rudder. The hull, with fore and after stages, is of the 'crescent type' usual in representations of the fourteenth and early fifteenth centuries.

The Bibliothèque Nationale 'Chroniques sire Jehan Froissart' (MS. français 2643) is work of the second half of the fifteenth century. It contains several miniatures showing ships, and one of these in which reef-points are seen (fol. 7) I have reproduced in 'M.M.,' August 1912, (see Fig. 28.1). This represents the arrival at Dover of King Edward II and his Queen Isabel of France in 1307; and in the same journal Mr. Morton Nance has published sketches of ships in other miniatures of this MS. (June 1913, p. 183). The illustration in the present article (see Fig. 32.7) reproduces the miniature of the Battle of Guernsey in August 1342 between the English Squadron and the Spanish and Genoese fleets (fol. 118). Single reef-points in several rows are represented in the same manner as in Queen Isabel's ship. In notes by myself, written at the time of examining the MS. (see 30), I agreed with Mr. Morton Nance in his conclusion that 'the artist responsible for these pictures was evidently no

Fig. 32.7 Bib. Nat, Froissart, *c*1470.

Fig. 32.8 Breslau Froissart, *c*1470.

Fig. 32.9 Hillesden Church Glass. Late fifteenth century.

Fig. 32.10 Gresford Church Glass, c1480.

sailor,' but with all his obvious faults he has usefully given us evidence confirming the conclusion from other representations that mediaeval reef-points were often sewn in rows covering most of the area of a sail. In a Froissart of about 1470, preserved at Breslau, a miniature of the Battle of La Rochelle, in 1372, again shows reef-points sewn in all over the sail, but in this case the points are double (see Fig. 32.8).

In Hillesden Church, Bucks, which was rebuilt in the last decade of the fifteenth century, there is a window depicting events in the life of St. Nicholas (for a description *v*. W. de Gray Birch, *Journ. Brit. Archaeol. Assoc.* 1888, p. 222) (see Fig. 32.9). In the lights representing the episode of The Child and Cup of Gold and The Miracle of the Corn Sacks there

Fig. 32.11 Vatteville Church Glass, 1528.

are ships, and that of the former has double reef-points in three rows sewn in all over the sail.

The window in Gresford Church, Denbighshire, illustrating the Life of St. Mary, is glass dating from about 1480. In the Presentation of St. Mary panel there is a small one-masted ship under way whose sail has two rows of reef-points, one in the head and the other in the foot (see Fig. 32.10).

In the south transept window of Vatteville church, on the left bank of the Seine, about two miles below Caudebec-en-Caux, there is, as in Villequier church on the opposite bank, a representation of reef-points in glass of the early part of the sixteenth century. I have described these examples in a previous article (*Camb. Ant. Soc. Communications*, vol. xv 1911, p. 31) and later in the work of my friend the Abbé Anthiaume, Aumônier du Lycée du Havre, *Cartes Marines, Constructions navales, Voyages de Découverte chez les Normands*, 1500–1650 (Paris, 1916). I am indebted to him for much kind assistance extending over many years in obtaining information as to mediaeval representations of ships in Normandy, and for now lending to me the block of my sketch for his book of the ship *La Roumaine* of the privateer *Billes* as she is depicted in the south transept window of Vatteville church. This sketch is of the ship only (see Fig. 32.11); in the glass we see the crew and on the poop a conventionally gigantic figure of St. Clement by which the artist displaced the mizzen mast the ship evidently carried, an artistic expedient which explains the incompleteness of the back-stays. The double reef-points and a suggestion of reef-bands are seen in the upper half of the mainsail. In the beautiful window of 1823 in Villequier church in which the chief picture is a naval combat one of the ships has similar double reef-points.

The latest example of early reef-points known to me is of about the same time as the Norman glass, for it occurs in Braun and Hogenburg's *Orbis Civitates Terrarum*, published at Cologne. Of this work there were several editions, the first bearing the date 1573. Mr. Morton Nance's sketch of a 'Turkish' *terrada* or *gelve* from the woodcut in this Cologne picture book appears as Fig. 32.12. Allowing for the time occupied in collecting the drawings, we may safely call this curious *terrada* a ship of about 1550. However exaggerated and fanciful some of her ornamental and other features may be there can be little doubt that reef-points are intended by the lines of short ropes on her fore and mainsails. This example from eastern waters must be accepted with some reserve in the absence of knowledge as to how the sixteenth century authors of *Orbis Civitates Terrarum* procured and reproduced their pictures. It is not impossible that the reef-points were introduced for artistic effect from sources much nearer Cologne than the Gulf of Aden and Levant, though

32.12

the care as to the details of the ships represented renders the *terrada* worth mentioning.

With the continuance of this puzzle of the disuse of reef-points in large vessels of the northern seas at least for more than a century it is natural to enquire if the tradition of reef-points was maintained in smaller craft. As to this I have to thank Mr. Morton Nance for some suggestive notes. He is inclined to think that square-sailed fishing craft are very likely to have continued the use of reef-points when they were discontinued in large vessels, though pictorial evidence of a reliable kind is wanting. Mediaeval reef-points are sometimes represented all over the sail, sometimes near its head only, and again, sometimes near its foot only. No doubt many representations still remain undiscovered, but in those we know the position on the sail does not exhibit any chronological grouping. Modern reef-points, *i.e.*, those since the fitting was revived, are in the upper portion of a square sail: those of fore-and-aft sails are in its lower portion. The latter may be neglected, as jibs were first fitted in ships of the Royal Navy only as late as 1705 and it seems likely that the reef-points of lateen sails were introduced as imitations from square sails at a comparatively late date. As regards square sails, Mr. Nance calls my attention to Dutch fishing boats having reef-points near the foot of the sail, while Norwegian boats sometimes carried a row of reef-points near the head of the sail as well as the customary rows near its foot. He also remarks on the

Lanvéoc fishing boat, a primitive Breton type, which still carries a row of reef-points near the head and two or three rows near the foot, the latter being very possibly inherited from her ancestors of a time before reefing at the head of the sail, *i.e.* modern ship fashion, was introduced. Mr. Alan H. Moore tells me that the Biserta fishing boats also carry reefs at the head and foot of their sails. Mr. Nance is inclined to look upon the sail reefing below as a survival of the ancient method of northern European waters, and such examples as square-sailed Norwegian boats and the Lanvéoc craft as transitions to the modern fashion of reefing a square sail above. Reefing below has survived in fore-and-aft sails by reason of their cut rendering reefing above impossible.

Mr. Nance has recently sent to me some notes on the possible meaning and use of the bight or ring, in some instances represented (probably incorrectly) as a knot, which is seen in mediaeval drawings of *double* reef-points at their insertion into the sail. I hope that he will publish his elucidation of this curious and hitherto unexplained detail of rigging in these pages. It occurs so uniformly and through so long a period that there can be little doubt that it is a real fitting and not merely an artist's fancy.

From Vol VI, No 3, §§77–85 (*March 1920*)

❡ 33   EARLY REEFING

One would almost think that amongst mediaeval draughtsmen there had been a conspiracy to conceal all the mysteries of the contemporary 'Shipman'—a sort of fellow-feeling, perhaps, for those who, like themselves were engaged in work that must savour of the marvellous to plain men.

One of the most baffling of these mysteries is that of the reefing-gear that they show; for if they are to be trusted—and from the agreement that exists among them on the point, trusted I think they must be—sails, during the long period from the first reefs to the earliest bonnets that afterwards for a time replaced them, had their reefs fairly evenly distributed over their whole surface, instead of being confined as in our day to their head or foot.

Those secretive draughtsmen seldom or never show such a sail reefed. The only exception that I can think of is that shown in Fig. 33.1 from the early 14th century copy of *Albumazar*, Sloan MS. 3983, in the British Museum.

This is not supremely satisfactory either; but I think it may give a hint as to how such reefs were used.

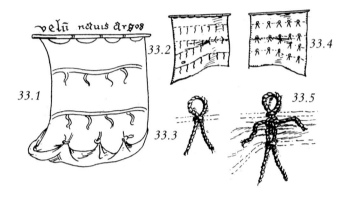

If I am right, this was quite different from our own reefing method; for it seems to me that in the reef taken in this 'sail of the ship *Argo*,' the engaging reef-points are not those on opposite sides of the sail, but that the points of a band at the bottom of the sail are tied to those of the band next above them, forming a bag along the sail. Such a bag-reef is still all that is ever taken in the mat sail of an East African *mlepe*, but we may suppose that a second tying, of the corresponding reef-points on the other side, was made on the sail of the *Argo*, reducing this bag to a respectable reef—a clumsy, but quite possible way of reducing canvas.

I shall not pretend to be absolutely convinced that the *Albumazar* artist knew what he was about in drawing such a reef, but *if he did*, he has explained the numerous reefs that we see on mediaeval sails, for a reef taken in this way might be made as readily in the middle of a sail as at its head or its foot. See Fig. 33.2.

Supposing this theory to be sound, it provides an object for another type of reef-point that we see in the period just before bonnets came into use—the time at which they were commonest being the early 15th century. This, which must be considered as an advance on the earlier single point, is composed of a loop from which dangle two reef-points, the whole being a length of rope stitched to the sail so as to leave a bight of it open—the loop—while its ends form the points, Fig. 33.3.

Now, supposing that reefs *were* taken in the way above suggested, there must have been considerable difficulty in reefing a flapping sail, for the jerking canvas would be tearing open the first tie of each reef-knot before the second could be made to secure it. Here we see how the loops and double points come to the rescue.

We will suppose that a reef is to be taken in the sail, Fig. 33.4, and that to save the readjustment of tacks and sheets this is taken not at its foot, as in the *Argo* sail, but right across its middle. The two points on the upper reef-band are passed over and through the loop on the lower band, thus at once obtaining a *purchase* by means of which the reef can be taken and held while the ends of the two points are being tied in a reef-knot over their own standing part, as in Fig. 33.5. The process would probably be repeated on the other side of the sail, making a very firm, if to our eyes awkward-looking, reef, across the middle of the sail. If a reef were wanted again, either above or below this one, the loops of one side of the sail would give a purchase for the two points of the other, either at the foot or at the head, which explains why loops are present at the uppermost reef-band and points at the lowermost, where but for this possibility they would be useless.

It is obvious that such a sail would never be 'close-reefed,' for if every possible reef were taken no canvas would remain spread, but the means given by such all-over reefs of reducing canvas at any part of it may have been valued by our sailor ancestors. However clumsy we think it, we have to remember that the mediaeval reef was replaced by that still, as compared with modern reefing, awkward method of reducing canvas by casting off a bonnet; so that there is no reason to believe that it was distinguished by any great handiness. There is a general absence from these sails of reef-cringles. These under any theory to reefing, however, must have been present, unless the reef-points were extended to the bolt rope itself, where we do not find them depicted, so that their absence does not affect the present suggestion in any way.

By R. MORTON NANCE, from *Notes*, Vol VI, No 3, §§85–86 (*March 1920*)

34

THE MEDIAEVAL ARTIST

HIS VALUE AS A WITNESS IN NAUTICAL AFFAIRS

By Gregory Robinson

Our knowledge of the mediaeval ship being so largely dependent upon the work of the artist of the time, it seems proper that the naval archaeologist should make some enquiry into that person's character and attainments, and the state of his mind. It seems especially necessary, since the evidence which has been brought to light of late years in the form of inventories and fragmentary writings, throws a great deal of doubt on his truthfulness. Although there are few means by which he can be checked in nautical affairs—there are no draughts, no models—we can fortunately check his statements upon matters with which we are well acquainted.

Serving as a headpiece to this paper is the shield of the Black Prince, (Fig. 34.1) and on it are six representations of the lion, the king of beasts. Here then, I think, is evidence enough to put the fellow on his trial. First will come into the witness box a gentleman from Regent's Park. He will tell us he has been for many years the keeper of the Lion House, and has never seen such beasts. Big game hunters will speak rudely of them. Zoologists and other learned folk (with whose names I am not acquainted) will all explain in their several ways how such beasts never have, and never could exist. And if the wretched artist can be persuaded into the box, how will he explain the varied proportions of his lions? And if at the last he is taxed with it, it is said to him, 'Sir, these are not like lions?' if he understands what is said to him at all, he will perhaps answer as Mr. Whistler answered when the likeness of one of his paintings to his sitter was in question—'Likeness, O that is the last thing I think about!' So on this count there is no doubt about the verdict, and the same thing will happen with the rest—his dolphins, his leopards, and his birds. He will be convicted. That will be the end of him as far as the public is concerned. But we will inquire into the state of his mind.

The mediaeval artist was a man who pleased himself, and it pleased him to decorate. The mediaeval public expected a story, so the artist and his public came to an understanding. They invented a language, it was

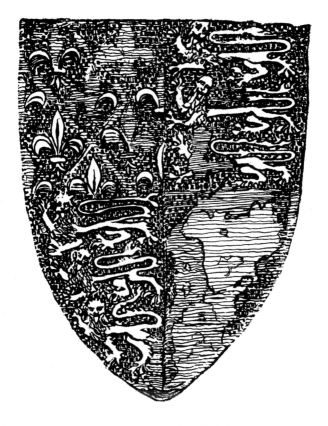

Fig. 34.1 The shield of the Black Prince in Canterbury Cathedral.

called Symbolism, it was a mixture of facts and decoration. In the fourteenth century it was mostly decoration, and facts were scanty. We can hardly doubt it, if we look at the Lions of England on the Black Prince's shield. There is a great deal of ramping and raging, but not much lion, reminding one rather of the Cheshire cat in 'Alice in Wonderland,' where only its grin was left.

It is plain, too, that everything was ruled by the shape of the space that had to be filled. The facts had to fit in where they best could. One cannot help thinking that had the arms of England been 'three ships passant' instead of the lions, we might have had articles in the MARINER'S MIRROR on the longships of the Middle Ages, and we might even have been led into discussions on the inordinate length to which bowsprits went in those days. Fortunately, we as naval archaeologists are not concerned with the 'morals' of the business, we are only concerned with the facts. It is enough for us to know that the mediaeval designer spoke in symbols to a people who understood symbols, a people whose knowledge of things both in Heaven and on Earth came to them by way of symbols. And Symbolism is a dead language in spite of many attempts at revival. Think what would happen today if the Mint were to issue a gold coinage with a representation of His Majesty, enthroned in the battleship *King George V,* and figuring as large as the funnels! It would never do. Yet the difference would only be one of degree between that and the gold coinage of Edward III.

The designer of the golden noble (Fig. 34.2, see 17 and 20) was no ship specialist, we may be pretty certain of that. He may have been the same fellow who designed the Black Prince's shield. He was told, we may suppose, that his design was to represent the King, a ship, and the sea, and he was given a very small space to work in. The King, of course, must come large in the picture, and the engraver cut him in first—there could be no distortion here—your mediaevalist had a fine sense of the 'Greater Proportion'; the lower orders and mere things could be twisted into any shape, but the King must be respected. So King, crown, sword, and shield took up most of his space, and there was little sea room left. Here your modern designer would have been beaten, but to the man who could draw lions there was no difficulty—the ship was cut in where there was room for her, and so the ship of the middle ages came by her wondrous sheer. The ship had to take that form, firstly because it suited his design, and secondly because he must find room for the fore-stage and after-castle, details which went towards the making of the symbol of a royal ship. It pleased the designer to put in a few more details, and his work was done. To the naval archaeologist it is of as much value as the work of a 'Futurist.' To the lover of beautiful things it is a little master-piece. If the shipwrights were anything like one of their successors—old Mathew Baker (he who, Mr. Oppenheim tells us, spoke ill of equals, inferiors and superiors during his very long life), they probably said hard things about the artist. They were men who used a plumb-line. The sailors I imagine didn't worry much about the ship they only laughed at it. As long as they had enough of the golden nobles to spend they were happy. It became the standard ship—I think Mr. Brindley has shown it ran through fourteen editions—and it must have had a wonderfully wide circulation, too. The designers far inland must have found it very useful when they were making their stained glass windows. The monks, il-luminating their service books and their lives of the saints, found it useful when, in the Psalms, the ships rolled to and fro like drunken men, and again when St. Paul was shipwrecked. Sometimes there may have been among the good brothers a reformed sailor, or a brother who had been to the Shrine of St. James in that doleful pilgrim ship—then we may be sure the stout Apostle was wrecked in a more ship-shape fashion.

So the little ship sailed on for many ayear. She sailed in company with other ships of course. Some with more freeboard, some with less sheer, and some with no stem ropes. They couldn't sail on for ever, they were repaired and patched again and again, and at last all were lost, driven on to the iron-bound coast of Realism; and with them perished the mediaeval ark filled with wondrous beasts. That I think is a not unfair presentment of the story of the invention and progress of the ship of the Golden Noble. It is true the lion is not on all fours (if the expression may be permitted) with the ship—not quite. Ships were more often seen, we may suppose, than lions, so that there were more opportunities of addition to the symbol of the ship. The artist did, however, occasionally come across a lion. There is a record of one of these meetings in existence—a thirteenth century drawing of a lion, endorsed—'from the quick.' Nevertheless it is, we are told, on very good authority, quite a conventional rendering. Seeing was evidently not always believing. So even supposing the artist did see ships, we cannot be certain he saw them clearly, and therefore, I think it would be as well, when we discuss these matters, to remember the Lions of England.

Mr. Brindley, in the many delightful articles which he has contributed to the MARINER'S MIRROR, I am sure, often has them in mind. But I'm afraid he sometimes forgets them. Perhaps when he tells us that the ship of the Golden Noble 'is more or less a portrait of the sailing vessel of the times,' he means very much less, and not more at all; but when later he tells us that in the reign of Henry VII, ships had become less crescent-shaped I begin to wonder whether that artist fellow of the middle ages hasn't been deceiving him—appealing to his sense of beauty, getting on the soft side of him, as it were. And then there are the stem ropes. Are we

Fig. 34.2 Golden noble of Edward III.

quite certain what their true position in the ship is? Did the oak planking really take that wonderful turn upwards? And isn't it just possible—and perhaps a little more than possible—that the engraver found his lines were going to make an awkward junction, and to avoid it, broke them with the ropes? And if I agree with Mr. Brindley that the doubtful ropes of the Bayeux Tapestry may be but an artist's convention, and I notice that the stem ropes do not appear until the Noble had obtained a wide circulation in England, and that in France, where the Noble did not circulate, there are to be found no stem-ropes, am I very unreasonable if I still doubt a little whether the stem-ropes had any existence in fact? And if I thank him (and I'm sure we all do) for that brave ship of Bourges, (see Fig. 3.1 and ¶ 5) will he forgive me if I take but little delight—as a naval archaeologist—in the pictures of the good Canon Mamerot?

We shall never know with exactness, what were the proportions of hearsay, written description, deduction, observation, and pure imagination which went to the making of the works of the mediaeval marine artist. We know that there is strong evidence of distortion, and that proportion was not the artist's strong point. Perhaps we might liken them to the reflection of a ship in very troubled waters. We may gain an isolated fact from them here and there—that is all.

We shall need stouter stuff than this if we would build a ship which will please the critical eye of Dan Chaucer's brown-necked friend, the Master of the Magdelaine, who went a-cruising from Gotland to the Cape de Finistere.

From Vol II, No 12, §§353–58 (*December 1912*)

35

AN ITALIAN SHIP OF 1339

R. Morton Nance

As a mediaeval ship of the Southern or Mediterranean, as opposed to the Northern or Ocean type, one could hardly choose a better example than the ship (Figs 35.1 and 35.2), sculptured by the Pisan artist, Balduccio, in 1339, upon the tomb of S. Peter Martyr, in the church of S. Eustorgio at Milan. Ships of her type are not rare in contemporary illuminations; but here we have, in uncompromising relief, details that as shown in these more or less crude drawings, are more open to misinterpretation.

In nearly all of these illuminated ships, for example, the sides seem to be decorated with bands, in some cases resembling the painted ports of modern merchant ships; in others, taking the form of a row of equidistant squares, with perhaps a painted design that connects them. (Figs. 35.7, 35.8 and 35.10–14).

In this sculpture we have them in something like the right proportion and without the coloured decoration, and it is evident that they are rows of projections from the hull beneath the wales, in all probability literally 'beam-ends,' that come through the outer planking of the ship. A reference to Egyptian ship-paintings will show us similar 'beam-ends;' we can trace them among the few records of the sailing ships of ancient Rome; and in some oriental craft to-day, living representatives of this ship-family that peopled the waters of the ancient world, we find these 'beam-ends' surviving. In the Mediterranean itself, as we see in Jacopo di Barberi's view of Venice, they were still to be found in the year 1500, together with the ancient twin rudders, in a two-masted lateener of pure southern type (Fig. 35.12); and, more unexpectedly even than this, we see them along the sides of great square-rigged carracks of hybrid type in pictures of almost as late a date (Fig. 35.14). In all likelihood this way of building could be traced back to a primeval paddled canoe; the beams representing thwarts that were lashed down on the gunwale, their ends outside and above it; not inside and below, as in the primitive rowed boat, that seems to have been the ancestor of our northern ships of concealed beam ends. Among ship-builders mainly occupied about the galley, with its *apostis*

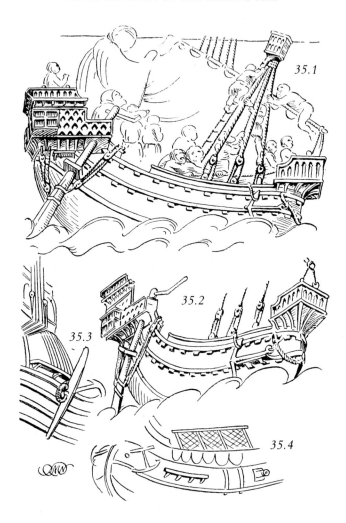

that spread out supported by beams projecting beyond the hull, it is less astonishing that such a method should have survived.

The hull of our Italian nef, following another ancient tradition, is carvel built: the stem and stern posts being covered over by the planking instead of being left projecting, as in the northern style, that originated with clinker-boats, and survived the adoption of the southern carvel-build. The wales that protect the sides here, and later become so marked a feature in all carvel-built ships, seem also to have been traditional in the southern type.

The chock of wood on the quarter, in which the rudder works, explains many vague drawings of the illuminators; the rudder-tackles, too, usually neglected or merely indicated by lines in these, are here given with such detail that we can even recognise that ancient type of block, always retained in galleys and long used for lifts even in square-rigged ships, with holes for the attachment of ropes instead of scores for a strop.

The rudder itself is of lozenge section at the blade, but rounded above, to allow of its working freely in the chock and in the hole through which it pierces the stern-castle, to offer its curiously jointed tiller to the hand of the timoneer. Such a broadside view as we have here, and in most of our illustrations, would suggest a doubt as to the number of rudders carried, but from other evidence it seems safe to say that two rudders were as much the rule in vessels of the southern type, from the steering paddles of its ancestral canoe down to the twin rudders of the modern boat of the Venetian lagoons, as the single starboard rudder, shifting later back to the stern-post, from whence, as a steering oar it had come, was the typical steering apparatus for ships of the north.

The elaborate stern-castle, with its rising stages and side galleries, reminds one more of that ancient terra-cotta ship found at Amathus, probably a far back ancestor, than of anything that northern waters had to show at the same time, although in detail the gothic arcades and the lattice work are nearly matched in contemporary ship-seals of the North.

The fore-castle is a feature not commonly seen in ships of this type, but it seems somewhat in advance of the fore-stage of northern ships at the time, and similar southern fore-castles may have suggested the later development of these fore-stages into fore-castles resembling it. A bulwark, except for a break in it aft, occupies the space between the castles.

The anchor is stockless and without the painter-ring at the crown that is so often seen on ancient anchors, the shank-painter passing round the fluke in modern style. The stout bow-rope, not a cable, will have a separate notice in Mr. H. H. Brindley's article on 'Bow-ropes' for the MARINER'S MIRROR, and need be no further mentioned here.

It will be seen, by a reference to Fig. 35.2, that the wale is expanded where the anchor rests into a sort of shelf for its reception. An anchor-rest of this sort seems to be shown in one of Carpaccio's carefully drawn ships of about a century and a half later (Fig. 35.3); and what may be the same thing appears in a ship of 1536, forming part of the decoration of a piece of plate in the Louvre (Fig. 35.4). These latter may, of course, be chain-wales gone astray, but such an anchor-rest, even if usual, might have escaped further record as an inconspicuous detail.

Beneath the side brackets of the stern-castle, and just abaft the rudder is another such shelf, except that here it stands alone, the wale running with too lofty a sheer to serve as a base for it. With unshipped tiller, the

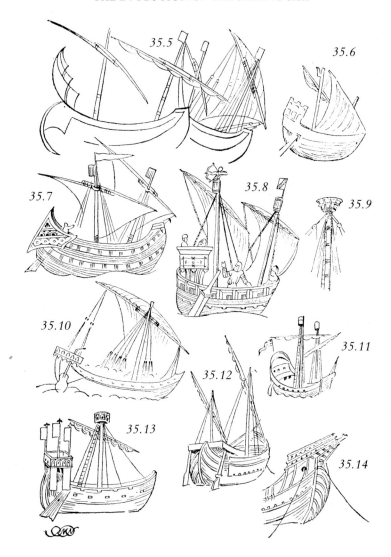

rudder, when not in use, may have been lowered free of its chock, and again hauled up to lie horizontally upon this shelf.

The fore-raking pole-mast, placed further forward than it would be in the contemporary square-rigged northern ship, is rigged as simply as that, but in quite another way. It follows closely the ancient southern tradition which, even to the very names of its parts, came down almost unchanged from the square-sailed ships of antiquity to the latest lateen galley, and, in a modified form, is still extant in the Mediterranean. The shrouds, not rattled in the northern style, are each set up by means of a tackle running in blocks instead of dead-eyes, and all leave the mast together from beneath a lashing. The ties, instead of running in the hounds through the mast and below the eyes of the rigging, as in the northern style, go through holes or over sheaves in an upright block, the *calcet*, that is morticed on the mast-head. This *calcet* here is hidden by the fore part of a top, the bulk of which stands abaft the *calcet*, and consequently above the eyes of the rigging. A square top, or half-top like this, frequently appears on the ships of contemporary northern seals, but always, reversing this southern practice, stands before the mast and below the eyes of the rigging. Even when in later years the northern square sail was adopted for large sea-going ships of southern ports, this ancient fashion of rigging the mast was not abandoned. It seems for a time to have prevailed even in the North over the native style; and one commonly sees great carracks represented with unratlined shrouds set up by blocks, tops set above the eyes of the rigging, and, as here, one narrow rope-ladder forming the means of access to them. (Fig. 35.9) Possibly the sailors inherited skill in swarming up bare shrouds caused them to leave the despised rope-ladder to the men-at-arms, who climbed to defend the top in fight, but it must be remembered that the huge sails could be worked almost entirely from the deck, and that they were lowered for furling.

The details of the sail in the carving are few, and may be better seen in some of the pictures that have been preserved (Figs. 35.5–8, 35.10). These shows sails that range in shape between the extremes of triangular lateen and high, squarish-headed lug, including some of the intermediate shape of the carved sail. Yards are shown composed of two parts, lashed together and furnished with parrels, halyards, vangs, and the ropes, called 'orse' and 'poge' in southern sea-language, that served somewhat as the mizzen bowlines of a 17th century ship. These latter ropes are the only details amongst those mentioned that find a place in the S. Peter Martyr ship; a rope is shown, however, between the middle and after shrouds that may be a truss fall, and from the peak six rope-ends run up, converging to a point that lies far beyond the limit of the carving. These might be supposed to be the legs of a lift-crowfoot, but if so it is difficult to see how such a lift, not otherwise recorded at this date, could run; for even assuming a top-mast, which was not a feature of this southern rig, these ropes tend away from the place where a top-mast would have stood, and they remain for the writer a nut which he must hand over for cracking to the united efforts of our Society.

From Vol I, No 12, §§334–39 (*December 1911*)

36

NORTHERN SHIPS OF
CIRCA 1340

By R Morton Nance

The sculptor of the ship upon the tomb of Saint Peter Martyr (see 35, Fig. 19.2) has given us there a typical ship of the South in 1339, with all its Mediterranean features as yet uninfluenced by the example of Northern visitors to those waters.

Of our Northern, or Ocean, square-rigged ships at the same date we have no single representation that is equally full and reliable; but amongst the ships that Mr. H. H. Brindley has already introduced to us, as illustrating the mediaeval use of reef-points, are some that, showing common features, seem to provide material from which we may get some idea of at least one type of Northern ship. These ships, to which have been added one or two others that seem to bear on the subject, have been repeated here for convenience of reference, and, in some cases, enlarged.

As a starting-point we cannot do better than take the miniature of Marco Polo's ships leaving Venice, reproduced by Mr. Brindley (Fig. 27.1). The date of this miniature, perhaps more to be depended on as such than those of seals, which may be taken from earlier designs, just forms a parallel to that of the St. Peter Martyr ship, with the Latin style of which we may compare her Northern build, for it was executed between 1338 and 1344.

It will at once be seen that vessels of two types are shown in this picture, four of the ships being one-masted sailing-ships, while two are two-masted, and have oars in addition to their sails. The latter type is evidently the galley of the South; but drawn by a Northern artist, who, unfamiliar with the actual vessel, probably worked from a verbal description. 'Beaked, with an *apostis* along which oars are grouped in threes; having a *batticopa*, or poop-tilt, astern; two-masted, with the lesser mast abaft the greater; the main-mast having a half-top.' Such a description of the actual galley of the time faithfully carried out in his work may yet have produced the result that we have here; for the artist, full of Northern notions, has grafted them on to each detail of his drawing. He places

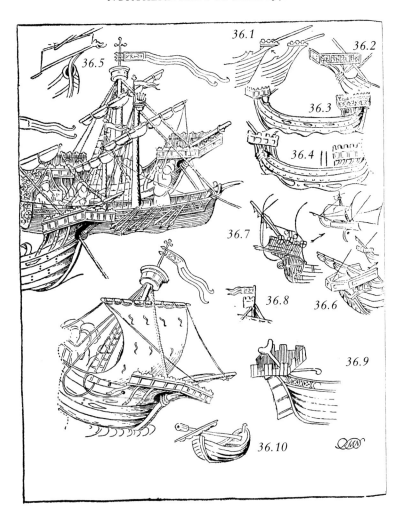

36.1
36.2
36.5
36.3
36.4
36.7
36.8
36.6
36.9
36.10

the main masts of his galleys upright and amidships, instead of making them stand forward and rake over the bows; the half-tops he places not, correctly, abaft the masthead, but before it in the scarcely yet abandoned Northern fashion shown in the Rye seal (Fig. 36.8). Abaft this mainmast, but so close as to leave no room for working its sail, is the mizen-mast, which, like the main-mast, is given Northern square sails instead of the triangular or lug-shaped lateen sails of the South. The beak at the prow, too, is quite unlike the real galley spur, and probably like nothing that ever existed. Were we in search of a typical galley, then, we should put this picture aside as without value; but when we consider it solely as a means of obtaining knowledge of Northern shipping, the very defects of these galleys serve to inspire confidence in the genuinely Northern character of their companion sailing ships.

These ships, as we see by the way in which their planks are shaded, are clinker-built; but instead of the clench-nails that we see joining the lapping edges of the planking in the seals (Figs. 36.2–4), the nails are placed in such a way as to suggest that the artist has paid more attention to the occasional vertically-arranged nails that fastened the butts of the planks and held them at intervals to the ribs, than to the nails that clenched them all together fore and aft. To get, then, a just idea of the nailing of these planks in either vessel, one would have to blend these two half-truths.

At both ends of the simple boat-like hull are 'castles.' These castles, or stages, when we first see them on Northern seals, are square or oblong platforms raised, quite independently of the stem or stern-posts, upon wooden props that seem to have stood on the deck, or perhaps went through it to rest upon the frame of the ship. Later we find them moved out, forward and aft respectively, so as to bring the stem and stern-posts into use as supports, and still later the 'castles' are projected beyond the ends of the ship so as to leave the stem and stern-post-heads, rising in their midst. Of these now useless survivals the stern-post head was the first to go, the introduction of the stern-hung rudder in place of the starboard steering-paddle necessitating the decapitation of the stern-post below the level of the tiller, and at the same time the stern-castle, now unsupported by the stern-post, was modified in shape, becoming lower and longer than the fore-castle which, before, it had strongly resembled. It is at this stage of development that we find our ships of 1338–1354.

In these no trace is seen of a rising stem-head, although they are still shown in pictures of later dates. The perspective leaves a little doubt as to the shape of the forecastles; but they are probably rectangular and have not yet acquired the pointed fore-end that came into fashion later; and eventually, by its growth aft, came to occupy the whole forecastle space, thus making it the triangular forecastle of the fifteenth century. The upright posts of the old fighting stage are still represented here by the curving struts or skids that join the rectangular 'castles' to the curving sides as they swell out from bow and stern beneath; but the spaces between these supports are filled in so as to form rooms below the 'castles.' The Rye seal (Fig. 36.3) shows a cabin window between such struts aft, and the miniature and some of the seals here given suggest that there was usually a great cable-way or hawse close to the stem-post. The ships in Fig. 36.1 show a slight upward projection from the bulwark which may have some bearing upon this hawse in the other examples (Figs 36.2–4). Assuming this to be a break in the bulwark, forming a fair-lead for the cable, we seem to have in the Rye seal (Fig. 36.3) a similar fair-lead, but one placed further forward, and in the others the fair-lead, now close up to the stem, forms the after edge of a great hawse-hole. That this was for long an approved form of hawse-hole is shown by the fact that two of the ships engraved by W. A. are fitted with semi-circular hawses close beside the stem (Fig. 36.5). A comparison of Figs. 36.2 and 36.4 shows that this great hole forward was also connected in some way with the 'bow-warp' with which Mr. Brindley has made us familiar; but, as two ships in the miniature are clearly anchored and have their cables put out of this hole, we see that, whatever the 'bow-warp' may be, this hole is, in part at least, a hawse-hole.

Along the sides of the clinker-built ships of the North, as displayed upon seals of the thirteenth and fourteenth centuries, we very commonly see projections of slightly varying form. These for the most part are three in number, and follow one another along the same strake, their shape usually inclining towards that of a spear-head with its obtuse end aft; but, occasionally, they are mere shapeless lumps, irregularly spaced. In our miniature we have them, too, and it seems evident that they are fender-cleats that perform for these 'clinkers' something of the service rendered to carvel-built boats by their wales, in protecting their sides, being sharp-ened forward to allow of an easier gliding past their surface, of the water. On turning again to W. A., we find that these fender-cleats were still in use in his day, as additional protections beneath the wales of the carvel-built ships of his prints (see 44).

Another feature common to the ships of the manuscript at the Bodleian Library and to those of W. A. is the comb-like arrangement beneath the bowsprit. This is rarely seen in mediaeval drawings of ships; it is none too plain here; and but for the ships of W. A. it might easily have been passed over. W. A., however, carefully as he has drawn it, leaves us in doubt as to its purpose; and it is only when, here, we see the bowlines leading out to it, and how they might at will be hitched on to an inner or outer notch, that we recognise it as a 'bowline comb' by means of which the bowline might be adjusted, much as the 'vargord' of a Cornish lugger was by its 'comb' or 'timmy-noggy,' according to the wind or the height to which the sail was hoisted. The artist, however, seems to have studied the rigging of these ships from a vessel with furled sails; for he has shown the bowlines of his ship under sail still leading down from the yard instead of from the leeches of the sail. Besides the excellent examples of 'bowline-combs' given by W. A., they are to be seen on the bowsprits of ships in a book of sailing directions of c. 1490 (Fig. 7, from *Archeologia*, vol. 57, pt. 1), where in some instances the artist has confused them with the somewhat similar lines of a furled spritsail. A manuscript in the Bibliothèque Nationale (MS. Français, 9199) gives us some ships with furled sails laced along beneath their bowsprits which seem to be the result of an ignorant copying of this 'bowline-comb.' (Fig. 36.6). A 'bowline-comb' seems in Italy to have been fitted above, instead of beneath, the bowsprit end. (See illustrations to Mr. G. Callender's article, *Ships of Maso Finiguerra*, Figs. 38.5 and 38.6).

The further details of these simply rigged ships continue to show us Northern features, quite different from those of the Saint Peter Martyr ship. Thus the shrouds here are rattled and their eyes are concealed by the base of the round-top that encircles the mast. Above the top rises a staff rather than a mast, whose chief purpose seems to be that of supporting a cross and a large streamer that swings vane-like on the staff and points to the wind with two or three barbs: The yard is a single stick, and its parrel is a single string of trucks; braces are shown leading to the after castle, and, as we have seen, bowlines are, wrongly, made fast to the yard arms; tacks and sheets, too, are clearly shown, the former leading in at a hole in the loof. In this connection it is interesting to notice that the words corresponding to our 'hawse' in other Northern languages apply to the tack, which would seem to indicate that the hawse or hals (literally a neck, or throat) was not originally appropriated to the cable alone.

The rudder in the portion of the miniature illustrated is not visible, only one of the ships, that of which the bow is seen, having its stern in plain view; but this is in the original of just the same shape as that in the Rye seal (Fig. 36.3) and like that, it has braces at each gudgeon.

In the same volume as the miniature containing these ships is another ship (by a different artist, but of similar date) where the rudder is drawn as it would appear beneath the water line, and we see that the stern-post was still at this time rounded off into the keel below, as in earlier ships; the rudder ending just at the point where the stern-post curved round. (Fig. 36.9).

In this last-named miniature we see the tiller and also another detail that would probably have been actually present in the other ships—the myke, or mast-crutch. This, however, is so rarely shown that, but for W. A., we might hardly look upon it as a permanent fitting of mediaeval ships: in his ships, even, it is usually a crutch for the mizen-yard, although in one instance, that of the 'trader' (see 44) it seems to be placed, like the myke of our illustration, for the support of a lowered mast. Fig. 36.10 shows, from the *Livre des Merveilles* (Bib. Nat. MS. Français, 2810), the

Ark of Noah with the mast lowered on to a myke which the artist has forgotten to put in; she is, however, not quite such a helpless hulk as the Ark of the Miracle Play of the Deluge, written in Lancashire about 1360:—

> 'Withouten mast other myke other myry bawelyne
> Cable, other capstan to clyppe to her ankrez
> Hurrock, other hande helme hasped on rother
> Other any sweande sayle to seche after haven.'

Most of these necessary ship-fittings, lacking in the Mother of all Ships, we have traced in these seals and miniatures, with some others that she wanted equally; but we have not been able as yet to trace a 'hurrock,' and although a capstan is probably represented in the merchant ship of considerably later date, shown in Fig. 37.1, we still have none to show of a date to fit the ships illustrated here. That the mediaeval 'hurrock,' was the same thing as the 'hurrock' of Shetland and Orkney fishermen, or the 'thurruck' of the men of Norfolk, seems doubtful, for if so it was merely the stern floor of the boat, the removal of which must have made the Ark a coffin-ship of the worst order, and the above quotation together with another example of the use of the word quoted in the N. E. D. (where Jonah is said to have held on by the 'hurrock,' while lying on a board in the bottom of the boat), both suggest that the mediaeval 'hurrock' was a fitting rather than a structural portion of a ship or boat, and, one would imagine from the *Deluge* quotation, an important one. Possibly, were all the dialect words used by the fishermen of all countries collected and examined we should find a better solution to this and other puzzles, for it is certainly amongst the traditional users of the most simply rigged boats that we should expect to find such ancient words surviving in their original uses.

From Vol III, No 2, §§33–39 (*February 1913*)

37

A TRADER AND A MAN-OF-WAR—LATE XIV CENTURY

R MORTON NANCE

The miniatures that illustrate a late fourteenth century *Livre de Merveilles* in the *Bibliothèque Nationale* (*M.S. Français, 2810*), show us, besides some fantastically imagined Oriental ships and almost equally impossible European vessels, drawn by other artists, the two more reasonable specimens here illustrated. These are intended to represent crusading ships voyaging to the Holy Land, but they are, of course, ships of the miniaturist's own time—late in the fourteenth century—and from the details shown would seem to belong to the northern, rather than to the Mediterranean, school of sea-architecture.

The bow of the first is not unlike that of W. A.'s 'fifteenth century trader' (see 44). The stem-head, though less curved and pointed aloft, still rises high and is flanked by similar staring hawse-holes; the bulwarks, too, are raised forward in a way that is suggested by a rail on the larboard bow of W. A.'s ship. With the bow, however, all likeness to this ship, nearer

37.1

to it in age, ceases; for the deep, square stern and skid-strengthened sides are far more suggestive of those other Flemish ships of the sixteenth century that were, perhaps, hulks. The uncastled bow, with its one curved skid to represent the many of the 'hulk,' would seem to bear out the idea that there may be more than a chance likeness between this ship and the 'hulk,' and that it may indeed be the 'hulk's' true fourteenth century ancestor.

The object seen in the after-castle would seem to be the head of a capstan with four holes for capstan-bars. At this time it is extremely doubtful if these holes would all be on one level, as the oldest capstans of which we know had their bars going right through the capstan at, of course, different levels, but where so much 'artistic license' has already been taken, perhaps we may allow this undue regularity to pass. The only other features that seem to call for comment are the knots upon the sail, that seem to represent the fastenings of a bonnet rather than reef-points, but may be either, and the anchor with its clear details of stock, ring, flukes and painter-ring. The unarmed crew or passengers, the absence of a forecastle, and the heavy build of this ship, proclaim her a merchant-man, and contrast strikingly with the armour-clad warriors and more warlike build of the other crusading vessel.

This is more like the ships that we are accustomed to expect in drawings of the time, the warship being usually demanded by the incidents to be illustrated in old histories and romances, but she, too, has her individuality. Both in this ship and that just described, there is some uncertainty as to whether their hulls are clinker, or carvel-built, the wales along the sides in the trader seeming to point rather to carvel-building and the lower portions of the warship seeming clearly by their shading to be clinker-worked. In the latter the hull seems to be heightened abaft the mast by a structure of upright planking strengthened by a wale above and below, and again with three heavy skids. The three projections below the upper strake amidships seem to be fenders, such as those on W. A.'s before-quoted ship, rather than beam-ends that project, such as are found usually on ships of the Latin type (see 35). The wide tiller-hole, perhaps, shows a fashion that preceded the long-lasting one of a hollow, horizontal counter, with a small arched tiller-hole cut in it, but it is also like that of the flights and other round-sterned craft of the seventeenth century, in which it may have been perpetuated. The after-castle with panelled sides has at each corner a post with a decorated cap. These ornaments a little suggest the lantern-turrets of some fifteenth century ships; but here nothing beyond decoration seems to be intended. The forecastle shows no similar ornaments and is even differently constructed; its shape, in plane resembling the pine-end of a house, shows a form earlier than that of the triangular forecastle that was in fashion during the greater part of the fifteenth century. Details of rigging are as scanty here as in the trader, but we see a parrel not shown there, and the fore-stay seems to lead not to the stem, but out on the bowsprit; this, however, would certainly be wrong at this date, so we may fairly safely conclude that the rope leading to the bowsprit is really a bowline. The 'jack' at the bowsprit end is certainly an early, if not the first, appearance of a flag in this position.

The first recorded date for the *Livre de Merveilles* is 1413, when it was presented to the Duc de Berry; but it is believed to be older by a good many years, and may almost certainly be ascribed to the concluding years of the 14th century.

From Vol II, No 6, §§174–76 (*June 1912*)

38

THE SHIPS OF MASO FINIGUERRA

By Geoffrey Callender

John Ruskin in 1873 bought for the sum of one thousand pounds a collection of some ninety-nine early Florentine drawings from the pen of an unknown master. Until 1840, they had lain in Florence, but in that year were purchased by Professor Schaeffer, of Heidelberg. They passed through various hands before Ruskin obtained them. But their pedigree was unimpeachable. Ruskin valued the pictures not alone for their antiquity but for their beauty. He had several of them framed to decorate his walls and made gifts of others to his friends.

Fifteen years after their acquisition the sketches came under the observation of Sir Sidney Colvin. He scrutinized them narrowly, set upon them an even higher value than Ruskin: in fact, very quickly convinced himself that they were of unique interest and a possession beyond price. He set to work to convince the great critic that the British Museum had a first claim upon them if ever he felt tempted to part with them. Ruskin rose to the occasion and very generously offered to sell the whole collection then and there. He refused to take a penny more than he had given for the drawings and enthusiastically set himself to recover all the fugitive sheets. The pictures had been numbered at some time or other; not by the artist, but by some other hand. This enumeration, though obviously at variance with the original scheme of the composition enabled the folios to be checked in some measure and set in some sort of order.

The pictures are drawn on paper measuring thirteen inches by nine. They differ in tone. Some are pale and some are dark. They display every shade of umber and sepia from yellowish or greyish to the richest brown. But they are all executed in pen outline, sometimes over a faintly visible sketch in chalk. The shadows are also suggested by the pen, but in many cases the strokes and cross-strokes are reinforced by the brush.

It seems evident that the artist intended to illustrate some compendium or epitome of universal history such as the *Historia adversus Paganos* of Orosius which King Alfred translated for the instruction of his people.

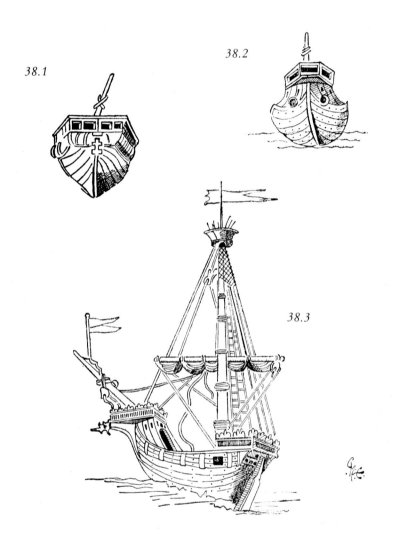

38.1

38.2

38.3

The pictures portray many of the well-known characters in sacred and profane literature, Jason and Medea, Adam and Eve, Daedalus and Icarus, Jeremiah and Ezekiel, Nimrod and Tubal Cain, Dido and Æneas, Theseus and Pirithous, Cain and Abel. There is a most ingenious architectural restoration of the Maze of Minos at Crete and a carefully modelled elevation of Noah's Ark. In several of the more ambitious drawings the artist gives a loose rein to his vivid imagination and intense delight in realism. Notably is this the case in the picture of Deucalion and Pyrrha raising a new generaiton by the simple process of flinging stones over their shoulders.

But the interest of nautical archaeologists is centred in the drawings of *Orpheus, Jupiter, Egeus,* and *Æneas.* Orpheus is depicted playing upon his lute and all nature listens to his music, the birds, the beasts, the fishes, the trees, the flowers, the rivers and the sea. And on the sea are two ships.

Jupiter is shown as a blustering, swaggering bully. He has just deposed his father and landed on the island of Crete. He stands there in a defiant attitude with head thrown back and legs apart: truly bombastic, for his island is hardly large enough to accommodate two people. But this enables the artist to give an unimpeded view of the sea, and close at hand are two ships in which presumably Jupiter has reached the island. Into one of these (Fig. 38.3) the artist has put some of his finest work.

The picture of Egeus shows the monarch's death. The forgetful Theseus returns home with the fatal black sails and the unhappy father casts himself with the most literal directness head foremost from the topmast battlement of his palace into the wine-dark sea. The ship of Theseus is a two-masted vessel and, for more reasons than one, a most interesting craft.

There are two illustrations to the story of Æneas. In the first the hero lands at Carthage and is welcomed by Queen Elisa. He appears to have brought his ship in a most unseamanlike fashion stern foremost to the shore and then sprung lightly from the poop or rather stern-castle to the rocky cliffs above. We must not quarrel with his mode of disembarking for it enables the artist to give a particularly detailed view of the stern works of the ship. In the second picture Dido kills herself while the false Trojan sails heartlessly away.

The entire series of ninety-nine pictures was in 1898 reproduced in facsimile by modern photographic methods and published by Mr. Bernard Quaritch under the name of *A Florentine Picture Chronicle.* This handsome volume contains a learned and interesting introduction by Sir Sidney Colvin, who makes it his business to answer two questions. When were the drawings executed? And by whom?

As to the first point there is happily no room for doubt. The evidene supplied by the architecture, the armour and the dresses makes it perfectly clear that the artist was a Florentine of the first half of the fifteenth century. More than that. It may be safely affirmed that he was the devoted admirer of Donatello whose *David, St. George,* and *Baptist* appear with little change in these pen and ink sketches. Like Donatello, our artist was a realist with a healthy and genial dependence on the facts of actual life.

It is one thing to date the pictures and quite another thing to establish the actual identity of the craftsman who produced them. We need not follow Sir S. Colvin into his reasons for believing that Maso Finiguerra was the man. It will be sufficient for us that Sir Sidney is himself quite convinced of the correctness of his attribution.

Maso Finiguerra was born in 1426 and died in 1464. He was at first a goldsmith as also at one time were Verocchio, Ghirlandaio and Botticelli. Like them, he developed into something greater. At one time it was thought that he and he alone was the inventor of the process of engraving on copper with the burin. Sir S. Colvin while robbing him of the sole credit for this, ranks him among the foremost pioneers of the new hand-maid of the arts. In fact, he believes that these unique drawings were the work of a goldsmith-engraver who preferred the role of draughtsman to that of metal-chaser, and desired to render permanent his finest efforts with the pen.

Being a pioneer, being perhaps the foremost pioneer in the art of copper engraving, it was not for Maso to know; it was for him to discover the limitations of the burin. We may question whether the most skilful of the early engravers could have copied one-half of the intricate beauty of his pictures. Were then any of the ninety-nine sketches that Ruskin bought ever reproduced by mechanical process? Sir S. Colvin has happily discovered a certain number of prints that look as if they were intended for reproductions of Maso's designs, and in the *Florentine Picture Chronicle* these prints are set on the pages opposite to the sketches with which they correspond. As we should expect, the modification is considerable, and what this involves may be seen by comparing Fig. 38.4 with Fig. 38.7. Fig. 38.4 is Maso's drawing. Fig. 38.7 is from an engraving which Sir S. Colvin believes to have been produced either by Maso himself or else by one of his pupils. There is one mark of identification which Sir S. Colvin himself has overlooked. Alike in the drawing and in the engraving the ship has two flags flying in one direction, and a third (contrary to nature) flying in the other.

The importance of identifying a certain number of engravings as the work of the draughtsman who produced the *Picture Chronicle* will declare itself later. For the moment it is more necessary to insist upon the unique character of the *Picture Chronicle* itself.

We have, it is true, drawings by the old masters. There are multitudes, for example, by that wayward and versatile genius, Leonardo da Vinci. But these drawings when extant are in the nature of sketches and studies: rough ideas for the general composition or careful delineations of some portion of a subject, the folds of drapery, a hand holding a sword, or the

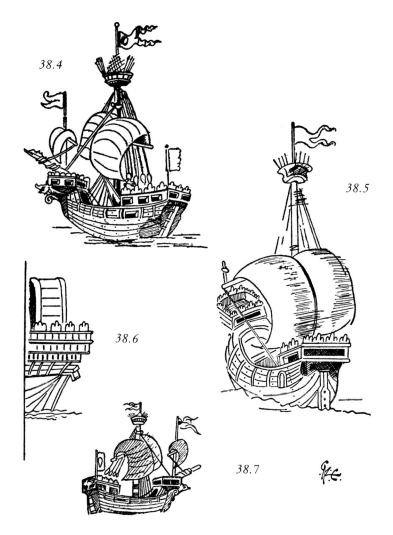

38.4

38.5

38.6

38.7

feathers of an angel's wing. But the drawings of Maso are entirely different. They are not rough sketches. They are in no sense incomplete. They are the finished works of a master who chose for reasons of his own to work in ink.

So far as our knowledge goes at present there is no parallel to this. Maso's drawings stand alone. They come midway between the miniatures of the illuminated manuscript and the drawings that were specially made for the earliest illustrators of books. Both miniatures and early engravings have this disadvantage. They treat the more minute details very much as they like. If the details are easily inserted, well: if not, then they are omitted. And this is especially true when the object portrayed is a ship. But Maso, master of his pen, had no reason for omitting detail. He revelled in it.

What a debt then is due to him from nautical archaeologists!

But while we honour him, we must not suppose that we have discovered a fifteenth century Van der Velde. Maso Finiguerra was no seaman. But at least he was a most careful and accurate draughtsman as a reference to the *Picture Chronicle* will testify. And I do not think it is too much to say that from the few little sketches of ships that he has left we shall gather quite as much as from seals and missals and painted glass. Nay, further: As Maso himself in the history of art belongs to a period of transition, so his pictures illustrate in an indirect way a transitional period in the development of ships, the period when the primitive vessels with a single great sail developed with such apparently startling suddenness into the glorious creations of the Henrician and Elizabethan navies.*

Maso was puzzled as all mediaeval artists appear to have been by the difficulty of representing the round ship of the period with its breadth of beam and great sheer. He drew a broadside view (Fig. 39.1) and put it aside unfinished, for his ship was not true to life. Her freeboard was too low, and her lines too fine. He drew two end-on views (Figs. 38.1 and 38.2), and caught successfully the breadth of beam. But these sketches failed to satisfy him. They gave no hint of the vessel's length. Finally he seems to have decided that the artist's point of view was best obtained by facing the vessel's quarter (Figs. 38.3–5). But here, though he struggled bravely, the difficulties of fore shortenings were insuperable, and his drawing is faulty and unconvincing, though in Fig. 38.5 he suggests the height of the bows, and in Figs. 38.4 and 38.5 the build of the stern.

It is difficult to form any estimate of the size of the ship which Maso intended to represent. What little evidence there is suggests that he had in mind a great ship. The vessel, for example, which illustrates the story of Theseus (Fig. 38.4) is accompanied in the full plate by an attendant galley. Above this the sailing-ship towers, like a modern *Olympic* beside a torpedo boat destroyer.

The top sides of Maso's hulls are protected by those timbers which Mr. Morton Nance calls skids (Figs. 38.1, 38.3–7). But there are no walings or rubbing-streaks, not even on the broadside view. In Fig. 38.1, however,

---

* I have redrawn from the photographic plates all the vessels that Maso has left us. These drawings may be considered facsimiles in all but one particular. The lines are of necessity clearer than the penstrokes of the faded originals.

the stem is surmounted by what appears to be a double cross. An exactly similar terminal occurs in a picture in the Academy at Venice, Carpaccio's *Arrival of St. Ursula*, where the device is clearly seen to be due to the junction of the lower and middle wales with the cutwater . It is, therefore, not unreasonable to suppose that Maso, by accident or design, omitted a feature which we should expect to find and which was actually present.

(To be continued)

From Vol II, No 10, §§294–300 (*October 1912*)

39

THE SHIPS OF MASO FINIGUERRA

(Continued)

By Geoffrey Callender

The shape of the fore-stage, or forecastle, varies in Maso's different sketches. In Figs. 38.1 and 38.5 it is obviously square. But in Figs. 39.1 and 38.3 it appears to be triangular, and in Fig. 38.2 hexagonal, like the stages of ships in the mediaeval gold coinage of England. I think that in his desire to do justice to a striking feature Maso over-accentuated the height of the forecastle archway. Certainly other pictures of a slightly later period, such as the frescoes in the Piccolomini Library at Siena, or the St. Paul's ship in King's College window, conflict with the evidence derivable from Figs. 38.3 and 38.4. It seems more probable that above this archway there was room for a middle deck with accommodation for offices of various kinds and cabins for the 'boteswain' and his mates. Such quarters would need light, and Figs. 38.2 and 38.3 show lesser apertures which should scarcely have been needed if the archway were as lofty as Maso makes it. There must have been some hatchway from here to the forecastle, seeing that there is no vestige of a ladder from the maindeck; and as we see in Figs. 39.1, 38.3–5, the forecastle was walled in on every side. The aft stage, stern-castle or poop was similar in this respect, as may be seen in a very interesting drawing at present in the Uffizi.

This drawing (1505?) is either a study by Pinturicchio for one of his frescoes in the Piccolomini Library, or (as seems more probable), a study by Raphael from his master's work. The study, exquisite in its detail, represents the embarkation of Æneas Sylvius (Pope Pius II) on his journey to the Council of Basle. The great ecclesiastic and his retinue fill the foreground of the picture, and in the middle distance is a three-masted bowspritless vessel, in dock (Fig. 39.3). The artist with minute and scrupulous care has attempted to show the size of the ship by including the figures of dockyard hands and seamen. Two of the latter stand on the port side of the poop. They cannot lean over the side of the ship, but their heads and shoulders can be seen over the edge of the rail. And the

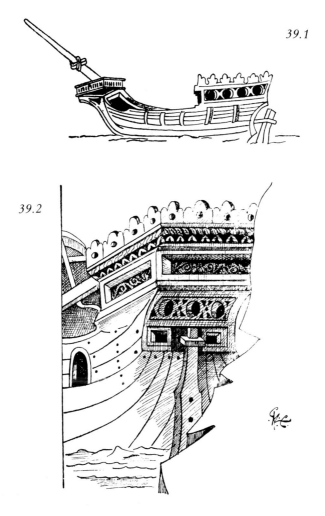

39.1

39.2

rail goes from one side of the poop to the other, cutting them off from the waist.

It will be noticed that Maso's ships on the whole are richly decorated. We notice first of all the prevalence of the Fleur de Lys pattern. It occurs in Figs. 39.1–2, 38.3–7. It appears to have been universally employed at this period for the embellishment of the poop, though not of the fore-stage. It may be traced in the illuminated MS. of Marco Polo's travels (Fig. 27.1) and again in Mr. Brindley's picture of the early sixteenth century glass in the window of Malvern Priory (Fig. 1.4). This last example would almost suggest an iron railing, very perilous to mariners in a seaway. But Maso's drawings make the matter quite clear. Fig. 39.2 shows the edging very plainly indeed. It does not bear the slightest resemblance to fleurs de lys, though the impression occurs in Fig. 38.5 and elsewhere. Evidently the edging was made of good stout planking, perforated and scalloped to please the eye at a distance. If the drawing by Raphael mentioned above may be trusted, if the scalloped border was some four feet high, then the ship in Fig. 39.2 pretty obviously had cabins between the main deck and the poop.

In this same Fig. 39.2 may be seen the 'egg and dart' moulding typical of the period under review. Other attempts to beautify the stern works show that the taste for ornament of this description was not the exclusive property of the sixteenth and seventeenth centuries. But perhaps the most interesting embellishment of all is the figure head (Figs. 38.3, 38.4, 38.7). There is indeed no diversity of pattern. The serpent-like head is almost exactly similar to that in an illustration to Rous's *Life of Warwick*, reproduced by Laird Clowes, *Royal Navy*, Vol. I, p. 376, save that Maso's figurehead is better drawn. It is not without interest to note in this connection that the figurehead first appears in the inventories of the English fleet just about the time that Maso drew his ships. Oppenheim, *Administration of the Royal Navy*, p. 15, writes, 'The *Trinity Royal* had a painted wooden leopard with a crown of copper gilt—perhaps as a figure-head.' The *Trinity Royal* was built in 1416.

I think it is more or less clear from Maso's drawings that the figurehead did not grow out of the bowsprit trophy. For in Fig. 38.3 we have both. Rather the figurehead appears to have originated in a natural desire to decorate the blunted finial of the stemhead when the stemhead was purposely elongated to support a triangular forestage. My meaning will be made clear by comparing Fig. 39.1 with Fig. 38.3.

But after all the most striking feature of Maso's ships are the portholes. There are large ports and small ports. There are ports square, circular, and oblong. They are cut in a multitude of shapes as if the device was a new one, and its novelty a thing to toy with. Maso is careful to show the thickness of the scantling in which they are pierced, not perhaps in the case of the round ports with complete success, but always with the same object (Figs. 39.1–2, 38.1–2, 38.4). And here we may ask whether or no our artist intended to represent an Entry Port. Judging by Figs. 39.1 and 38.5, one would certainly answer in the affirmative, for there is in the port quarter of the vessel what can only be an arched doorway. But in Figs. 38.3 and 38.4 this has changed its shape to that of a window, and in Fig. 38.7 (an engraving be it noted, and not of necessity from Maso's hand at all), it has shrunk to the merest indication of a horizontal hole or

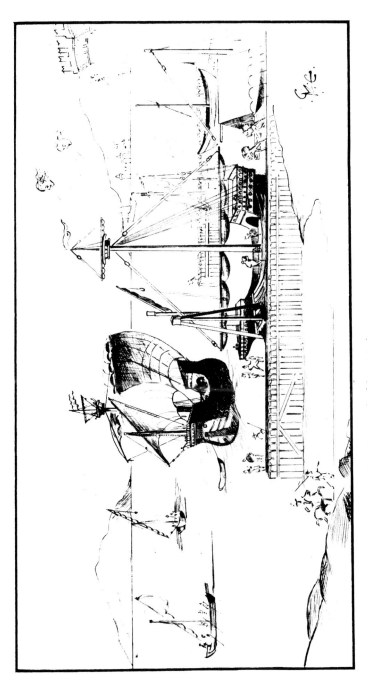

Fig. 39.3 The embarkation of Pius II. Drawn from photograph of the original.

slit. Perhaps in any case it would be misleading to refer to it as an archway. Perhaps it was a man-hole through which returning seamen might struggle up a rope ladder let down to their boat from the deck. And yet if the aperture were roomy enough to admit a man at all, surely it would be made sufficiently commodious to admit the ship's commander without obliging him to bend his head.

Of the window-ports, holes pierced primarily for light and air, it will be remarked that they have, so far as we can tell, no port-lids or any form of substitute for port-lids. And yet some of these openings are enormous. Those in Figs. 38.3 and 38.5 may of course, be carelessly drawn. If truthful representations, one would imagine that the poop cabins would be quite uninhabitable in stormy following seas. Probably the early popularity of these windows led to over-production, and the resulting discomfort and inconvenience diminished in time their number and size. Certainly the ships of the second half of the fifteenth century are hardly comparable to Maso's in this respect, and in the British Navy the use of gun-ports was not adopted till the following century, although, of course, this does not mean that ports were not pierced for purposes other than artillery. It will be noticed that in Fig. 39.2 the large oblong port in the stern is filled with a fanciful decorative scheme. At first one might suppose this to be wood-carving; but the depth of the surrounding framework almost precludes the possibility of this. It seems more likely that the artist was intending to represent ornamental metal work. If this was intended to beautify the officers' quarters it would certainly be in keeping with the general scheme for the embellishment of the stern.

Among the most interesting ports are the two shown in the end-on view of the ship, presented in Fig. 38.2. From their size it is quite evident that these like the others are intended for light and ventilation. Yet the question instantly arises, were they used for anchor work? The seal of Winchelsea (1290) shows us quite clearly that the forestage was not used for hauling in the cable. The seamen are hauling away over the bulwarks somewhat forward of amidships. Now if apertures such as those in Fig. 38.2 are faithfully drawn, their usefulness for anchor work would immediately suggest itself. At least one would think so. Perhaps as the first novelty of big windows wore off, and the ports all tended to diminish in size these forward windows shrank into hawse-holes. Some authorities, I know, trace hawse-holes back to antiquity. Mr. Cecil Torr, I believe, though I have not his book beside me as I write, identifies them with the human eye represented on ancient ships. This, I always thought, was the symbol of watchfulness. At any rate, in regard to mediaeval ships, the state of our knowledge at present leaves room for the supposition put forward above. For there are no hawse-holes in the Bayeux Tapestry, nor in the seals of the Cinque Ports, nor in pictures of ships in illuminated MSS. nor in stained glass windows.

Maso does not give a very clear notion of the rudder. In fact, the steering-gear seems different in every sketch (Figs. 39.1–2, 38.3–7. After comparing the drawings one with another we may, however, presume that the rudder itself was shaped like a church buttress. It is safe also to argue that it was hung upon the stern-post by pintles (Figs. 39.2 and 38.5), and that its component parts were riveted together by iron clamps (Fig. 38.4). Fig. 39.2 shows the tiller passing through the midmost of three square ports on a level with the rudder-head. But the most interesting particular that Maso supplies about this part of a ship's furniture is his sketch of the Whip Staff in Fig. 39.2. Our evidence as to this fitting is exceedingly meagre. It is known to have been in use in the Royal Navy by the end of the sixteenth century, but Maso, I think, puts its introduction earlier than any investigator of inventories has yet dared to do. Another interesting feature in connection with the Whip Staff is the cross-plank or helmsman's bridge. One would gather from Fig. 39.2 that the vessel was undecked. And if this were the case we should have a motive for the bridge. But the impression is corrected by Fig. 38.5 in which the relative positions of bridge and main-deck are shown. If the helmsman had been on the deck itself he would have lacked the leverage necessary to hoist the Whip Staff before putting it over to starboard or port. But apart from this there is another possible reason for the bridge. Does it not appear from Fig. 38.5 that without some elevation the helmsman would not have been able to see anything owing to the height of the bulwarks? If this surmise is correct, then I think it follows with something like certainty that the capacious opening on the vessel's quarter (Fig. 39.2) is, after all, a full-sized Entry Port, and that its sill gives the level of the Main Deck. The drawing of the forecastle archway in other pictures lends considerable support to this idea (Fig. 27.2). For even the least skilful of draughtsmen suggests that the base of the archway is situated at some depth below the gunwale.

These ships of Maso lend no countenance to the theory that three-masted vessels were common in the first half of the fifteenth century. In only one of his drawings (Fig. 38.4) does the artist show a two-masted ship, and even here the additional spar does not seem to indicate any corresponding increase of tonnage. It is stepped very far forward and carries a very small sail. In this connection we may note that Henry V.'s *Grace Dieu* of 1418 'had one great mast and one mesan or foremast' (Oppenheim, p. 14), a description which exactly accords with Maso's drawing in Fig. 38.4.

Certainly, the 'great mast' was tending at this time to become disproportionately taunt, and the peculiarity we know prevailed until after the beginning of the sixteenth century. In Fig. 38.3 we are shown wooldings, but these are drawn in a manner that suggests that the artist did not quite understand what he was drawing and inserted the feature purely for its decorative effect. The great mast is surmounted by a top and the top, as we should expect, is filled with spears, some of them (Fig. 38.4) very carefully drawn.

So far as one can judge, there is in Maso's ships no single example of a topmast. In Figs. 38.3 and 38.5 for example it is impossible to believe that the artist intended anything but a flagstaff. In Fig. 38.5 the flag-staff appears to be quite separate from the mast, but its very slenderness precludes the idea that it could support a yard and sail. In Fig. 38.4 the matter is more doubtful. Here we find repeated in a careless way a peculiar fitting which Maso drew with loving care in Fig. 38.3, a network or mat of ropes encircling the mast and shrouds. What this is I cannot say. It appears to be intended as some kind of chafing-gear, perhaps to protect the standing rigging from the yard. But if so, then we should expect to find a topsail yard in Fig. 38.4 to account for the repetition of the chafing-gear. Of course, it may be argued that the upper mast in Fig. 38.4 too closely resembles the flag-staff in Fig. 38.5 ever to be mistaken for a topmast proper, and that as this same diagram shows the manner in which the mainsail was set it would have been quite impossible to have sheeted the topsail in the manner in which we know that it was sheeted in after times. But as late as the second decade of the sixteenth century it is possible to point to examples of ridiculously small main topsails sheeted in the tops. In the map of Constantinople drawn by Giovanni Andrea Vavassore, and published in Venice in 1520, we find an example of this. Of great ships Vavassore represents four galleys and two round ships. Of the latter, one has all her sails furled and the other all her sails set.

From Vol II, No 11, §§328–34 (*November 1912*)

40

THE SHIPS OF MASO FINIGUERRA

(*Concluded*)

By Geoffrey Callender

In one way I think the representation of sails is the most valuable feature of Maso's drawings. He does not make absolutely clear for us the exact cut of the canvas in vogue at his day, but there are sufficient suggestions and hints to enable one to know in what direction to pursue one's researches. And first I would like to call particular attention to Fig. 38.5. Here is an extraordinary sketch; a vessel apparently head to the wind with the great mainsail bellying out over the poop. There is but the roughest attempt to indicate rigging: shrouds, chafing-gear, a starboard brace and a starboard sheet. There is no vestige of a mainstay which Maso religiously includes in Figs. 38.3–4 and 38.7. And yet the mainsail is divided into two hemispheres, just as if it were straining its convexity against a stay. More than this, we can see quite clearly a band like a reef-band running from the head to the foot of the canvas.

I do not know whether this was a strictly localised rig. It seems to me a very interesting one, and one that explains many mysteries of ships in the fifteenth century. But first it is necessary to enquire whether there is any support for Maso's rig in the drawings of others besides himself. In the pavement of the Cathedral of Siena there is a figure of 'Fortune' attributed to Pinturicchio. The fickle goddess has one foot on sea and one on shore. She holds above her head a ship's yard with a bi-lobed bellying sail akin to Maso's. This figure has been tentatively dated at 1504. In the National Gallery, London, there is a famous picture by the same artist, entitled *The Return of Ulysses*. Penelope sits at her web, distraught by the attentions of the suitors, and the ship of Ulysses is seen through a window at the back. The picture [No. 911] is not very easy to study, as it is skied in a corner of Room VI, but as it is painted in a flat level tone it comes out very well in a photograph, and supplies evidence of the kind that we are seeking (Fig. 40.2).

But the most valuable witness in this connexion is an engraving reproduced by Sir Sidney Colvin in the *Florentine Picture Chronicle*. He sets it

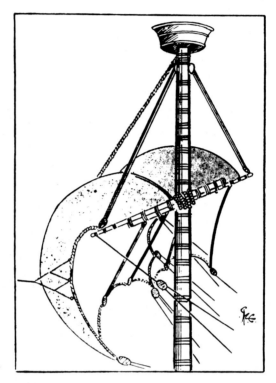

40.1

alongside of Maso's drawings of ships in order thereby to derive additional support for his contention that Maso was responsible not only for the drawings, but also for a school of engravers who carried on his traditions after his death. In this engraving which Sir Sidney Colvin describes as the 'earliest extant engraving of a ship' there is as a matter of fact but very slight resemblance in build to any of Maso's craft; certainly none of the similarity that there is between Fig. 38.4 and 38.7 which is a contemporary engraving. But in the 'earliest print extant' there is not only confirmation of the *bi-lobular* theory, but an almost complete representation of the rigging which such a sail required. The engraver in his desire to be correct and complete has evolved a most complex and intricate design which could only be accurately reproduced by photography (Fig. 40.1).

The bi-lobular sail according to this nameless engraver was an attempt on the part of the quattrocento seamen to supply their vessel not with a sail as we understand it, but with a capacious double-power air envelope or balloon. Mention has already been made in the MARINER'S MIRROR

Fig. 40.2 *The Return of Ulysees* by Pinturicchio.

of the preference of even sixteenth century mariners for the bellying sail. We need not wonder then that a century earlier the pioneers of sailing-ship construction pinned their faith to progress by balloon. Sir Sidney Colvin's earliest extant print shows a very taunt mast which would allow the sail full power to swell without chafing against the stay; a double yard with its component parts very strongly lashed together; a tremendous parrel of four-fold strength; lifts, braces, bolt-ropes, sheets and sheet-blocks, and a port bowline and bowline bridle. All these we might perhaps expect to find. In addition we can count quite easily seven extra blocks with their tackle. Of these blocks, three are fixed to the bi-lobular band which is seen so clearly in Maso's Fig. 38.5, and less clearly in Figs. 38.4 and 38.7). The lowest of the three like a sort of central sheet block is made fast to the foot of the sail, the other two apparently at equidistant intervals along the band between the foot and the yard. W. B. W. in a contribution to the MARINER'S MIRROR (Vol II, p. 188) pointed out that in the sixteenth and seventeenth centuries the courses were bowsed down by a tackle at the middle of the foot. Perhaps this was a relic of the bi-lobular system.

The remaining blocks in the engraving are placed in pairs along the foot of the sail between the central bowsing tackle and the sheet blocks at the clues. But the ropes, instead of leading aft, lead upwards; apparently to opposite and corresponding pulleys on the yard. Perhaps they were intended to constrict the mouth of the balloon and complete its capacity for holding a wind!

If this bi-lobular balloon sail really existed as pictured by Maso and others, it supplies as it were the missing link between the primitive one-masted craft of the fourteenth century and the galleon of the sixteenth. It is the peculiar product of the earlier Renaissance. One can readily under-stand that the mariners at the end of the 'Round Ship' epoch were groping blindly forward on the dark path of development. They recog-nised the wind as their motive power, and like the legendary heroes of the Greek myth attempted to imprison the breeze in a wind bag depend-ent from their towering mast. The new design must have had a singularly brief career, extending perhaps over the third quarter of the fifteenth century. The bi-lobular sail must have been almost unmanageable. At best it can only have been suitable for the Mediterranean, and only possible there. And the third quarter of the fifteenth century robbed the Mediterranean of its predominance. Men began to turn their attention to the western ocean, and those of the Mediterranean mariners who took part in the work of exploration must quickly have learned that their chief requirement was power at will to control their sail, and reduce its bulk in an emergency. But there was no retrograde movement. The canvas carried by one mast had reached its maximum. Experience would complete the education of the pioneers. In our own day, like da Vinci in the fifteenth century, men have endeavoured to construct a flying machine by studying the wings of a bird. Some have found the canvas area necessary to support their weight as unmanageable as a double balloon sail, and they have been led in consequence to evolve the biplane and even the triplane. By analogy we may reason that the late fifteenth century constructors resolved at last to divide the canvas of the great sail among two masts and afterwards more than two. If this was the process of evolution it was the most natural thing in the world seeing that the ships of the Mediterranean had possessed for three hundred years (in addition to their *mast* proper) flag staves of varying number for colours and kites. We can see from Maso (Fig. 38.4) that one of these lesser spars had already attained considerable dimensions. But henceforth the foremast was no longer a subsidiary appendage, a doubtful auxiliary. Henceforth it was to halve the burden of the main, sharing its proportions and developing step by step.

If the fifteenth century mariners did actually evolve and use a bilobular balloon sail they must certainly have abandoned all their reefing gear. At least one would think so. They were accustomed already perhaps to wait for a favourable wind. Such a sail as that described would prevent them from venturing out at all if the wind were likely to increase. Mr. Brindley, in his investigations into the subject of reefing gear, (see 26, 27, 28) has shown that there is a strange hiatus in its history, that is between the beginning of the sixteenth century and the beginning of the Second Dutch War. Perhaps there is some relationship between the disappearance of reef-points on the one hand, and on the other the coming of this monstrous sail and its subsequent distribution into smaller parts. This, at best, is perhaps a fanciful conjecture. But at least we may predicate with some certainty that so long as the fashion of the abnormal sail endured, there was little chance, if any at all, of mariners learning to tack.

In the matter of rigging, as we should expect, Maso's drawings are unsatisfactory. So much is omitted either accidentally or on purpose. There is, however, sufficient to make one wish for more.

It will be seen at once that in the rigging of the mainmast Maso's ships must be classed with those of the fourteenth century rather than with those of the latter part of the fifteenth. There are no shrouds, properly so called. The standing rigging seems to consist in chief of the mainstay, clearly shown in Figs. 38.3, 4 and 7, and of a number of backstays. Fig. 38.4 makes the mainstay appear of considerable thickness. This drawing also shows the method of its attachment to the mast. The stay appears, as a rule, to lead to the deck of the forestage, but in Fig. 38.4 to the bowsprit. In Fig. 38.5 the stay is omitted altogether. The backstays, either three or four in number, seem to lead to the deck of the poop, and in this confirm the impression which one obtains from a study of mediaeval seals from 1309 onwards (cp. Keble Chatterton, *Sailing Ships and their Story*, p. 155; Holmes, *Ancient and Modern Ships*, Part I, p. 75; and 'M.M.,' Vol. II, [see 18, 19 and 26]). Fig. 38.3 shows no more than the seals show; but Figs. 38.4 and 38.7 show blocks at the masthead and blocks just above the level of the bulwarks.

Like the seal of John Holland, Earl of Huntingdon, in the British Museum (Fig. 18.19) Maso's vessel in Fig. 38.3 shows a rope-ladder, evidently leading to the maintop. There are two differences. In the seal the ladder is single and hangs limply. In Maso's drawing the ladder is double and taut, suggesting that the rope-ladder was introduced at first for its own sake, and was afterwards retained and multiplied as its usefulness for support was recognised. It is worthy of notice that the early engravers continued to rig their ships in this fashion long after the adoption of shrouds and ratlines. To mention one example only: Alciati, in his *Emblems*, has a ship which might have been copied direct from one of Maso's vessels.

Before leaving this part of the subject I must point out that in Fig. 38.4 there is an assemblage of ropes leading immediately forward of the mainmast, some of them through the archway of the forestage. These do not appear at all in Fig. 38.3. The pair leading aft may very possibly be the centre sheet for bowsing down the foot of the mainsail. But what of the rest? They may possibly be intended for the rope ladders which otherwise are unrepresented. But, on the other hand, they may be some sort of shrouds. In any case there is not a tittle of evidence to show that any of the rigging of the mainmast led outboard.

It will be noticed that where Maso includes a second mast he gives it no support at all.

One of the most interesting details that the artist has preserved for us is the fitting attached to the bowsprit. This evidently caught his fancy, as he repeats it in every picture except the two stern views where its inclusion would be impossible. The most careful drawing, however, occurs in Figs. 39.1 and 38.3. In the latter it will be seen that this collar has a block attached to it on either side. From one, both parts of the rope fall into the forestage; from the other a rope leads aft to the main yard or to the sail furled under it. What may very well be a corresponding rope for the near side of the bowsprit may be seen underneath, leading to the forestage at a more acute angle. What then was the purpose of all this tackle?

From an examination of the different plates some idea may be gained of the bowsprit which Maso intended to depict. It was long and had considerable steeve. It had a zigzag ornament similar to that in the 'Fifteenth Century Trader,' which appeared in 'M.M.,' Vol. 1, (see 44) with this difference, that the zigzag is placed on the top side of the bowsprit instead of being underneath as in Mr. Morton Nance's drawing. In Fig. 38.3 this attachment, which the artist shows to have had considerable breadth, supports a jack-staff. In Fig. 38.4 it is repeated without the jack-staff, and one would gather that its principal function was to prevent the bowsprit collar from riding up the spar.

It seems clear at any rate from the drawings that the bowsprit existed for rigging purposes only, and had no sail of its own. Maso, it is true, probably saw his ships in harbour when spritsails and spritsail yards might be stowed away. But judging from Figs. 38.3 and 38.4 one would say that the bowsprit collar was not in any way connected with the rigging of a spritsail yard. Unhappily these two drawings do not agree. In Fig. 38.4 the bowsprit receives the fore braces. In Fig. 38.3 there are no fore braces to receive. On the other hand, if Fig. 38.4 be carefully examined it will be seen that the fore brace appears to lead to the zigzag, and that the bowsprit collar is there also, for some unspecified purpose. Perhaps it existed for the setting of the bowlines which must have claimed considerable attention when the vogue of the bellying sail was at its height.

Maso leaves us in some doubt about the main braces. In Fig. 38.5 the port brace is shown, and it is single. In Fig. 38.3 the port brace also appears single, but the starboard is double, and has an enormous block at the yardarm. This arrangement is exactly repeated in one of the ships in the *Embarkation of Marco Polo* (Fig. 27.1), the third ship from the lower right-hand corner. This vessel bears many points of resemblance to Maso's ships, but is somewhat earlier. The starboard brace is double. One rope leads aft, and its attachment is hidden by a tree. The other leads forward to the bowsprit. This brace apparently is lashed securely to the yard arm. The opposite brace on the weather side is also double. The forward rope leads to the very end of the bowsprit. The aftermost is hidden by the sail. But unlike the starboard, this port brace seems to pass through an enormous block. Perhaps this is what Maso tried to represent. But in Fig. 38.4, his only picture of a ship under sail, he omits the braces altogether.

Of the remainder of the rigging the representation is hazy and indistinct. One should not however fail to notice the curious attachment to the lee clue of the mainsail in Fig. 38.4, and the lifts in Fig. 38.3. The flags flown are of two kinds: the 'gitton' flown at the masthead and the jackstaff; and the 'standard' as in the Earl of Rutland's seal flown on an ensign staff at a corner of the poop.

From Vol II, No 12, §§371–77 (*December 1912*)

¶ 41 THE SHIPS OF MASO FINIGUERRA

I have just been reading Mr. Geoffrey Callender's interesting article under the above heading in the November issue of the 'M.M.' I should like to offer one or two suggestions with reference to the port holes which he discusses.

He is inclined to think that the large ports on the quarter of the ships in Figs. 39.2, 38.3–5 and perhaps 38.7, are intended as 'entry ports,' but is not sure. May they not have been intended for putting out a 'steer-board' or additional steering oar to supplement the rudder upon occasion? The rudder was a comparatively new invention, and the seamen of those days may have wished to be able to fall back on the old and proved method of steering in an emergency. As regards the very wide ports in Figs. 39.2, 38.2–3, 38.5, 38.7, and the decoration shown within them in Fig. 39.2—which the author surmises to represent ornamental metal work—I would suggest that these were cut entirely for military purposes, so as to have two tiers of men-at-arms or bowmen, and that where shown shaded and not solid black, as in Figs. 39.2, 38.3, 38.5, 38.7, shutters or pavises were fastened in position to render the deck or cabins weather-proof, those in 39.2 being elaborately decorated in colour. Fig. 38.5 puzzles me. The sail appears to be hoisted abaft the mast, and I do not see how the cross-plank could have been a position for the helmsman, as it is close under the high sheer of the bows, and he could see nothing.

I must presume to disagree as to the figure-head having such a comparatively late origin. Figure-heads are distinctly portrayed in the Bayeaux Tapestry; they would appear to have been in use among the nations of antiquity, and Baring Gould, in 'Strange Survivals and Superstitions,' says, in reference to figureheads in very early times in Northern Europe, 'The figurehead of a warship was designed . . . to strike terror into the opponents and scare away their guardian spirits. An Icelandic law forbade a vessel coming within sight of the island without first removing its figure-head, lest it should frighten away the guardian spirits of the land.' But we can go very much further back. Dozens of distinct figure-heads are to be seen among the Egyptian carvings or inscriptions in the British Museum.

By C. F., from *Notes*, Vol III, No 6, §§184 (*June 1913*)

¶ 42   THE SHIPS OF MASO FINIGUERRA

In these ships introduced to our notice by Mr. Geoffrey Callender we certainly have a valuable contribution to our stock of material for the study of mediaeval ships, for they are of a type and of a period none too richly illustrated elsewhere. Personally, however, I find it difficult to believe that the artist, as he drew these designs, was originating; for, in many cases, the detail bears the stamp of having been copied without understanding, from the free sketches of another hand.

In Fig. 38.5, for instance, Maso has made the ship sail stern first, and the rudders in this and in Fig. 39.2 meaning nothing to him have become mere bottle-shaped balks bolted flat against the stern. In Fig. 38.3 the rudder and tiller-head are again made meaningless, and a bowsprit turns the stern into an apparent bow. Again the cross-hatching shown in Fig. 38.4 is obviously a defensive top-netting (as in Fig. 38.6), of which the outside lines are omitted, but the reversed print of this subject (Fig. 38.7), with slightly improved proportions, has the containing lines of this top-netting without the cross-hatching, a strong indication that we have here two copies of a drawing in which the top-netting was complete. Fig. 38.3, with its netting below the top (this is hinted at in Fig. 38.5 also), suggests that the same top-netting, when not set up, was stowed at the head of the lower rigging.

The bowsprits of Figs. 38.3 and 38.4 are remarkable as having each a 'bowline-comb' in a position the reverse of that usual. In Fig. 38.3 bowline blocks are also present on the bowsprit and in Fig. 38.4 the single bowline (drawn as a forward-leading brace) is wound about the spar quite independently of this 'comb,' so that we could not from this artist learn of its use to hold fixed a turn of the bow-line round the bowsprit.

The lines in Fig. 39.1 that Mr. Callender would interpret as a 'whip-staff' and 'bridge' seem to me to be nothing more than a muddled version on a larger scale of the detail in Fig. 38.5; the 'bridge' being the beam across the forecastle arch; the 'tiller' and 'whipstaff' being the larboard brace of the stern first sailer, the upper part made to pass behind the 'cross-plank or bridge' beam and the lower to waver away in the direction of the poop. In Fig. 39.2 the arch of the forecastle is still plain enough, but it has been turned, by added lines and shading, into a round bow, while the forecastle is left out. A tiller of the length required to meet such a 'whipstaff' would not only have to work across the space occupied by the foot of the mainmast, but would reach so far forward that without sweeping far out over the waist bulwarks it could not have play enough to turn the rudder; on the whole the 'whipstaff' idea does not seem to me to be admissible. I would suggest that Figs. 39.2 and 38.5 had a common original, a ship with sail furled as that in Fig. 38.3, for it will be noticed that the yard in Fig. 38.5 is lowered to about the same point; and that Maso Finiguerra, if it was Maso Finiguerra, has made use of his copy twice, each time giving absurd alterations in his result.

Further, the 'portholes' of this artist are in many cases not holes at all, but mistaken representations of the panelling often seen on mediaeval ships, and in all are so disproportionate as to be quite misleading if taken literally. Compare, for instance, the round holes in the poop of Fig. 39.1 with the more reasonable round ports of Fig. 39.3 and the probable amount of exaggeration with which we have to reckon becomes obvious. The 'entry-port' thus is seen to be only a magnified cabin light, such as we see on the quarters of later ships (see Figs. 48.1, 48.3, 48.4), and the hawse-hole's apparent size no longer astonishes.

In fine, the original artist, ignorant of shipping but delighting in the beauty of ships, has enormously exaggerated all the ornamental details of them in order to conceal his want of knowledge of their construction, or because he was indifferent to all but their decoration; and the work of this man is probably seen in these drawings in a more or less bungled imitation of its first form. In spite of all which their value is sufficiently great.

Of quite a different order seems to be the ship whose mast and sail are shown in Fig. 40.1. This would surely be worthy of an article to itself if the detail is all so fully and faithfully shown.

By 'R.M.N.', from *Notes*, Vol III, No 6, §§184–85 (*June 1913*)

43

A MEDIAEVAL SHIP IN THE ASHMOLEAN

By Geoffrey Callender

In the galleries of the Ashmolean Museum at Oxford is a picture of a mediaeval ship painted in oils upon a panel. I have not measured it, but should estimate its size to be about thirty inches by eighteen. The name of the artist is at present unknown, but the picture is assigned to an Italian master of the fifteenth century.

This picture has never been reproduced at any time by any sort of process. But Mr. C. F. Bell, the Curator of the Fine Art Department of the Ashmolean, has very kindly had the panel photographed, and the thanks of the Society are due to him for the illustration which accompanies this article.

The scene which the artist has chosen is evidently intended, like the glass in the Jerusalem Chamber, to illustrate one of the miracles of Saint Nicholas of Bari, the patron saint of sea-farers. A great ship is struggling helplessly in a gale. The mariners cannot say with Shakespeare's boatswain in the *Tempest*, 'Blow till thou burst thy wind, if room enough!' For they have failed to take in their sail and their ship is at the mercy of the storm. The sky overhead is black as pitch and the hunger of the sea is symbolized by monstrous fish, the largest of which has the teeth of a wolf, the eyes of a lynx, and the mane of a ravening lion. Everybody on board has come on deck. One or two endeavour to make their voices heard above the noise of the gale. One man with a high forehead and resolute look stretches out an arm and points to something in the distance. Others gaze in a stupefied fashion at the fate that awaits them. Some are busy with efforts to lighten the ship, struggling to cast the freight overboard. A man in a broad-brimmed hat rests his box of merchandise or treasure on the gunwale, wistfully gazing at the depth below as if loath to part with his belongings. Another attempts to lean overboard and place his bundle on the surface of the water like a mother who confides her baby to a stranger. These are human touches and afford striking testimony to the growing panic.

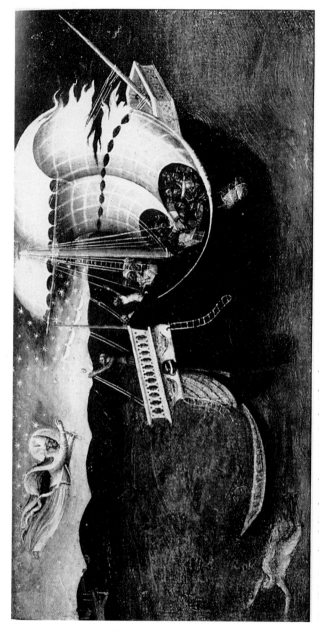

Fig. 43.1 A medieval ship from the painting in the Ashmolean Museum.

The waist of the vessel is crowded. The forecastle is deserted. The poop, or after-stage, is the refuge of a select few. One of these, a man, dressed in a white robe with short sleeves, may possibly be one of the ship's company. He is perhaps the boatswain. He throws his eye up aloft and beckons with one uplifted arm as if he gave directions to the mariners. Perhaps he cries, 'Fall to 't yarely, or we run ourselves aground. Bestir! Bestir!' Perhaps in a minute he will address himself to the little knot of well-dressed men who stand directly in front of him and presume upon their position to harry him with questions. If so, we know what he will say. 'You mar our labours. Keep your cabins. You do assist the storm.'

The principal figure in this little world afloat stands apart from all the rest. His frock and shaven crown proclaim him a monk. In an attitude of humble veneration and fervid belief he stretches both his hands to heaven and beseeches the good Saint Nicholas to take pity and come speedily to the succour of sinful men.

His prayer is heard. Saint Nicholas comes. And at his coming the darkness lifts and the evil spirit of the storm glides away over the surface of the waters in the guise of a sea-maiden with scaly tail and long flowing masses of golden hair. At the coming of the saint the thick clouds pass and the dawn of a happier morning breaks over the rolling eastern hills. The stars of heaven shine again in all the glory of their multitude. And a calmness falls upon the sea.

The figure of the saint is an impressive one. The artist has been at pains to suggest the sublimity of the revelation. St. Nicholas is of a dignity and majesty more than human. He wears a mitre and a cope, an alb and a stole. His left hand bears an emblem of some kind. His right hand is raised in benediction. He opens his mouth to speak words of comfort. There is a halo round his head.

The hull of the vessel is in such deep shadow that no details can be gathered from the starboard side—the side which faces the spectator. Nor is there any stern-post visible; but the rudder is seen in all its length, both above water and below. There is a large semi-circular hole cut in the concave counter for the fitting of the tiller. At the sides of this the artist has represented diadems or crowns which he has drawn with the utmost carefulness. These ornaments were perhaps fashioned of metal and affixed to their stern partly for the decoration of the ship and partly for ease of identification. The vessel in all likelihood may have been called *The Two Crowns*.

Swinging out over the vessel's quarters are a pair of ladders. These are attached to iron pins of a peculiar shape. The pin to starboard is easily discernible against the light paint of the ship's counter. The corresponding pin on the other side is less easily detected against the darkness of the sea. To judge from the shapes they assume as they swing with the motion of the ship, these ladders were doubtless made of hempen rope. But to be useful they must have had a rigid crook to slip over the pin.

What were these ladders for? The oddly shaped long-boat towing astern with its sweeps tucked under the thwarts supplies an answer. But it is difficult to see how anyone desiring to come on board could do so from the boat by means of these ladders with any facility, unless we are to suppose that the figures in the ship are drawn to scale and that the concavity of the counter is too slight to impede a climber. To argue that the figures are drawn to scale is to neglect the evidence afforded by almost all other representations of mediaeval ships. And if the aftermost angle on the port side of the poop be carefully examined, it will be seen that the overhang is considerable.

The long-boat seems to suggest an Adriatic build. The Venetian seagoing boats of to-day are remarkable for their very slight draught forward. And the artist who painted *The Two Crowns* may perhaps have been a native of Venice. The clue provided by the shape of the boat together with two other scraps of evidence—the illumination of the background with eight-rayed stars arranged symmetrically diamondwise and the largeness of the hands in all the human beings represented—make it just possible that the painter was Quirizio da Murano. I have proffered this conjecture to Mr. C. F. Bell, who tells me that a well-known living cognoscente once remarked that the picture seemed to be clearly connected with, if not actually copied from, another in the Vatican gallery. Mr. Bell does not recall anything in the Vatican at all resembling the panel under consideration. But, with one sidelight and another to aid research, the identity of the artist may some day be revealed.

The vessel is a two-masted vessel. She has a large mainmast and a small mizzen. In this respect she differs from the two-masted vessel of Maso Finiguerra [see Figs. 38.4 and 38.7] which in many other respects she resembles. The sail set upon the mizzen is furled, and the rigging of this mast is scanty. But there are one or two points that call for comment. In the first place the mizzen yard is composed of two spars lashed together. I do not know if this is unusual. I am inclined to think that it is. In the case of a great spread of canvas like the mainsail, a double spar, we know, was common enough. But I do not remember ever to have seen a mast, apparently so small, honoured with so pretentious a yard. There is certainly only a single stick in Pinturicchio's study for the *Embarkation of Pius II* (see Fig. 39.3). If the artist has not made a mistake we are justified in assuming that the mizzen sail of *The Two Crowns* was a sail of considerable size. And if the mizzen sail was large, how much larger must have been the mainsail!

The mizzen yard has no lifts, but the port and starboard braces are carefully drawn, and it will be noted that the blocks are not stropped, but are drilled with holes for their attachment.

The main mast is taunt, but hardly taunt enough. Exigencies of space have compelled the artist to shorten it unduly, with the result that the stay appears to pass through the canvas in order to reach the bowsprit. The mast is without wooldings of any sort. It is supported by shrouds; but there is no suggestion given of the method by which these are set up. A Jacob's ladder appears to lead from the starboard side of the after stage. This may, however, be due to an error of perspective. The mast is surmounted by a top; but this part of the picture has incurred some damage and the details are not so clear as they might be.

The sail is nothing less than monstrous in size. It resembles in many particulars the bi-lobular balloon sail which I described in my article on Maso Finiguerra's ships. Thus it has the unwieldly voluminous expansion forward that seems to fill the entire ship from the mainmast to the forestage. It swells upwards above the yard in two distended lobes. There is not the same evidence as in Maso's ships of a medial band. The artist may or may not have intended such a medial band to be shown. There are no vestiges of tackles at the foot and in the belly of the sail. But the canvas is bowsed down at the centre of the foot in exactly the method shown in the early engraving included by Sir Sidney Colvin in his *Florentine Picture Chronicle* [See Fig. 40.1] and by Pinturicchio in the *Return of Ulysses* [see Fig. 40.2]. It is to be noted that neither here nor at the starboard clue of the sail is there any sign of a block. The sheet might be composed of a welding together of the bolt-rope along the foot and along the starboard leech of the sail. Only that there does not appear to be a bolt-rope at all. Perhaps its place was supplied by a broad hem. This, if present, has not been sufficient to save the sail which, as the artist shows in a most graphic fashion, is being torn to ribbons by the wind.

The sail is composed of large rectangular pieces of canvas, and the broad seams that join them together are shown with perfect distinctness. This method of making a sail is shown very clearly also in the central ship in the *Expedition of the Knights of France and England under the Duke of Bourbon to Africa in* 1390 [Harleian MSS., 4,379, folio 115] which Nicolas had engraved as a frontispiece to his second volume. I think it is arguable, too, that this method of making a sail is the feature seized upon by the engraver of the seal of La Rochelle [twelfth century], which we have learned to regard as the earliest example afforded by pictorial evidence of the occurrence of reef-bands and reef-points. In the impression of this seal in the 'M.M.' for May, 1912 (see Fig. 26.1), the horizontal and vertical lines seem clearly intended to be equal in thickness and to divide the canvas into squares of equal size. These divisions of course only occur in the lower half of the sail. But the engraver may have been purposely distinguishing the course itself from the bonnet.[1]

I cannot help feeling myself that this chequer method of making a sail was an ancient method. The fact that the evidence for these rectangular divisions seems, so far as we know at present, to occur in the fifteenth century by no manner of means proves that the method was not employed at an earlier date. There is, for example, the analogy of the 'Veil of the Template.' This was made long before the Christian era in exactly the manner adopted by the sail-makers of *The Two Crowns*. Those who are interested in the subject will find the matter discussed by Edersheim in the second volume of *Jesus the Messiah*, page 611, though I can find no reference to it in Hastings' *Dictionary of the Bible*. Solid strength was the quality aimed at and achieved by the Jews. And it does not seem altogether probable that the knowledge died out suddenly, not to be revived again until the fifteenth century. The vogue of the bi-lobular balloon sail would doubtless at that period call for the exercise of much ingenuity in the fashioning of iron-bound sails. But we must not forget, as Nicolas reminds us, that the earlier accounts and inventories show that great numbers of women were employed and charges entered for an unconscionable supply of needles and thread for the making of the sail for a King's ship. The substitution of cloths for rectangular patches must have led to a saving of labour. And the service of the army of women may have been on that account discontinued.

Not by any means the least interesting feature which this picture supplies is the bonnet of the main-sail. The artist gives us no real information as to the manner in which it was laced to the course. But obviously he has been at pains to depict with faithfulness the look of the thing as he saw it. Round each of the gaping interstices may be traced the horizontal hems which bound the head of the bonnet and the foot of the course; and their presence, be it noted, supports the contention that a hem took the place of a bolt-rope. But as to the connecting link between the two parts of the sail there is no ocular evidence, although it is plain enough to see where the points of attachment are placed, because the vertical hems

---

[1] Cp. also the drawing taken from an ancient lamp which illustrates Κερουχοι in Smith's *Dictionary of Roman and Greek Antiquities*.

in the bonnet correspond in the nicest way with the vertical lines in the course.

The main yard, like the mizzen yard, is composed of two spars lashed together. The parrel is clearly shown. And the artist has put a world of care into his rendering of the manner in which the sail is bent to the yard, the ends of the seizings flying loose in the breeze. He shows us also both port and starboard braces and has not forgotten the lifts.

The fore stage and the after stage are clearly part and parcel of the fabric of the hull. Their construction is simple enough. The after stage is square. The fore stage has a pointed foreend and is perched well over the bows of the ship, in order to derive additional support by resting on the stem-head. Above and below, these stages receive a finish from bevelled pediments and cornices and the wooden entablature between is pierced by an unambitious scheme of decorative fretwork.

The bowsprit with its extravagant steeve forces itself upon our notice. It is long and tapering and looks very naked. Its function, at any rate in *The Two Crowns*, is clear enough. It elongates the upward curve of the bows to a height sufficient to receive the rigging. The artist shows us plainly that, with so distended a sail, it would be impossible to set up the stay on the after side of the forecastle rail. And so it is led to the bowsprit, which rises to meet it and which is nothing more and nothing less than a forward outrigger. The bowsprit also receives the bowlines. But there is no sign of the 'bowline comb' which Mr. Nance has traced in more instances than one (see 46) and which I found to be present in reverse among the ships of Maso Finiguerra (see 40, 41, 42)

From Vol III, No 7, §198–203 (*July 1913*)

44

A FIFTEENTH CENTURY
TRADER

By R Morton Nance

The fact that an artist, working during the last quarter of the fifteenth century, held ships to be in themselves subjects worthy of his skill, would give all his ship pictures an unusual interest. Such an artist was the Fleming who is known to us only by his signature 'W. A.,' (see 45 and 46) and among his productions is the curious print of which a rough copy is here given. A copy of this print is in the nautical collection at South Kensington; but, as it is skied in a dark and inaccessible corner, and is not catalogued, it can hardly be said to be exhibited.

At first sight the ship seems so strange as to be incredible but on further examination one is disposed to take her as a serious attempt to show the distinctive features of some actual vessel.

Perhaps the first thing to strike us will be the absence of a forecastle, which allows us to see the bowsprit stepped into a chock on deck, beside a very strongly curving stem-head, much as we find these features in the hoys and other small craft of a later date. The bowsprit is decorated above with a foreshadowing of the spritsail topmast, here serving only to raise the hoop adorned with fleurs-de-lis, which may have been a mark to distinguish the service of the vessel, as were the armillary spheres, borne in the same place by East India ships of the following century. The fitting beneath the bowsprit, if not mere ornament, may have served as a lead for the fore-tacks, as did the comb beneath the beak in ships of a later date.

The poop is raised above the stern by stanchions, leaving a free passage for air and light between them, a feature more clearly shown in other contemporary drawings. Turrets such as those shown may be seen also in other fifteenth century ships, and notably in that painted by Benozzo Gozzoli in his 'Rape of Helen,' in the National Gallery. Possibly they served as lanterns.

Between these turrets is a crutch or 'myke' which, in other prints by the same artist, is shown as supporting the lowered peak of the lateen

44.1

mizzen yard. In this instance there is no mizzen, the little spar being clearly a flagstaff, so that we must take it that either the mizzen has been forgotten, or the crutch is intended to support the main mast when that is lowered.

This brings us to the consideration of the use of such a vessel. If we could be sure that the main mast lowers we might feel disposed to consider her as a deep-sea fishing boat, and the presence of so many barrels on the poop and slung over the side, would lend colour to this view, but she seems rather large for this, and there are still the apparent awning supports to be accounted for. On the whole she seems more likely to be a 'flute' or 'hulk' of the time than a mere 'herring buss.'

Some very interesting structural details are shown in the bulwarks; the round ports, however, are put in on the starboard side only, while the building up of the bulwarks at the bow is left out on that side, possibly to give a better view of the deck forward.

Beneath the middle wale are several rounded timbers serving no doubt as fenders; somewhat similar projections are shown on mediaeval seals.

From the rigging we can learn but little. The setting up of the shrouds is difficult to understand, and although things are not glaringly wrong in the rig all is sketchy. This is the more remarkable, inasmuch as the plate that 'W.A.' has left us of a 'Kraek' or carrack is the most complete and convincing record of the rigging of his time to be found. In other respects also this carrack is very different, being engraved probably, from a drawing by a different hand from that responsible for the present print.

It is to be hoped that it will prove possible to give reproductions of all these designs in some future number, but meanwhile those whose interest is aroused in this nameless Flemish artist will find the print here illustrated framed and hung on the wall in the ship model department of the Victoria and Albert Museum. Another may be seen in the print-room at the British Museum, and two more are reproduced, from originals in the Bibliothèque Nationale at Paris, by De la Ronciere in his 'Histore de la Marine Française.' It would be interesting to know of any other existing work of this old-time ship lover.

From Vol. I, No 3, §§65–67 (*March 1911*)

ℱ 45   A FIFTEENTH-CENTURY TRADER

It is worth considering whether the ship reproduced by Mr. Morton Nance from the work of W.A. (see 44) does not represent a flute, which seems to have been the typical medium-sized ship of burden both in the 15th as well as in the 16th and 17th centuries, though latterly the term fly-boat may be held to have become more common. As is well known the term flute survived till the end of the great French Wars in the expression *en flûte*, which implied a man-of-war partly disarmed and used as a transport.

It is perhaps hardly correct to say that the 'poop is raised by stanchions.' The drawing seems to show the beams of the poop laid across the original gunwale, with their ends exposed, as though the poop had been added as an after-thought. Exactly the same arrangement will be seen in a large ship illustrated in a French manuscript of 1402, or very shortly after, which is among the MSS. at the British Museum. (Egerton 2709). The ship there shown is probably conventional in many respects; for instance, though she is meant to represent the first-class fighting ship of the period, she has but one mast. She has a long poop with pavesades, much as is seen in the W.A. drawing, but she had in addition a short, high forecastle.

By 'S.G.', from *Notes*, Vol I, No 4, §119 (*April 1911*)

SOME OLD-TIME
SHIP-PICTURES

I.—The Kraeck of W Ꙫ

R MORTON NANCE

The *Kraeck*, engraved, and by a lucky chance named also, by the crafts-man who hid his own name from us under the initials W.A., has so often been mentioned in this journal (see 6, 7, 27, 37, 44, 45, 58) that it seems desirable that she should make a personal appearance. Here, accordingly, she is, redrawn; but in such a way as to preserve the detail that gives her her chief value.

To the forgotten artist who supplied the original drawing from which this plate was engraved, the correctness of this detail was clearly, as it is to us, a first consideration, for he has left us such a record of the carrack of his day as could never be matched by the most patient piecing together of the scattered and fragmentary evidence available elsewhere; and in an artist of the late fifteenth century, a time when drawing was as much as writing an indoor occupation, this accuracy would seem to imply more than a wharfside sketcher's knowledge of shipping.

From her name it seems fairly certain that the carrack originated in the Mediterranean, and although she was in the main but an enlarged version of the northern type of ship then naturalised there, she retained many features inherited from a southern ancestry. If this *Kraeck* of W. A. be, as seems probable, a Flemish carrack and not a Southerner seen in a Low-Country port, she shows that these Latin characteristics were maintained in the carrack even when she was built by people with Northern tradi-tions behind them. That this should be the case with regard to the hull is, perhaps, not astonishing; but the retention of Mediterranean features is even more apparent in the rigging.

In order to give as complete an idea of her as possible, the artist has made free with the laws of perspective and shows more of her bow than is in strict accord with his assumed point of view; by this 'artistic license' we are enabled to see how the widely-spaced wales are continued out on

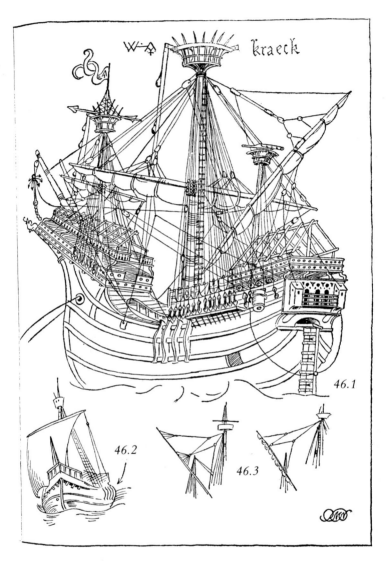

the stem and there cut off bluntly. As we scan her sides coming aft, we notice successively a great hawsehole; a single curving skid beneath the forecastle; a chess-tree; and then a group of skids of unusual form. The fact that the first few shrouds are set up to the sides, independently of the broad chain-wale that spreads those shrouds that are abaft these skids, probably implies that boats and goods were hoisted up here by means of tackles from the masthead; for such awkwardly guided burdens, before they were safely lodged in the waist, would be likely to tear away a channel here, were one present, or to damage the sides, but for the thickset skids that protect them. Apart from some copies of this *Kraeck*, mentioned later, a small (Flemish ?) ship in Coverdale's Bible shows similar skids. (Fig. 46.2)

It is a little surprising to find on the shrouds here modern-looking, three-holed deadeyes in place of the blocks more commonly shown in the best ship-pictures of the time, or the more mysterious devices that may be hinted at in less skilful drawings; but were there many such searchingly drawn fifteenth century ships as this *Kraeck*, we should, no doubt, find deadeyes in plenty.

The chain-plates are represented by lines that are at short intervals crossed by smaller lines. In this arrangement (which looks here like a feeble attempt to indicate by breaking the line, that it is composed of separate links and is, in fact, a chain) we seem to have a convention not of the careful draughtsman who drew the chain of the bowsprit grapnel, but of his engraver, W. A., who has furnished the shrouds of ships in others of his prints, designed perhaps by himself, with similar cross-strokes that form their only visible means of tension. That these strokes or knots in themselves may represent some forgotten method of setting up shrouds, has been well shown by Mr. H. H. Brindley (see 7), but the *Kraeck's* shrouds have already their deadeyes and lanyards, and were there any meaning in these cross-strokes here, her loving recorder would surely have allowed us to see it as he saw it.

Lashed abaft the main-chains is a barrel, probably the steep-tub (see 47). Apart from the testimony of W. A., whose ships usually carry such a 'steep-tub' on the quarter, we find a barrel in the same position, to give examples, on one ship in the Warwick MS.; in some coarse early wood-cuts of ships, where the technical difficulty of cutting its fine lines has left it barely recognisable, the often-reproduced *Oceanic Classis* being one; while two of these 'steep-tubs' are lashed side by side in the chains of that ship of Bruegel's that was copied later for Cresentio's *Nautica Mediterranea*.

Coming now to the stern we pass a great open port-hole, perhaps placed there, as in modern wooden-built ships, as a timber or cargo port, and arrive at the rudder. The stern-post upon which this is hung is not visible (it may be that, like the stern-post of Latin ships, it does not project from the hull), neither are any pintle-irons in sight; but the three gudgeon-irons with fishtail ends; the seven wooden clamps that bind together the two timbers of which the rudder is composed; the wide tiller that fits over the rudder-head; and the ring to which are fastened the rudder-ropes, are all clear enough. Over the rudder-head hangs the con-cave counter, usual in ships of the time, and almost their only feature, that passed on to nineteenth century ships; this is pierced by an excep-tionally wide tiller-hole to fit the tiller. Above the counter the stern is extended yet further aft by two structures, each covered with its lean-to roof, but open between its supporting brackets below. These are exactly like the machicolated bartizans of mediaevel stonework, as seen, for example, at Compton Castle, Devon; and no doubt they served the same ends, possibly as a means of annoying boarders at the stern by pouring hot water or molten lead upon them, but far more probably as garderobes only; for such conveniences were commonly placed as far as possible astern until quarter galleries came into use, and the counter below their openings seems to be protectively leaded. These two sanitary offices are joined by a little open gallery, the high rail of which only partly conceals the three round-headed windows that with their simple tracery fill the remaining space aft. The solid structure ends here beneath a row of gun-muzzles, but raised upon it (much as the older 'castles' were raised upon the simpler hulls of their day, except that curving stanchions, or knees, take the place of upright posts) is the poop with loop-holed bulwarks; and higher still is a high-pitched framework to extend an awning or, in fight, nettings. From the poop the posts and rails of a stout pavesade run forward hung with shields. The bearings on these shields might be ex-pected to yield a clue to the *provenance* of this *Kraeck*; but in the absence of colour their simple heraldry is mute; the engraver's initial 'A' upon one suggests that the rest too are fancifully blazoned. On both sides, at the waist, are gangways that rise towards the forecastle and join to form an arch as they meet it. This arch is universal in ships of the time, rising sometimes, it seems, from the deck, at others from a gangway. Here in forming it the gangways alter their horizontal direction so little that, assuming that the original *Koebrug* or 'cowbridge' was such a gangway, it is easy to imagine that thus arose our old sea-term, 'cow bridge head.' The Dutch *Koebrug*, now the lowest deck, was in the sixteenth century the gun-deck; so that by a similar process of change we might conceiv-ably work back to a fifteenth century *Koebrug* that was a gangway, built much after the manner of the bridges by which the Dutchman's pied cattle passed over their dykes. That *Koebrug* was ever so used, however, or that *Koebrug hoofd* was ever good Dutch for what, in later times, was a *beschot* remains to be proved.

The arched 'cowbridge head' is continued upwards by the after breast-work of the forecastle which, with its round loopholes, matches the poop in style. To the sides of the forecastle the fore rigging is set up with deadeyes, and below it are the butt-ends of many beams that support it as it launches over the bows: its main support, however, is the long knee that, prolonging in an outward direction the stem itself, ends as a gargoyle-like dragon with a curling tongue of metal. Beneath this 'knee of the head' is, almost its last appearance, the mysterious 'bow-warp' that Mr. Brindley has shown us in so many mediaeval ships. It seems not unlikely, even here, that it is the setting-up of the main-stay; for it will be noticed that no dead-eyes are used for the fore-stay as yet. If not that, we are almost forced to conclude that it is the gammoning of the bow-sprit. Over the forecastle rises another stage, like the poop raised upon curved knees, and covered like it by a skeleton roof. The ledges of this roof all join the roof-tree at the same pitch, shortening as they approach the bow. The low bulwarks of this 'top-gallant forecastle' are pierced with a fretted pattern and in the midship aft they are interrupted, like the breastwork of the lower stage, with an embrasure.

Visible as they rise through the slight structure forward are the bowsprit and foremast. From the bowsprit-end hangs a chained, six-armed grapnel, ready to drop at will and grip the foe. The lashing of the block of this; the collar or lashing of the fore-stay; a woolding; and the lashings of the bowline-blocks, complete the clothing of this spar; but it seems likely that the grapnel is temporarily taking the place of the spritsail just as the netting that covers the fore-top in battle trim has ousted the topsail, and that both these sails would be carried at ordinary times. With the coming of larger topsails, top-nettings were soon driven out of use and very few drawings show them, but they were an obvious form of defence for top-castles at a time when nettings were found on the lower fighting platforms of bow-and-stern-castles, and were the maintop mast present in our *Kraeck* we should no doubt see them there also. The omission of this mast and its fittings is probably due simply to the reluctance of W. A. to use a bigger copper plate for the sole purpose of getting them into the scope of his engraving. Around the fore- and main-tops darts are ranged at intervals, the fore-top bearing also a mighty barbed and feathered shaft. Top-cranes, too, are seen with their 'crane-lines' and 'crane-line-pokes' attached. These were, when single, usually abaft the top; but when double they seem to have been at its sides, and, in spite of the forward-leading cranelines, this seems to be the position intended here.

How the fore-top was reached by armour-clad soldiers is not plain, neither can we see how those who manned the mizen-top's wooden-stocked swivel gun got aloft. The fore-top man might be hauled skywards in one of the 'crane-line-pokes;' but even this is denied the gunner of the mizen-top, and neither of them have another such wood-runged jacob's-ladder as that by which the main-top men-at-arms so easily reach their post.

It is unfortunate for our purpose that the ship is shown with furled sails, for had they been set we might have seen the solutions of some difficult problems that are raised by contemporary inventories and imperfect pictures. Of all the details of rigging the lifts of the main-yard will perhaps be the most surprising. To serve the purpose of a double block at the yard-arm, two single blocks are lashed there at some distance apart, so as to give the appearances of two lifts on each side. Martnetts as we know from other sources were then in use, but it is a surprise to find them already so complicated. In later times we usually find them hanging in festoons beneath the furled sail, but here we see them taut and trim in the older fashion, still shown in some of Bruegel's prints of c. 1560.

Another interesting fitting is the mizen lift. In principle the same as the lift that was in use until the introduction of square mizen-topsails, it resembles, too, that shown in ships by Carpaccio and Jacopo di Barbari, of about 1500 (Fig. 46.3), but it differs from all those in that its pendant is single, with a double block; while they have two pendants, each with a single block. The yard, as usual with this lift, is slung within the rigging. A temporary fashion, made necessary by the high awning roof, is seen in the double mizen sheets; these rise from the garderobe roofs and lead in again on the quarter. The introduction a few years later of an outlicker made a single sheet serve their purpose. The bowlines of this *Kraeck* all run in blocks on the bowsprit, those of the foresail passing first through the bulls-eye of a long horse (O strange sea-lingo!) attached to the fore-stay. Only one bridle is seen. It is noticeable that the falls of the bowlines and of the fore braces and sheets lead into the waist. The sheets and tacks, both single ropes, are not knotted into the clews, but on to a short rope that hangs therefrom. All blocks seem to be drilled with holes for their attachment and not stropped; it is doubtful even whether the shrouds encircle their dead-eyes. The later fashion of stropping blocks and turning in dead-eyes seems to have been suggested by the fitting first of a sheet block into the clue of a sail and noticing its increased strength.

One fitting is a mystery to the writer; this is the rope that leads down from the main parrel to a block and thence in three branches to the fore end of the mizen yard, to which it may serve as mizen-bowline. The truss-tackle seems to be shown coming down before the mast. The parrel itself is very modern, with ribs and trucks in perfect order instead of the loose necklaces that we expect to see. The alternating wide and narrow wooldings, too, are far more ship-shape than usual, and show that we must put down much of the slovenly look of early ships to the account of the artists who drew, rather than to the sailors who rigged them.

The flattery of imitation has not been denied this *Kraeck*; for some manifest copies of it exist. The best of these is, perhaps, the wood-cut in the *Alciati Emblematum Libellus* of A. Wechelus. (Paris, 1537). That this was a direct copy from W. A.'s print on to the wood-block is shown by the fact that it is reversed in printing; in spite of this, however, it is but a bungling version. Another copy was engraved as the coat-armour of a North German early in the sixteenth century: in order that the ship should face to the right in accordance with the laws of heraldry, it was re-drawn on the plate backwards, and its porportions were at the same time made to fit neatly into the shield; it is also a mastless hull, so that it is altogether much altered from the original, but the crest of a mast and sail above this shield show the influence of W.A.'s other ships, and there is small doubt that it is copied from him. Still another sixteenth century borrower of our *Kraeck* was the artist who executed the miniatures in the *Book of Hours* of Henry II of France. (MS. Lat. 1429, Bib. Nat.) In one of these Jonah is jettisoned from a carrack, of which the rigging is copied loosely from W. A.'s; although, judged by the comparative size of the prophet and his unwilling shipmates, a single mast and sail would be enough for her.

These several copies, if there were more, go to prove that, perhaps until Bruegel's ships began to appear, this *Kraeck* was regarded as the last word in ship drawing, and make it seem unlikely that any finer or fuller delineation of a fifteenth century ship will ever come to light.

From Vol II, No 8, §§225–32 (*August 1912*)

ᛈ 47 SHIFTER

The Shifter was a sort of 18th century nautical equivalent of a kitchen maid. Falconer (1769) describes him as 'a person appointed to assist the ship's cook, particularly in washing, steeping, and shifting the salt provisions.' Hawser Trunnion, it will be remembered, boasted that he had 'served all offices on board from cook's shifter to the command of a vessel.' ('Peregrine Pickle,' (Chap. ii.). In that case he must have been roughly contemporary as a Shifter with the Henry Noble who got into trouble for mis-interpreting the duties of his office.—S.G.

'There came to the ship's side (the ship being the *Richard* of Arundell on her voyage to Benin in 1590) 'a monstrous great fish (I think it was a gobarto) which put up his head to the steepe-tubs where the cooke was in *shifting* the victuals, whom I thought the fish would have carried away.'

The steep-tubs (see 46) in this case I take to have been lashed without board, either in the main-chains or on the quarter, in both of which positions they are frequently shown in ship pictures of the XV and XVI century, and the 'shifter' here was the cook himself. According to the 'Vade-Mecum' of Wm. Mountaine, 1778, the cook was 'to have charge of the steep-tub' and was 'answerable for the meat put therein,' he was also 'to secure the steep-tub, that it may not be washed overboard.'

The 'shifter' of the *Chichester* was evidently an understrapper to the cook, and his opportunities of 'diminishing' the meat in the steep-tub would be increased by the fact that the steep-tub was lashed, if not without board, at least, as we see by the 'Vade-Mecum,' in a place where it was peculiarly liable to be washed overboard and where it would probably be to some extent out of view of the cook and others of the 'shifter's' shipmates. Bailey's Dic., 1735 ed., gives:—'Steep Tub [at Sea] vessels for watering Beef, Pork, or Fish.' Watering means softening and freeing them of salt.

By 'S.G.' and 'R.M.N.,' from *Notes*, Vol I, No 12, §349 (*December 1911*)

48

SOME OLD-TIME
SHIP-PICTURES

II   A MEDITERRANEAN CARRACK

By R Morton Nance

The *Kraeck* of W. A. gave us a view of a northern carrack presenting her larboard quarter (see 46). Our present example (Fig. 48.6) shows us a southern carrack that offers us her starboard bow, so that between them we should have a fairly comprehensive idea of carracks in general.

We have here an enlarged copy of a ship which M. Bourel de la Ronciére has reproduced in his *Histoire de la Marine Francaise*. It is to be found in a manuscript that was brought by Charles VIII, of France, from Naples. (MS. Latin 6142 f. 1. Bib. Nat.).

The drawing of the *Kraeck*, although it formed the high-water-mark of mediaeval ship-drawing, is not perfect in perspective and proportion, and in this drawing, obviously less good, we must expect to find such imperfections multiplied. The very elementary notions of perspective held by its creator are shown by the fact that he has, in order to express the roundness of her sides, made the skids curve, indeed; but so that their convexity is toward the bow instead of outwards. This is so common a form of error with inexperienced draughtsmen, that it is scarcely necessary to refer to other drawings of the time to satisfy ourselves that her sides were not built concave, as, from this simple mistake, corrected in Fig. 48.1, they appear to be. Skids like these are usually present on contemporary ships, but in hardly two specimens are they disposed alike. Here we have three of the curved timbers usual beneath the forecastle, two skids at the 'loof,' perhaps a duplicated chess-tree, and two more at the main-chains. These skids seem at this time to have served a double purpose in strenghtening the weaker parts of the quickwork, as well as defending the sides from abrasion.

Besides these skids a side-ladder is seen; this is not perhaps a fixture, for although, allowing for the curious reversed perspective, it accommodates itself perfectly to the curve of the hull; yet as it stands it is in shape like the

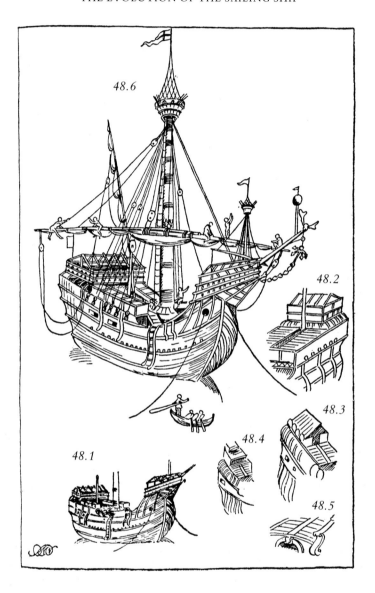

ladders that flank the poop of a galley of the time, and the draughtsman, inconsistent even in his errors, may have drawn this correctly.

Resting their butt-ends upon the middle wale for the greater part of its length are the projecting beams that, as already noticed in a previous article (see 35), form a typical feature of ancient Mediterranean and

Oriental ship-building; their position, if correct, implies an enormous sheer forward in the deck that they support. The fact that the wales are so much more numerous on the larboard bow shows that we have careless, as well as ill-trained, drawing to reckon with.

Perhaps the drawing, as such, is at its worst in the forecastle, which from this cause seems tilted over so as to show the whole of the supporting structure beneath. This forms, with the sides of the forecastle, the central timber, and connecting cross-beams, a triangular projection very like the *echelle* that, without any superstructure, forms the beak of such lateen vessels as xebecs and tartanes. The faulty perspective makes it difficult to see exactly how this joins the bow; but the central timber is here not a prolongation of the stem, for it seems rather to rest upon the stem-head. The loop-holed bulwarks of the forecastle are very like those of W. A.'s *Kraeck*, and the roughly indicated figure-head would probably have been another wide-mouthed dragon; the 'top-gallant forecastle is absent, however, and the tilt-roof or netting-frame rises directly above the forecastle.

The tiny foremast should, probably, have been drawn bigger; but it would be too much to expect of our artist that he should keep to any particular scale. His men would certainly not be able to get inside the fore top-netting; but, large as they are, they are in far better proportion than we have any right to expect at this early date, and the size of the boat, with its rowers, is not so very far from the truth. The rigging of the foremast is very slight and the fore-stay is left out.

In contrast with this tiny foremast we have a great bowsprit that supports the weight of an enormous grapnel, chained and slung just as we saw it in the *Kraeck*. As if this grapnel were not in itself burden enough, the bowsprit carries also a staff at its end that would be quite capable of supporting a sail, had the notion of a spritsail-topsail struck the sailors of the time as being desirable; but the presence of what seems to be a stag's antlered skull, nailed as a mascot to the bowsprit end, where it would inevitably tear such a sail to ribbons in a few minutes, disposes of the idea that this staff is intended for any wiser purpose than that of carrying the globe that, with its little flag stuck in, looks like a Christmas pudding. This globe, gilded like the flower-de-luces on the bowsprit of our *Sovereign* of 1495, would perhaps inspire the same sort of half-superstitious pride as was felt for the figure heads of their ships by later sailors.

The half-deck, or after-castle, shows an arrangement not altogether unlike that of other ships of her time, as we find them recorded. It is very difficult from the crude nature of all these early drawings to judge of the arrangement of the decks in the ships represented, but we shall probably not be far wrong in allowing such a carrack as this, a lower-deck and a main-deck, both of which would be continuous, unless, as in many sixteenth century ships, there was a fall of two or three feet astern to give cabin-room. Above these, in the waist, gangways would run along on each side, leaving an open space amidships that formed, as the gangways rose forward, the great arched opening under the forecastle. These gangways ended at the break of the aftercastle, and there probably communicated by ladders with the deck beneath, although we are unable to give any example of this. The ladder seen in this particular ship is probably unique, and seems, from its position, to lead down from the half-deck, inside the unseen gangway, to the deck beneath it.

Of the half-deck itself we see little more than of the assumed gangways; but we can here infer its position, not only from the ladder above mentioned, but also from the curious semi-circular gangway that embraces the foot of the mainmast much as one sees a seat built to encircle a tree-trunk. At either side of the half-deck of our Italian carrack is a frame-work exactly answering with its timbers to the 'waist-trees,' 'roof-trees' and 'ledges' of the waist-nettings in Elizabethan ships, and like these and the roof-like frames at bow and stern, it was no doubt 'contrived a double debt to pay,' serving in peace for tarpaulins and in war for nettings, as defences against the elements and the enemy. The half-decks chosen from other sources to elucidate their arrangement seem to show an advance on this simple framework, for in each case these timbers support a deck that, like the waist-gangways of the time, is planked athwart-ships. These side-decks, too broad to be termed gangways, seem still to leave a narrow interval between them in the deck-view shown in Fig. 48.2; but in Figs. 48.3 and 48.4, their thwartships planking is joined so as to form one deck by a single plank that follows the middle line of the ship. That this was the actual construction seems the more likely, for the reason that De Bry, many years later, in representing Columbus on shipboard, makes the decks of the *Santa Maria* take the same character (Fig. 48.5). His notion of a ship was, indeed, vague; bow and stern get mixed a little in his work, and he makes masts, rigging and sails into mere decorative adjuncts; but he gives us swivels on the bulwarks and breech-loaders mounted on carriages and sledges; pavesades with their shields loopholed; ladders and hatchways and deck arrangements generally, with a *vraisemblance* that induces one to think that, at least as a passenger, he was well acquainted with a ship's deck, and that he had himself seen a half-deck with this thwartships planking. The *Kraeck* of W. A., unfortunately, shows us nothing of her half-deck, but it is evident, from the pavesade that runs forward on the level of the poop, that the side-decks or gangways are planked like those other examples, and not as here in the Italian carrack, mere *ponts-a-cordes*.

Immediately below the raised poop the bulwarks that screen the half-deck cease abruptly, and for the rest of the distance aft their upright stanchions are replaced by curving knees, struts, or stanchions that connect the beams of the flyaway poop with the wider, solid structure of the hull. These curved struts, below the poop will be noticed in Figs. 48.2, 48.3 and 48.4, also, but they are seen, perhaps, at their best in W. A.'s *Kraeck*, where they are of a slightly different shape. In others of W. A.'s prints these struts seem very slightly elevated from the bulwarks and look more like the ends of the actual beams of the poop; possibly they originated as beam-ends only. (See 45.)

Whether the deck below the poop would be continuous with the half-deck or not, it is difficult to determine, possibly this varied actually as it apparently does in our various examples. The presence of light-ports on the quarter, just below the resting-place of these struts in Figs. 48.3 and 48.4, seems to imply that the space lighted by these windows was decked in at the bulwark level. The other drawing, Fig. 48.2, and also the *Kraeck* of W. A., seem to show us, on the other hand, that these struts do not rise from a deck-level, but from the top of bulwarks, upon which in the *Kraeck* guns are mounted, and it seems likely that the light-ports in all would, correctly, have been placed lower down as they are in our Italian carrack where, with their sliding shutters, like those fitted to Chinese junks or in the deckhouses of European ships, they are much more convincingly drawn.

The poop of this carrack is almost exactly like that of the *Kraeck*, but with the important exception that, with its crowning framework, it is placed athwartships, reversing the direction of that in the *Kraeck*. Examples of these two methods of placing the poop are sufficiently frequent to show that both were common; possibly the whole stern was wider in ships that had the thwartships poop; but it seems more probable that the only difference lay in the comparative shortness of the poop itself, which was, if narrower fore and aft than across, roofed athwartships. The little ensign staff at the side of the poop is interesting, for this remained the place for it long after this crab-legged poop with its open space beneath had given place to one that formed an integral part of the ship.

The rigging of this carrack, comparatively good as it is for its time, shows a great falling off from the standard set by W. A.'s *Kraeck*, but with some more or less important exceptions, it tallies as far as it goes with that shown there. The main mast shows wide and narrow wooldings, but they are quite irregular. The top shows no crane or crane-line, but there is a top-arming round it, with what seem to be guns pointing through, although the drawing is not precise enough to make this certain; each side of the top bristles with darts, and the comparatively high topmast has a netting that stretches from the top-rim almost up to the cross-flag at the mast-head. Beneath the top are lines suggesting futtock-shrouds, but these may roughly represent such brackets as we see supporting the great maintop of the *Kraeck*. Abaft the mast is a jacobs-ladder, and the eyes of the shrouds all come in below the top and spread out without ratlines towards the chains quite in the manner of those in the *Kraeck*, except that blocks seem to be used instead of deadeyes to set them up. The parrel is roughly indicated, but is evidently composed of several rows of trucks with, perhaps, ribs also. The main yard in the *Kraeck*, rightly or wrongly, gives the impression of being a single spar; but here the more usual yard of the period is shown, composed of two spars lashed together like those of the *antenne* of a galley; possibly this yard, which seems to have been a loan from the old Mediterranean rig, was not universal even for the largest of Northern ships at the time, but we have ample evidence that it was general.

This yard is shown lowered to half-mast, where at this time it usually remained, except when the ship was under sail; unless, in bad weather, its great weight made it desirable to steady the ship further by lowering it a-portlast.

One detail in this ship reminds us of an important omission from the *Kraeck*. This is the great block of the main tye and halliards. Two tackles, too, run aft from almost the same place; but they are so mixed up with the shrouds as to make it impossible to identify them. The starboard lift has its upper block in place; but there is none at the yard-arm, and the lift itself seems to be made fast to the yard in two places. As it stands this lift would not work, but it seems likely that we have here a simplification by the draughtsman of such a double lift as that of the *Kraeck*. The lift on the other side is slackened down, apparently by lowering the pendant of its upper block; it may or may not have been possible to do this, but the lift itself must obviously have been a running part, too, or the yard could never have been hoisted higher than we see it here.

On the yard are several sailors, on a much less enlarged scale than we usually have them in pictures of the time; they are straddling along the yard in the old way and are thus far true to life; but it is difficult to see whether they are about to make sail or have, perhaps, just finished furling it.

The mizen we have left to the last and it seems to have been a little neglected by its original draughtsman also, for he has given it no shrouds or rigging of any sort. He has left no doubt as to the existence of a *calcet* at the head of this dwarfish stick, however, and we see that it has a single sheave-hole through its olive-shaped bulk. The mizen-yard is peaked up, but no lift is shown, and its single *oste*, or vang, seems to indicate that the mizen is rigged in galley fashion. There are instances of mizen-lifts on Mediterranean ships of 1500 and, perhaps, earlier; but everywhere the liftless galley-mizen was more common until some time later, and the 'Flemish hulk' kept it as part of her ship-rig until past the middle of the sixteenth century.

The boat, already referred to as being in unusually true proportion, shows in her upturned bow what may have been a southern fashion. She is rowed with three oars a side, and guided by a long steering oar astern. The rowers do not stand and push as Mediterranean sailors would to-day, however, but sit and pull in northern or, perhaps we should say, galley style.

From Vol II, No 10 §§309–15 (*October 1912*)

49

SOME OLD-TIME
SHIP-PICTURES

VI   A GROUP OF FLORENTINES

By R Morton Nance

In the Mariner's Mirror, Vol. II, (see 40), Mr. Geoffrey Callender, drawing attention to the balloon-like character of the sails in ships drawn by Maso Finiguerra and other fifteenth century artists, gives, in support of the 'bi-lobular theory,' by which he accounts for the shape of these wind bags, a diagram of a mast and sail in a ship reproduced in Sir Sidney Colvin's *Florentine Picture Chronicle*.

A reference to the Florentine Picture Chronicle shows that the ship as given there, although complete in itself, is but part of a larger print, and, tracing it to its source, it proves to be one in a company of three ships, and not the most elaborately designed of these.

The original print, perhaps unique, is preserved at the Albertina Museum at Vienna, but a *facsimile* at the British Museum gives all that need be wished for of its nautical detail, and from this the sketches (Figs. 49.1– 3) have been made.

This print of 'Three Ships at Sea' is unsigned and undated, but it is held from its style to be Florentine, and from the type of ship alone it may safely be said to belong to a period not very far removed from that of W. A.'s set of ship-prints, say, 1460–1480.

The vessels contained in it, probably themselves carracks, are in no way unworthy of being placed alongside of W. A.'s great *kraeck* herself, (see 46) for they show with equal care the character of hull, spars and rigging with which their Florentine engraver was familiar, and in the matter of sails the *kraeck*, with her furled canvas, does not even hint at the complications that we find in them. That these existed much as they are shown here, however, there need be no doubt, for we have at least one other print, either Florentine or North Italian, B.M., E.III.J., that gives us practically the same details (Fig. 49.5), and in other pictures, such as Pinturicchio's 'Return of Ulysses' (Fig. 40.2) and the ship (Fig. 49.4)

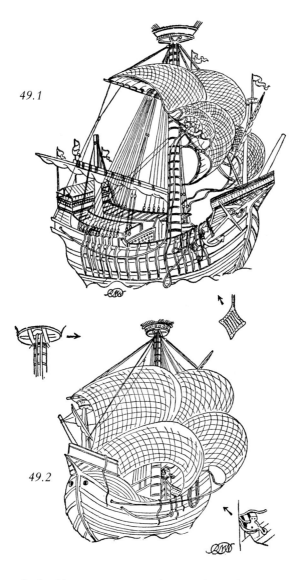

49.1

49.2

from Breydenbach's *Journey to Jerusalem*, we have the same rig more or less completely shown; while the prints of Peter Bruegel show us that sails of much the same sort that we see here were still bellying out on Flemish ships of nearly a century later.

The hulls of these three ships are of the same general type, but Fig. 48.1 either represents a vessel of larger size or is more fully delineated. All have along their sides, counting downwards, three single wales, and a double one that reaches the water line amidships. Beneath this double wale one single wale shows at the bows of Figs. 49.2 and 49.3, but two are visible here in Fig. 49.1, while the waist is also built up a little higher in this ship, but an even greater difference in her appearance is made by the sixteen skids that protect her sides, none being present in the other two vessels. The half-deck gangways too (see Figures 48.1–6), so clearly shown in Fig. 49.1, are not, apparently, fitted to Fig. 49.2 or Fig. 49.3. These are drawn as though composed of overlapping thwartships planking and rise to meet the poop much as the waist gangways of W. A.'s *Kraeck* rise towards her forecastle, but without forming an arch abaft the mizzen mast.

The stanchions that support the poop at its sides are straight, and planked over, in contrast with the curved, bare poop stanchions of the *kraeck* and other ships (see 46); but even here they still fall in at a considerable angle, owing to the small comparative width of the poop, which they connect with the wider deck beneath. Above the poop in Fig. 49.1 is a thwartship tilt-frame, drawn as though roofed with boards; in Fig. 49.3 we have no tilt-frame, which makes it seem most probable that this addition to the cage-work was made only to vessels of the largest class, and that Fig. 49.3 with her skidless sides is not included amongst these.

The simple forecastle is in all three without a tilt-frame, and the post in each forbids our seeing any detail of the forecastle cowbridge-head, but we get a distorted view of the ladder-like under frame upon which its forepart is resting and also of the curved planking (perhaps, with that beneath the poop, clinker-worked) that fills in the space between the top-wale and the forecastle.

The after cowbridge-head, as seen abaft the main mast in Figs. 49.1 and 49.2, seems to be pierced with rows of loop-holes. This is apparently divided into two parts by an upright pointed structure, of which the purpose is not clear, but if this is so, the further half is not shown, and instead of it we have a slight indication of the framework of the sides. In Fig. 49.3, where no cowbridge-head is drawn, this side-framing is more clearly shown. It is unfortunate that all three ships give much the same view of their hulls, leaving their sterns unrecorded. This deficiency cannot be entirely made up, yet Fig. 49.5, with her stern towards us, is at least suggestive of what we might expect to see if these three other ships were sailing away from us. The upper part of the stern, indeed, shows important differences, for the poop instead of being narrower than the after castle beneath it and raised upon inclined timbers, as in Figs. 49.1 and 49.3, is here of the same width as the aftercastle, upon the bulwarks of which it rests, and the tilt-frame runs alongships; but beneath this level

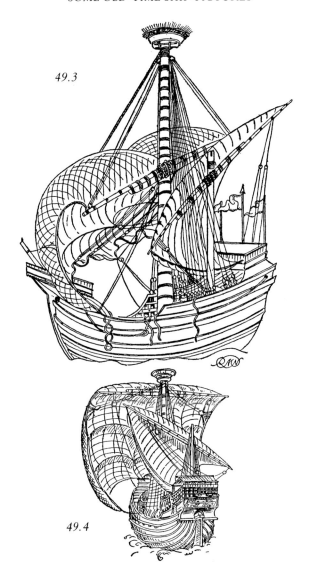

49.3

49.4

we find some striking likenesses in the form of the skids and the disposition of the wales. Three of the latter again surmount a double one, and this double wale, starting astern just beneath the tiller-hole, is again the lower limit of the row of skids. The number of wales in sight beneath the double one is here increased to four (or three, on one side) and between two of these on either side is what must be a rudder stopper (*braga del timone*) leading in at a hole near the stern-post. The ornate, leaf-shaped tiller-hole is exactly like that shown in yet another Italian ship-print of the late 15th century (B. M. E., III, 8, Fig. 49.6) and it is at least probable that this would find its match in all these Florentine ships. The forecastle arch, too, is indicated in Fig. 49.5, although too roughly to be of much use. A beam that, apparently, stretches right across the opening to project from the loof at each side is, I believe, unique; although a projecting beam that may well represent its outboard part is to be seen in a few 15th century ships, and the two 'devettes' standing at the 'louffelawes' of the *Sovereign* of 1495, must have had the same use and appearance. In front of this beam are two irregularly skittle-shaped objects, perhaps intended for bitts, but their meaning is not clear and it would be difficult to find their like elsewhere.

Although foremasts were of no long standing at the date of these prints, and we have evidence that some Mediterranean ships were without them at a period but slightly, if at all, earlier, there is yet no reason to suppose that any of these ships have less than three masts, excluding their bowsprits. In Fig. 49.1 the foremast is very small; in Fig. 49.2, still more modest, it lurks beneath the swollen mainsail, and in Fig. 49.3 it seems safe to assume that it has concealed itself entirely behind this sail, as it has done in Figs. 49.4 and 49.5. Where the whole foremast is seen, in Fig. 49.1, we see a flagstaff above its round top; Figs. 49.1 and 49.2 give us a furled foresail, and we get shrouds and, perhaps, a fore-stay from Fig. 49.2. With these we exhaust the small dole of rigging allowed the foremast.

The bowsprit is short, and, except as an attachment for the main-bowlines, seems to be made use of but little as yet.

The mainmast is without even a flagstaff above its round top in any of these pictures, which leads one to wonder whether the small topmast of those days may not have been unshipped from its place and sent down to leave more fighting space in the tops, or perhaps to reduce top-hamper in winter navigation. It is curious that top-masts, or at least flag staves, should remain at the fore masthead, while none were carried above the main-top, in both the Florentine (Fig. 49.1) and W. A.'s Flemish carrack (see 46); but possibly the size of the plate may have had something to do with it both here and in the case of the *kraeck* (see 18). The round-top itself is in all these ships slightly different in pattern. In Figs. 49.2 and 49.3 trestle-trees and crosstrees are plainly shown, and in Fig. 49.2 we can even see the hole through which the ties run up; the radiating arrangement of supporting brackets shown beneath the top of Fig. 49.1 is therefore, in all probability, an error. All the tops are more or less well provided with darts, Fig. 49.5 having these ranged in groups of three alternating with round shields. The florid decoration around and beneath

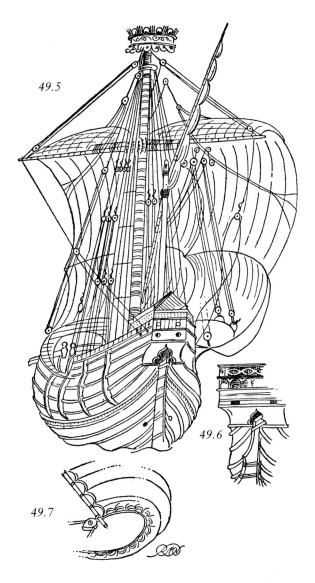

49.5

49.6

49.7

this top, unless mere engraver's flourish, may be set down as a representation of top-awnings of cloth.

The great mainmast, common to these ships, is closely woolded from deck to top and has a stay of enormous thickness, how set up we cannot see, but, unless the artist is at fault, not, as in the *kraeck*, to the projecting stem-head.

The shrouds in Figs. 49.1 and 49.3 are fitted aloft in galley-fashion, as might be expected in a Mediterranean ship, *i.e.*, with their eyes beneath the trestle-trees; and the greater number of them, to the tale of nine on either side, are set up below also in galley style, blocks taking the place of dead eyes; while in Fig. 49.3 the blocks of the lower row are not only without a chainwale, but are even out of sight inside the bulwarks. The aftermost three of the dozen shrouds on each ship, however, although still without a chain wale, are in both Figs. 49.1 and 49.3, set up ship-fashion with dead eyes (three-holed and heart-shaped in Fig. 49.3), all of which are in sight. Besides all these shrouds, and coming down just before them on either side of the mast of Fig. 49.1, we see a pair of tackles, 'pollankres,' perhaps, or 'swiftying takles.' In Fig. 49.5 these tackles seem to be more numerous, but they are evidently of the same form here as in Fig. 49.1, and it is by a mere chance that the artist has insisted upon them at the expense of the shrouds. No obvious Jacob's-ladder is shown in Fig. 49.5, though the widely-spaced lines that cross the larboard shrouds may represent either the treads of such a ladder or ratlines. The three ships (Figs. 49.1–3) show no sign of ratlines or Jacob's ladders, and although Breydenbach's ship (Fig. 49.4) has rattled shrouds, we must remember that this is doubtful evidence of Mediterranean practice, for, careful as he seems to have been to give true pictures of the galleys and sailing ships of the Mediterranean, his sketches were perhaps 'worked up' by an engraver, who might easily have added Northern ratlines to his carrack. In any case this carrack of Breydenbach is of a different build to that of the Florentines, her sides showing 'beam-ends' beneath the second wale and no skids or double wale, while her poop and after-castle are on the whole more like those in W. A.'s *kraeck*, with their bare, curved stanchions, *garderobes* and gallery right aft; even the detail of the steep-tub on the quarter seems to be there (see 47).

All these ships agree in having the main-yard composed, like the *antenna* of a galley, of two spars lashed together. For a short period this scarfed yard seems to have been used in Northern ships, for example the *Regent* of 1487; but it was evidently not admired in the North and remained essentially a Southern feature. The parrel that holds this yard in to the mast of Fig. 49.3 half hides a clumsy mistake of the engraver, who has drawn the yard upon the wrong side of the mast; the parrel however, is clearly seen to be an arrangement of ribs and trucks, as it is also in Fig. 49.5.

(To be continued.)

From Vol III, No 8, §§238–45 *(August 1913)*

SOME OLD-TIME
SHIP-PICTURES

A GROUP OF FLORENTINES (*Continued*)

By R Morton Nance

Coming now to the sails we can hardly fail to be struck by the sail-maker's share in giving these windbags their character. Each mainsail, with the exception of Breydenbach's (Fig. 49.4) shows its cloths arranged vertically abaft, in what we should call normal style; but wherever the foreside of a mainsail is visible we see lines that cross one another so as to give the appearance of a network over the whole surface. Whether the lines of this network are intended to run diagonally in contrary directions across the sails, or whether they should not actually have been made to run vertically and horizontally, is not certain. From the sails of Fig. 49.1 and 49.3 alone one would not hesitate to pronounce for the former view; but Fig. 49.2 on the whole lends more support to the latter, in favour of which Figs. 49.4 and 49.5 give their decided testimony. Similar reticulated sails are by no means rare in ship-pictures of the 15th and 16th centuries. In some of these we find the spaces within the network variously coloured, forming crosses or checker work, which suggests that the reticulation was mere ornament. In others the lines are double, suggesting that the sail is strengthened by means of bands of inkle or webbing, like the sails of Roman sailing ships. It is hardly satisfactory to decide that so much trouble would be taken, however, to decorate these sails, without the interest of variety to enliven the task, and it would be natural to expect that other patterns would appear sometimes; the Romans, too, had a purpose in their reticulated sail-bands that did not exist on these later ships, for they coincided with the numerous brails then in use and had, at each point where they crossed one another, the ring through which the brail passed. Neither of these explanations being satisfactory, there remains another solution of the problem: that they are double sails.

That sails were, in the 15th century, made double or single, according to their size or use, we know from inventories of the time, and it is reasonable to suppose that such double sails were at first actually two sails stitched back to back to make one. Assuming that the cloths in each part of such a sail were arranged in opposite directions, we should have, when they were stitched together along the vertical, back-seams only, a result like that in Fig. 49.5; while if stitched together in both directions a sail like that in Fig. 49.4 would be formed.

If we accept the more rarely shown diagonal lines as being correct we shall have more difficulty in explaining them; a quilting of the sail would of necessity show at the back also, and if the sail is double, or treble even, we still have to assume that it is attached to the back cloths only at the boltropes, and possibly down the middle, a method of joining the parts that seems very inadequate. Bartolomes Crescentio in his *Nautica Mediterranea*, 1607, describes a simpler method of doubling sails than that suggested by these reticulated windbags. In his day the sailmaker folded each cloth down the middle and seamed them all together with, of course, a corresponding increase in the number of vertical seams, but, unless he has forgotten to mention these, without any horizontal seams such as we see here. One thing at least all our sources of information seem fairly decided upon, that this doubling of sails belongs properly to square sails and not to lateens.

Another feature of these sails is the depth (at least half that of the sail) of the bonnet. This bonnet seems to have been removed, but seldom, and is sometimes (as in Fig. 49.4) shown with another bonnet beneath; so that the entire sail, perhaps as Mr. Callender suggests, by reason of a central band, or possibly by the central downward pull, alone, of a tackle at the foot of each course and bonnet, becomes not merely bi-lobed, but four or even six-lobed.

The tackles that produce this effect are in all cases attached to the foot of either a course or a bonnet, a point that is not well made out in Mr. Callender's diagram, and in the ships Figs. 49.1 and 49.3 tackles, like the similar gear in the same position on the great mainsail of a *Nordlands jaegt*, brings the middle of the sail in towards the mast. In sixteenth century ships, Peter Bruegel's evidence being strong on this point, such tackles were fixed to the feet of courses invariably; generally to the feet of bonnets, and more rarely to those of under-bonnets, or drablers. The name of these tackles or lines (they are sometimes a single rope) was perhaps in English 'bowge'; for this word survived long enough to get into *Bailey's Dictionary*, where it is said to mean 'a rope fastened to the middle of the sail, to make it stand closer to the wind.'

The four other tackles attached to the foot of the bonnet, in Figs. 49.1, 49.3 and 49.5, are obviously used in taking in the sail, and would no doubt be made fast to other cringles at the foot of the course, when the bonnet was cast off, possibly these are the 'strikes' of old inventories; similar tackles are made fast at the clews and in Fig. 49.3 we find in addition to these a single 'central clew line' attached at the same point as the second 'bowsing tackle' and the 'central sheet.'

To take in this enormous windbag, martinets were also needed; these are omitted from Figs. 49.1 and 49.3, but they can be made out in Fig. 49.2, branching down on either side of the sail from a block that hangs right over the yard. In Fig. 49.5 they are still more clearly shown with their 'legs' made fast to the leech, and Fig. 49.4, although showing them only on the after side of the sail, gives us the crow foot blocks also.

The tacks and sheets, both single ropes, lead in at holes, in the loof and on the quarter, respectively.

A bowline, with a single bridle is shown in Fig. 49.3, and less clearly in Fig. 49.2.

Ties are seen leading up from the yards in Figs. 49.1 and 49.2, but beneath the tops they vanish; their passage through sheare scores in the masthead or *calcet* is hidden, and their re-appearance abaft the mast is forgotten by the engraver.

The brace, clearly shown in Fig. 49.1, has the branching pendant seen also in Pinturicchio's ship at the National Gallery. (Fig. 40.2) The position of the brace blocks in Fig. 49.4 suggests that Breydenbach wished to give his ship a branching pendant also; but Fig. 49.5 shows braces with very long single pendants of a more modern type.

The lifts, too, show some variation in the attachments of their blocks. The upper of these in Figs. 49.1–3 is lashed close to the mast, while in Fig. 49.5 it is held by a short pendant; and the lower block is close to the yard arm in Fig. 49.3, and more loosely attached in Fig. 49.5, by means of a double seizing.

The mizzen-mast in these ships is treated with hardly more care than the foremast, and we have nothing to show how their shrouds were set up; although even where the shrouds themselves are left out the woolding-like *capelage* of their eyes at the mast head is not forgotten. Above this the mast itself seems to be provided with a sheare-hole for the mizen-tie; but perhaps this is only a faulty rendering of the *calcet* of harder wood usually set on the mast heads of the Mediterranean.

The mizen yard is made of two spars, clearly shown in Figs. 49.1, 49.3–4, while Figs. 49.3–4, where the sail is set upon it, show us the *ostes* or vangs, attached to the *penne*, the upper spar, and the *orse* to the lower spars, the *car*, quite in galley style.

This mizen is a single sail without cross-hatched seams. The seams in Fig. 49.4 are horizontal; but in the position here taken by it to reverse their true direction would be an excusable error. The foot of the mizen in Fig. 49.3 gives at the boltrope a detail that is seen less clearly at the foot of the bonnet of Fig. 49.1. This is of some importance as it shows another effort of the sailmaker towards producing a perfect windbag. In the 17th century we know that square sails were cut to the full width of the yard at the head, and gathered in to such an extent as to have the yardarms free. Boltropes, too, were made of well-stretched rope to which the canvas was stitched without being stretched; the result, of course, being a well-bagged sail. The sails in this print show in these two places an exaggeration of this method, the cloths being attached to the boltrope only at their seams, leaving the cloth slack between these points. A sail (held by a *Venus*, or it may be a *Fortune*) in an Italian woodcut of similar date shows such gatherings along its leech, Fig. 49.7. Another method of bagging sails, used for those of gallies, was that of allowing an additional overlapping to their seams for some distance at the head and foot; at the head only the same treatment was applied to ships' mizens, so Crescentio tells us, and such an overlapping of seams is apparently indicated along the mizen yard of Fig. 49.3.

It is not easy to give their separate names to the raffle of writhing ropes that dangle over the sides of the 'Three Ships at Sea' (Figs. 49.1–3); some of them may, from their eye-spliced ends and the positions in which we find them, be of use in fishing the anchor, the rest seem mere picturesque slovenliness, without definite meaning.

An anchor, by no means ill drawn, is shown in Fig. 49.1, held by its shank-painter and having one of the eye-spliced ropes wound about its arm. The object near it, if it is not a flat fender of worked rope, may be a shoe for this anchor.

The curious fitting abaft the main mast of Fig. 49.2 may be a capstan, or, if not that, a knight; another rendering of what is apparently the same thing is given in Fig. 49.3.

The suggestion is made in the British Museum Catalogue that these three ships on one plate may be copied from a certain painted picture that is known to have formerly existed. The little pennon that shows behind the mainsail of Fig. 49.1 certainly seems to belong to another ship, the rest of which has been left out by the engraver; and the omission of some important ropes, taken with the satisfactory delineation of some other parts, perhaps points to the same thing:—That we have here a good, but not a perfect, copy of a larger picture. It seems strange that this copy, if such it be, was not, like the *kraeck*, made use of in turn by other copyists; for it certainly seems to have been the highest achievement of 15th century Florentine engraving in the nautical direction.

From Vol III, No 9, §§276–79 (*September 1913*)

¶ 51 BELLYING OF XV CENTURY SAILS

References have been lately made in the 'M. M.' to the bellying sails shown by artists of the 15th century, and Mr. Morton Nance, in his paper in the August number, (see 49) again refers to this. It is a matter which has always puzzled me. If it has any semblance of truth the 15th century seamen could never sail 'by the wind,' or work to windward. But, surely, this was not so. Columbus, Cadamosto, Diego Cam, Bartholomew Diaz were all 15th century seamen. Could they have accomplished their wonderful voyages with vessels which—if we are to believe contemporary artists—could not work to windward? For, most certainly, the vessels pictured for us could not do so.

The solution of the mystery seems to me to be that the painters of that century exaggerated.

Another thing is that perhaps nine-tenths of vessels pictured were, even up to the middle of the sixteenth century, drawn with the wind abaft the beam.

Now, speaking as a sailor, I am aware that no one can appreciate this matter in all its bearings unless he has had charge of square-rigged vessels with no steam power. I do not wish to appear dogmatic, but, as a sailor, I know this to be true. I do not believe that Columbus went along with a flowing sheet when close hauled.

By the time we reach the middle of the 16th century, enough pictorial examples can be found to show that sailors of that date boarded both tack and sheet when by the wind and did not ease off their topsail sheets as artists of the time would have us believe.

L. Arte Del Navegar (1554) shows us on the title a vessel close hauled, tacks and sheets boarded.

Bruegel (1564) gives, in his series, two vessels with tacks boarded, but with sheets flowing, these vessels must be at least seven points off the wind and, taking leeway into account, could not work to windward.

In his plate of various craft is a vessel with yards sharp up, but though the tacks are *meant* (?) to be boarded they are not so. Bruegel was not a sailor.

In Civitates Orbis Terrarum (1575) there is at least one vessel closed hauled, main tack and sheet boarded, yet fore tack flowing though sheet is aft (probably an engraver's error).

In Lant's funeral of Sir Philip Sidney (1586) the *Black Pynnes*, though not well drawn, has her main yard sharp up and no belly to topsail. But her foresail is shown trimmed to a quarterly wind (another engraver's error, probably).

In all this carelessness, or ignorance, there is one exception known to me, and only one. This is Ribero's *Mappa Mundi* of 1529.

Here it may perhaps be supposed that, drawn as it was for such a tremendously serious purpose (the dividing of the world between Spain and Portugal), pains were taken to have things accurate. Be that as it may, the ships which embellish it are the only ones of that period known to me which to the trained eye of a sailor carry full conviction.

The ships are of the same rig as Columbus' *nave*, the *Santa Maria*, except that some of them carry fore topsails. There are nineteen vessels in all, depicted sailing in different parts of the seas. *Only one* of these has bellying sails, with flowing tacks and sheets in the case of the *mainsail only*, for her topsail sail is set flat though the sheets do not come home; no top-sail sheets did in those days. She is running down to Saint Helena with a quarterly wind, having rounded the Cape, *Vengo de Maluco*. Between Saint Helena and Ascension a ship is shown with her tacks boused down, but sheets flowing; this seems to have been the custom with the wind a little abaft the beam, and is to a less extent the custom still. In the case of vessels of that date, the weather main lift was in these circumstances slacked and the yard allowed to cant down to windward to allow the tack of the sail to be brought right down to the chesstree overside.

Vessels with the wind in all directions are shown, some with the wind dead aft, both main sheets hauled aft, and the mizen yard (mezana) right athwartships, some with wind quarterly, several close hauled all sails trimmed flat. As before said there is only one out of the nineteen with bellying sail such as mediaeval artists have generally given us, and in her case it is only the mainsail which is set thus flowing.

The date of the map being 1529, and the rig being the same as that of Columbus' day, we may safely say that these ships represent those of the end of the 15th century, and yet we find artists for at least another 50 years giving us these balloon like sails. What is the truth of the matter? My own answer is that artists thought bellying sails more 'artistic' in a picture and exaggerated on purpose, but that, in fact, the great seamen of those days were not such arrant lubbers as these artist would have us believe.

The quadrant and astrolabe on this map are also interesting; these are referred to in Vol. lxxvii of the *Nautical Magazine*.

By 'W.B.W.', from *Notes*, Vol III, No 11, §§347–48 (*November 1913*)

❡ 52   XV CENTURY SAILS

It may seem that, on a matter of sails, those who are not seamen should at once bow to the opinion of one who is not only a sailor of the old school, but also keenly interested in the history of his craft; but when W. B. W., as in his note on the above subject (see 51) has his hand upon practically the whole of our hardly-won little pile of pictorial evidence concerning mediaeval shipping and is about to pitch all these ship-drawings overboard as careless, lubberly, and even 'artistic' rubbish, it seems impossible not to try to defend their makers at least against that last accusation of wilful falsification for purposes of 'Art.' They may have been no sailors, but 'Art' at all events, they were innocent of: the thing had not been invented. We may find their naïve drawings 'quaint' or 'artistic'; but in their eyes, uninfluenced by realistic pictures, photographs, or even direct work from Nature, they were the nearest conceivable approach to 'the real thing.' Children draw in just the same way to-day, putting on paper what they *know* of their subject, and overleaping all difficulties of perspective and proportion by getting things to *look* right—to themselves if to no-one else. But, like children, these old fellows of the 15th century were absolutely sincere, and it cannot be for nothing that whatever their differences of style, of medium, or of nationality, they all agree in giving 'windbags' to their ships. Many of W. B. W.'s criticisms one is bound to agree with, especially those referring to the inconsistent way in which tacks and sheets are often drawn or engraved, and, no doubt, one must allow for a certain amount of unconscious exaggeration in these bellying sails, as one does in judging of the actual build of a ship from the same pictures (for example, they usually show too much of the vanishing side of their bows or quarters.) These, after all, are simply human weaknesses, and any art student knows how incredible reality may be, and of how many prejudices one may have to empty one's mind before one can truly see what is before one's eyes.

But, granting that there is even *relative* truth in the *best* of these pictures (and we can hardly refuse this, though we may say that many are worthless and none absolutely truthful), with no more faith than this, it yet seems impossible to doubt that, exaggeration apart, sails were made on the *principle* shown in the 'windbags' that illustrate Mr. Callender's articles (see 38, 39, 40) on Maso Finiguerra and my own remarks on the Florentines. We are all entitled to hold our own opinions (and they differ already (see 49, 50) as to the way in which these 'windbags' were put together, and what particular advantage was to be gained by them; but that they represent more or less faithfully a reality of the past, cannot be doubtful.

Wanting a more perfect knowledge of all their fittings it would probably be impossible to test their qualities fairly by experiment with actual sails made upon their model, though it would be interesting to try. Their balloon-like, shape was certainly, as much as might be, done away with when they were set on a wind, by what I have supposed to be a 'bowge' (see 50). This tackle has evidently, in Fig. 49.2, pulled the middle of the sail close in to the mast, and would probably flatten the sail more than this picture would lead one to believe. As it is still a familiar fitting on the one-masted, square-sailed boats of Norway, it may be possible to get from that quarter an idea of the extent of its help in working these survivals of mediaevally rigged boats to windward.

Apart from the 'bowge,' there are names of gear belonging to sails of this type that are not yet identified, some of which may have been vital to their windward sailing powers. 'Loof-hooks' and 'wartakes' we know, but what was a 'lych hoke?' Was it hooked on to the leech, and, if so, why? 'Stedyngs' and 'dryngs' we may think that we understand, and even 'strikes,' but what were 'trejets,' and how did one tail on to the 'tayling ropes?'

There is much work to be done before answers can be found to these questions, and we cannot afford to let 'W. B. W. give up the whole 'windbag' as 'artistic,' and refuse to help us to grapple with it. (see 51)

If nothing that I have yet written has power to move him, I would ask him again to look at the sail of the Florentine ship, Fig. 49.1. Does not this momentary glimpse of a rising, flapping sail convince him that the man was drawing something that he had seen, and seen well, and that he was not simply perpetuating a convention? I willingly admit that his ship demands too many 'vanishing points' to be praised for its perspective, and I think that the relative proportions of its parts may be drawn to as many scales, but, unless we should be so unfair to him as to blame him for neglecting sciences that were unknown to his contemporaries, we cannot deny him honesty of intention, and, granting it in his case, why should we deny it in the others.

By 'R.M.N.', from *Notes*, Vol IV, No 1, §§51–52 (*January 1914*)

❡ 53   A CARRACK OF 1482

In August, 1914, Mr. Nance gave us (Fig. 53.1) what he described as a third-hand copy of a Southern Carrack from a Venetian book of 1547. The original of this drawing is a map of 1482 by Grazioso Benincasa, now in the University Library at Bologna (No. 280). It is reproduced in facsimile in Fincati's 'Le Triremi,' 2nd edn., 1881, and on a reduced scale in 'L'Arte Nautica ai Tempi di Colombo,' by d'Albertis, 1893 (p. 90). Except for the loss of two figures, one aft and one amidships, the drawing

53.1

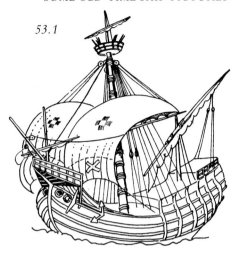

has suffered wonderfully little in its series of copyings. There are many other very interesting reproductions in the book by d'Albertis mentioned above.

By R C Anderson, from *Notes*, Vol VI, No 3, §§88–89 (*March 1920*)

A HANSEATIC
BERGENTRADER OF 1489

By R Morton Nance

Just as in the seventeenth century the fine merchant-ships of the Dutch, and in the nineteenth those of the British and American shipbuilders, showed examples of masterly ship-construction that were so widely copied as to make their style well-nigh universal, so in the fifteenth century, while the Hansa ports of North Germany were sending forth the greatest and best found fleets of merchant ships in North Europe, the influence of German fashions must have been felt by the shipbuilders of all countries that came within their range, and the absence of any trustworthy model or picture of a German ship of this time would leave a sad gap in ship history.

Failing such a record of these vessels amongst the treasures of the *Schiffergesellschaft* of Lübeck, or of the Bremen Rathaus, one might well despair of finding it; but the fates that preside over nautical relics have in this matter been kinder than we had any right to expect, for in the Marienkirche at Lübeck is to be seen a painted panel dating from the fifteenth century that shows us several ships flying the white-and-red of Lübeck (Fig. 54.1).

The principal amongst these ships, as an inscription tells us, came to her end by shipwreck in the year 1489; but fortunately for us the gratitude to Heaven of a survivor took the happy form of this *ex-voto* painting, which preserves for us not merely his own sentiments, but the scene of his danger and the ship herself, as yet showing, beyond some losses in masts and rigging, no signs of her impending dissolution.

The hull of this ship, though intact, shows us between the water-line and the castles very little detail; we see, indeed, the mighty curve with which her stem sweeps up from her keel beneath the break of the forecastle, answered by the bold sheer of the wales as they run fore and aft along her sides; but her stern is so blurred that only from her age, and from the sterns of other ships painted in the background can one infer that it is round. Above this meagre hull, however, there is much interesting detail in the 'cage-work' of the fore and after castles. There are, of

Fig. 54.1 Painted panel in the Marienkirche, Lübeck.

course, no lidded port-holes cut for guns in the hull, a round dozen of years must pass before this could be possible if Decharges of Brest rightly has the credit of inventing them in 1501 (Jal disputes this, p. 1302, of his *Glossaire Nautique*), nor do we see any guns mounted in the waist, where perhaps they would be carried by warships only; but each castle has its tier of round-headed, lidless ports, and from each port runs out a long, many-banded cannon, so that, without counting the half-dozen or more of them that might be in the cowbridge-heads and right astern, we can bring their tale up to thirty-eight. The arrangement of these port-holes seems to show a marked advance upon that in some other ships of supposedly similar dates, and from these less developed vessels we seem to see how such rows of round-headed ports came into being. Two of these, the *kraeck* of W. A. and a Mediterranean carrack, already illustrated in THE MARINER'S MIRROR (see 46, 48), have the light superstructure of their poops and forecastles supported on curved stanchions that, standing quite bare, are obviously but a development from tilt-frames such as we see in these and older boats, a light deck with bulwarks, and in turn defended by nettings, taking the place of the earlier netting or tilt. The Warwick MS. (B. M. Julius E IV) shows some ships with cage-work of this type (Fig. 54.3); but another type is also shown there, one that is even better exhibited in the pictures of Carpaccio, and is probably the Genoese carrack, and in this (Fig. 54.4) we can see the next stage in the development of these round-headed ports; for here, by the addition of spandrels at their upper corners, the free spaces between the curved stanchions have become arched openings that need only to be a little reduced in size, by blanking that still further covers the original stanchions, to become a tier of round-headed ports arranged like those of our Lübecker. Through the sixteenth century, and until the beak-headed galleon had finally prevailed over the ship of mediaeval tradition, we see in the 'cage-work' of high-caged sea-castles, like those of Peter Bruegel (Fig. 54.5), tier over tier of these round-headed ports; and even when their origin was long forgotten they remained as a favourite form of decoration.

In the after castle of the Lübeck ship we have a great advance upon the arrangements seen in the above-mentioned carracks, such a simpler and heavier poop would hardly seem out of place on a ship of even fifty years later; but although the pavesade runs unbroken along the bulwarks above, we seem to have, in the disposal of the portholes, a hint that, below and within, this stern castle may still be divided, like those of the carracks, into halves that are differently decked or fitted, for, abaft and forward of a solitary shield, we have, respectively, three large ports and five smaller, the smaller ones coming just where one might expect to find the lighter transversely planked 'half deck' that would necessitate guns of smaller calibre. The space in which the smaller gun ports are cut, like the corresponding part of the forecastle and all the shields that defend and decorate the after-castle, is painted in the white-over-red colours of Lübeck: the chainwale, with its tangle of shrouds and deadeyes, would probably have come immediately below it, but this has been left out, an omission which allows one to suppose that the single skid in that position, looking alone so unequal to its harbour duties of warding off the bumpings and raspings of wharf-piles and dangling freight, may stand as representative of a cluster, like that fixed below the chains of W. A.'s carrack.

The waist of this ship, owing partly to the over-sized figures that sliding to safety along the mainyard, hide from sight what might be there, shows us neither guns, *Kubrugge*, nor any other detail, and the forecastle cowbridge-head hides itself entirely. This lack of interest in the waist is, however, well made up to us by the forecastle, where we have, all painted with care, a paveside, forechains, and a remarkable figurehead. The shields of this paveside are painted with the arms of the Bergen traders, who, remembering in their pride the humble foundation of their fortunes, chose as their arms, dividing the honours with half of the imperial eagle that we saw on the *Adler*, (see 60) a silver stockfish that, actually, they crowned with gold, although on this paveside the crowns seem to be missing. It was, then, upon a Bergen voyage, after the savoury stockfish, that this unlucky ship was engaged when she got among the rocks.

The modern-looking, round deadeyes, each with its chainplate of iron held by a single bolt to the ship's side, are not, as they stand, sufficient to set up the rigging; either the shrouds should have passed through them to be again made fast to their own standing part; or, and this seems more probable, the upper of two deadeyes with the connecting lanyard has in each case been left out here, as in other instances, (see Fig. 8.3 and Fig. 8.5) but no holes are shown in them.

The figure head takes the form of a warrior, armed cap-a-pie, (Fig. 54.2). He seems at first glance as swarthy as a Saracen, and what is probably a wreath around his helm might well be a turban; but these suggestions are belied by the Lübeck colours of his lance-pennon and

54.2   54.3   54.4   54.5

even more strongly by the eight-pointed (St. John's) cross upon his shield. He stands between us and the bowsprit, upon the other side of which some brush-marks may faintly indicate a second figure. Were this the case, we should have a purely decorative anticipation of the more utilitarian 'Knightheads' that were to take up a similar position in eighteenth century ships: against the probability of twin figure heads, however, is the fact that the bowsprit would not at this time have been stepped in line with the keel, but would have had its heel abaft and beside the mast, and passing beside the stem head would have come out just where the second figurehead should stand, in the lop-sided fashion, shown in Figs. 54.3–5, that was only abandoned in the early seventeenth century, upon the removal further aft of the step of the foremast. Behind this figure head the sides of the forecastle meet at a sharp angle, the timber that forms their profile showing a series of well-contrasted curves.

Coming now to the rigging, it is clear that the artist was in too great haste to paint that of the foremast, perhaps because the foresail that flaps its parted sheet into a figure-of-eight knot gave him another opportunity to display in its folds the knack of painting floating draperies that he had acquired by long practice at sacred subjects such as form the chief motive of this picture. He has, at all events, covered, in painting the upper part of the forecastle, a considerable part of this sail and also obliterated part of each shroud. His haste perhaps, has prevented us from finding here any detail beyond the commonplace. We note, though, that, in contrast with the carrack's bare shrouds and jacob's-ladders, the shrouds here are rattled, and that the usual halliards are present at the bowsprit end.

The disorder of the main rigging is left to our imagination; but we see, circling the main mast where its rapidly tapering girth is greatest, the parrel of the main-yard, and we can almost hear the crash of the heavy main-top as it tumbles into the midst of the aftercastle.

The main-mizen snapped off just above its lateen yard by the falling wreckage of the mainmast, bears a small round-top with a short topmast and white-and-red vane like those of the foremast; besides the slackened shrouds there are some ropes that fly off into caligraphic flourishes, one of which, starting beneath the top, maybe a parted stay.

Right aft is the bonaventure-mizen, headless, and without visible means of support, in the shape of shroud or stay; its yard, like that of the main-mizen, has depending ropes that may be brails or vangs. The bonaventure sheet runs down to a long, low-placed outlegger, around which winds some gear that gives handhold to one of the shipwrecked crew. All the yards, like those of W.A.'s carrack, are painted as single sticks.

In the mind of the painter the figures, of course, provided the chief interest, and of these the ships company were of secondary importance. We reverse his process and, putting the ship first, come now to the sailors. The chief amongst these seems to be the person having a bonnet upon his head and around his neck a chain, perhaps the golden chain by which the whistle of command should hang, a lighter weight than that of the mariner who is seen clinging to it with the grip of one who has but one hope of life. Behind and supporting this be-capped officer is a man who also has round his neck what may be a chain, by which we seem to see that the old rule—captain last to leave the ship—was adhered to by the Easterlings of 1489. It is remarkable that no boat appears in the picture. Ship boats, when not towed astern may have been practically useless in an emergency, with such tackle as they then had, for they would probably lie deep down in the waist, covered with gratings that might become in turn cumbered with a jumble of gear and merchandise; the vessel, too, is so closely beset by the rocks of the shore, that the mainyard dropped aportlast makes a bridge to one of them; yet many of the crew, including the ship's dog, are afloat on boxes, barrels or hatches, while many more are swimming or drowning unaided. One wonders if a law such as those by which sixteenth century Spanish and Portuguese Indiamen were forbidden to carry boats, as an incentive to greater care of the ships, was in force in the Hansa fleets of the fifteenth century.

Although the air-borne figures furnish, with the shipwreck and escaping crew over which they hover, the main interest of this panel, no part of it is allowed to remain empty. The painter, following the convention of his day, seen at its best perhaps in the tapestries that it produced, has, without any attempt to delude the spectator into the belief that he is looking at an actual scene, tried rather to fill as pleasantly as he could the space allotted him. To avoid great sky-spaces he has placed his horizon very high, and has distributed the interest as evenly as possible over his panel without care for exact perspective. The small space of sky is here reduced still further by the two scrolls that bear legends descriptive of the wreck and the pious conclusions to be drawn therefrom. The sea with its high set horizon gives room for more ships, of which we have several in various postures. Of these lesser ships none would seem to be a sister ship to the wreck, which with her bonaventure-mast seems to be the most important of the fleet, but they are of some value as giving a few of the details that are wanting in the great ship ashore, one, stern-on, showing not only the rudder and the full-length of the outlegger, but also a glimpse of the forecastle arch, while others supply such missing parts as the main rigging with its chainwale, the mainstay (in one ship having a

54.6

stay-tackle upon it), and some braces and lifts that are not shown in the wreck. The mizen lifts are led to their own mast heads and seem to be used in conjunction with vangs, an arrangement that in the light of other evidence seems improbable; but we have a bit of correct detail that is warranted by other pictures in the short staves, fixed at the fore part of the tops, from which float the great white-and-red streamers.

In all these Bergen traders we see nothing that at once distinguishes them as merchant vessels, and in the larger class of traders at this time there would probably be no such distinction. If they are 'hulkes of the Easterlings' they in no way resemble Bruegel's 'Flemish hulks,' unless, indeed, the heavy build of their poops would be thought enough to give them a common name; for all have forecastles and are rigged in the height of the fashion of their day. That ships of such size should be engaged in a coasting voyage of no great length seems strange; but the rocks, shoals and storms were not the only foes that they might meet between Lübeck and Bergen, and the stock-fish trade was one well worth guarding. If an early seventeenth century model in the Church of St. Mary at Bergen is, as there is every likelihood of its being, a Hanseatic Bergen trader, our *Bergenfahrer* of the fifteenth century is neither greater nor more warlike; for this model, in a wonderful state of restoration ahead and aloft, has two tiers of guns and upper and lower quarter galleries with side turrets, the latter being decorations rarely found on any but the largest ships (Fig. 54.6).

From Vol III, No 6, §§161–7 (*June* 1913)

❡ 55   THE BERGEN MODEL

The little tail-piece of this model (Fig. 54.6), introduced only as hinting at the possiblity of large ships having been used in the Bergen stockfish trade, was made from a tracing of part of a woodcut in Eidem and Lütken's *Vor Somagts Historie*, p. 313, the left-out portions consisting of an impossible suit of sails, a figure-head and stern-davits that disfigured her. Possibly I should have been right in removing the foremost turret on the quarter gallery and the lower masts with their tops might have been retained, but the engraving itself is too small, and at the same time coarse, to allow of very critical examination.

The galleries are roofed in with a scale-patterned roof, the round ports of the upper tier seem to be wreathed, and *between* the ports below are lions' faces that one would have been less surprised to find on the port *lids*. Like most church-ships she has practically no underwater parts, and she is not built to any sort of scale, so that interesting as she is in other ways no measurements taken from her would be of any value.

Beneath the illustration is the title '*En hanseatisk Bergenfarer. Modellen hang i mange Aar i St. Mariæ Kirke i Bergen.*' The fact that Saint Mary's was the special church of the Hansa at Bergen seems to make it probable that the ship was in some way connected with the League; but it is of course possible that she may have been, as R. C. A. suggests, with much reason, a Danish-Norwegian warship. There is always a doubt in my mind whether these ex-votos were in all cases models of actual ships, or simply 'ships,' made to order by professional modellists, perhaps, or even kept in stock by them, to be sold to pious merchants and sailors. They are so similar in their style, and their faults, that they must belong to a school of model-craft, one would think, and not be the individual attempts of sailors, although no two are exactly alike.

If she is still in existence, a photograph of her would be most interesting, there are so many things that one would like to see more of. Perhaps some member who has visited Bergen can tell us the latest news of this model.

In the same Danish book, on p. 311, is a half-tone reproduction of a print by K. Moller, of a great man-of-war of similar date to (*c.* 1610) and not unlike, the Bergen model.

Her very elaborate and carefully-drawn rigging follows very closely the engraving of a great ship of 1594, after Barentsoen, with modifications that bring it up to date. This rigging is unfortunately the only part of the print that is clear, however, and although turrets on the quarter like those of the Bergen model can be made out, and it is almost possible to number her guns, it is only a vexation to attempt to trace the detail of her hull. I fancy I see a sun that may be the Stralsund emblem on her flags, but even these are blurred. The original print may be known to some of our members; if so, a large and clear, photograph of it would, I am sure, be much appreciated by all students of old shipping, coming, as it does, between the before-mentioned Barentsoen picture and those of the *Navire Regale* by Hondius and of the *Sovereign* by Payne.

By 'R.M.N.', from *Notes*, Vol III, No 11, §346 (*November 1913*)

56

A SHIP OF HANS
BURGKMAIR

By H H Brindley

*N*avicula *penitentie per excellentissimum sacre Pagine doctorem Joannem Key-serpergium Argentinensium concionatorem Predicata. A Jacobo Otthero Collecta. Ecce ascendimus hierosolimam,* is a work published at Augsberg in 1511, most of whose title page is here reproduced from the example, a small quarto, of which copies are at the British Museum and in the Cambridge University Library.

Its author, Johannes Geiler von Kaiserburg, was born at Schauffhausen in 1445, and became Doctor in Theology of Freiburg in 1475. He has been described by the Abbé Dacheux as 'un réformateur catholique à la fin du XVe siècle.' The *Navicula penitentie* was reprinted several times and also appeared as '*Das Schiff der Penitentz*' in 1514. It followed the same author's *Navicula sive speculum fatuorum,* in which he has been described as dealing with the shortcomings of the Church, while in *Navicula penitentie* he suggested remedies. The copy of the former work possessed by the Cambridge University Library is not illustrated by a ship. The signature H.B. is without question that of Hans Burgkmair, who was born at Augsburg *c* 1473, and died in 1559. The present woodcut is not mentioned by A. Bartsch in 'Le Peintre Gravure,' but in Vol. vii, p. 221, he describes a cut by Burgkmair in a book of sermons of J. von Kaiserburg. A. M. Hind ('A Short History of Engraving and Etching,' ed. 2,1911 pp. 35, 109, 346) points out that Burgkmair greatly influenced the engravers of his time; and John Jackson ('A Treatise on Wood Engraving,' ed. 2, 1866, pp. 277–281) expresses the opinion that as a designer on wood he is second only to Dürer, though there is no positive evidence that he ever actually engraved wood blocks himself. It is known that several of the original blocks signed H. B. have on their backs the names of the cutters, as for instance the well-known Triumphs of Maximilian series. So we may regard the *Navicula penitentie* as a design of Burgkmair cut by one of his pupils. Regarded as a picture the work is admirable; clouds, sea and rocky coast are disposed in a most pleasing manner, and if we overlook

56.1

the technical shortcomings of the ship she is a thing of life. Though far less rigging is shown, and some of it seems inaccurate, this ship of Hans Burgkmair has certain features in common with the *Kraeck* of W.A. illustrated and described by Mr. Morton Nance, (see 46). It will be convenient for comparison to take the various features of interest in generally the same order as Mr. Nance has adopted for the *Kraeck*. The ship of Burgkmair is shown much more end on than the former, so we miss the stem and the part of the hull immediately connected with it.

Whether there are skids is uncertain, there is some suggestion of one or perhaps two as the curve of the hull runs forward out of sight. There are four wales as in the *Kraeck*, and they are apparently continued to the stern post. But here the hull differs markedly in its square tuck from that of W. A.'s ship. The extension of the wales over the stern is either only for strengthening that part, or may be merely an ornamental continuation of the lines of the hull. As in the *Kraeck*, we do not see the stern post, and the tiller hole is very large, another resemblance, but the counter is not concave, or else is only slightly so. The rudder has much the same form as the *Kraeck's*, and we see no pintle-irons. The three pairs of bolts may indicate gudgeon-irons or possibly clamps, for perhaps the artist intended the two short vertical lines to show that the rudder is built up of two timbers, as in the *Kraeck*. The poop is built solid with the hull, and its side is a pavesade hung with oval shields. From the waist forward there are strong resemblances to the *Kraeck*; we see gangways rising towards the forecastle and joining thereat to form an arched doorway. Probably the gangways do not really slope more sharply than in the *Kraeck*, their apparent steepness seems an effect of perspective. The arched 'cowbridge head' of Mr. Nance is continued into the after breastwork of the forecastle, and, as in the *Kraeck* also the rail at the break of the forecastle has a gateway or embrasure amidships. Whether the bowsprit carries a grapnel we cannot see, but the two slack ropes outside the forecastle look very like part of its tackle when we compare them with what is shown in the *Kraeck*. The bowsprit end is decorated with a 'spider's web' or armillary sphere, as in the ship of W. A., drawn by Mr. Nance from the engraving at South Kensington and described by him in THE MARINER'S MIRROR, (see 44). Similar bowsprit ornaments are seen in some of the ships in the *Nuremberg Chronicle,* and in a one-masted ship in an engraving by Israels van Mecken, who died in 1503. This engraving is reproduced in W. Y. Ottley's 'Facsimiles,' 1828, pl. 37. Another instance is in the oil painting by an unknown German master of the XVth century from St. Severin's Church, Cologne, now at South Kensington, the ships in which are illustrated in THE MARINER'S MIRROR (see 9). It seems likely that the practice of fitting such symbols or ornaments to the bowsprit was especially a practice in Germany and the Low Countries in the XVth and XVIth centuries. The only piece of bowsprit rigging we can identify is the forestay with its collar. Below and just forward of this lashing a piece of gear is indicated too obscurely to make anything of it. The masts have the usual wooldings. The mainmast has two Jacob's-ladders, and these are forward of the mast, not abaft it, as is the single one in the *Kraeck*.

The shrouds of the foremast are led outboard, and those of the mizen mast inboard, but how they are made fast we cannot see. The inboard lead of the mizzen shrouds seems to have been still common practice of the age of the picture. The method of making fast the main shrouds, as far as any method is shown to us in this ship of Hans Burgkmair, is one which I do not recollect having seen in any other picture. There are no chain wales and the eight starboard shrouds are led to stout pegs projecting from below the gunwale. Round these pegs the shrouds are secured, apparently with several turns. Forward of the eight pegs taking shrouds are six more pegs which seem purposeless. The whole arrangement suggests confusion with a row of 'serpentines,' *i.e.*, the small cannon then in use afloat, thought it is unlikely that an artist of the capacity of Hans Burgkmair would be guilty of such a muddle. How could shrouds led as here shown be set up? Is it possible that the pegs are really drums, and that the shrouds were made taut by some windlass-like gear of ratchet and pawl? Search among early German representations of ships may show that Hans Burgkmair engraved in an imperfect or faulty manner some forgotten method of setting up shrouds.

Besides those mentioned above, the only spars we see are the lower yards without sails. The fore yard is outside, but the main and mizzen yards are slung within the rigging, as is only the mizzen yard in the *Kraeck.*

The foreyard is considerably topped-up. No parrel is shown, the yard crosses the fore-mast at the level of a woolding. The main yard is two spars strongly lashed together, as, to quote present day instances, we see the yard in a Trinidad lighter or in a *tartane* anywhere from Cette to Marseilles. This building up of the main yard in two pieces is common in the larger vessels drawn for the *Nuremberg Chronicle*, but we do not see it thus in any of W.A.'s ships or in the *Nuremberg Chronicle* ship of Ulysses, referred to by Mr. Nance in THE MARINER'S MIRROR (see 8). The practice in this respect is another point on which examination of early German prints may throw light. I do not recollect any vessel with the main yard in two pieces in pictures of the XVth or XVIth century by French or English artists. The main parrel is shown clearly, save that there is confusion between the ribs and trucks: the drawing falls far short of that of the *Kraeck* in this respect. In Hans Burgkmair's ship the mizzen yard is represented very like the crossjack yard of much later times, not only in its being so much squared, but also in having the same length on either side the mast. This feature of the woodcut greatly shakes our faith in the technical knowledge of the artist. In the blocks at the yard arms and the ropes coming down from them he seems to have had braces in his mind, and so he represented both tack rope and peak down-haul as braces. There is little other running rigging. From the foremast come down two ropes to the starboard aft end of the forecastle bulwarks, which are perhaps the fore halyards. The tackle at the top of the picture just outside the main shrouds may be meant for a lift, but it is led so far inboard from the yard arm that we are reminded of the martnetts of the *Kraeck*. The starboard main brace is seen led to the fore end of the pavesade, and the corresponding brace of the port side is obviously intended in the doubling of the ropes where we see the brace-like mizzen peak downhaul. The rigging is certainly the weak part of this picture. Mr. Nance has pointed out that the *Kraeck* was copied by several artists or woodengravers, but the Augsberg ship does not fall into this category, the differences from W.A.'s carrack are too great for this. Hans Burgkmair has given us the German merchantmen of his day imperfectly in many respects, but he has put on record features which are at least suggestive.

I have to thank Dr. W. M. Fletcher, of Trinity College, Cambridge, for calling my attention to Burgkmair's ship, and Mr. Charles Sayle, M.A., of the Cambridge University Library, for information on the work it illustrates.

From Vol III, No 3, §§81–84 (*March 1913*)

57

SOME XV CENTURY SHIP PICTURES

By A H Moore

The MS. from which the accompanying plates have been taken was described in Part I of Vol. LVII of Archaeologia, where the pictures were reproduced. Our Society is much indebted to Lord Hastings for permitting the editor to get fresh photographs.

The article states that the "manuscript, which is written on vellum, consists of fifteenth century copies, with some illuminations of various treatises dealing with chivalry, state, &c. These have been bound in one thick volume, which from external evidence we may suppose to have at one time belonged to that distinguished Prince, Henry, son of James I." The book thus described is said to contain twenty treatises of which the pictures whence the accompanying plates are taken belong to No. 9. This is a Pilot's Guide chiefly for the coasts of England and Wales. The article continues:—"9. Folio 130b is filled with the representation of shipping shown (see Fig. 57.1), which is followed by directions on the course to be followed in sailing round from Berwick-on-Tweed to Holyhead. These begin on fol. 131, 'Berwik lieth southe and northe of golde stones,' and end on fol. 137b, 'The redbanke in Chester water northe and southe.' Also by sailing directions for the Bay of Biscay. These begin on fol. 137b, 'Opyn o geronde there is wose and sonde togedir,' and ends on fol. 138b, 'than goo est north est a long the see, &c.' The greater part of fol. 138b is filled with an illumination of a ship taking soundings."

The article also tells that the contents of several of the treatises are to be found in Landsdowne MS. No. 285, including that accompanying the ship pictures.

This MS. is written in a XV century hand, and its contents are as those of the Hastings MS. described above.

The sailing directions are rather obscure in places, and a good many names round the coast seem to have been different in the days when it was written. Beachy Head, for instance, is not named, though Dunge (Denge) Ness is. Other familiar names are the Spits, the Horse Shoe

57.1

Beacon, the Brake, the Goodwins, the Needles, the Runnel (Reynolds) stone, the Seven stones, the Longships. I have used modern spelling.

The use of the word slade, still found on the Essex coast for a channel in the sand is worth noting, and so is the curious expression, 'half tide under Rothir.' Why the 'under rudder' particularly is not apparent.

In Fig. 57.1 four ships are completely represented and part of a fifth, together with three boats, probably the great boats of the ships.

To what extent may we take these pictures as supplying trustworthy likenesses of the shipping of their time? They were certainly drawn by a man familiar with ships or copied from an original by such a man. It may be objected that the pendants are blowing from two or three directions, but to insist on this is, perhaps, demanding too much realism from the artist. The general direction of the wind is clearly shown by the ship coming into port under a pair of courses, and the ship towing out with her yards pointed to the wind; true, her streamer and that in her boat seem to show a fair wind, but if the artist troubled about it at all, we may take it that he ascribed the contrary pointing of the flags to the same eddying puff that blows the smoke from the beacon seawards, while the windmill across the valley faces the true wind. Further, who that has sailed under high land is not familiar with the way in which the wind may in a comparatively small space be fair on opposite courses? The writer remembers sailing down the North Kentish coast to the Foreland with a fair wind and there seeing two vessels approaching one another stem on each before the wind on courses roughly at right angles to his own.

There are a good many omissions from the running rigging, but the undoubted mistakes are few.

Beginning with the ship in the top left hand corner of Fig. 57.1, we may note that she has the bluff bow and the convex stem that seems almost an arc of a circle, together with the long overhanging forestage, that are marked features of many of Le Testu's ships in the middle of the XVI century (see Fig. 57.3–8). The vessel immediately below her presenting her port bow shows the same characteristics more clearly.

It will be noticed that all the ships, with perhaps one exception, have their forestages considerably higher than their after castles. They are all 'great ships of forecastle,' to use a phrase that occurs in the Paston letters and to which they add significance.

In the ship we are particularly considering, the after castle, half deck, summer hutch, or whatever it should rightly be called, reaches to the mainmast, and aft it overhangs what is apparently a transome. It appears also to project on either quarter.

57.2

The bulwarks of both forestage and aftercastle bear small dots, which may represent ports or rather holes for serpentines, but which may well be only for ornament. There would scarcely be room for the smallest ordnance at the forward end of the forestage in the narrow angle made by the bulwarks of either side, encumbered with the bowsprit and at times with the spritsail yard as well. The four nearly circular holes that appear in the ship's side, one just beneath the anchor, and the other three from just before the main mast aftward may well be gun ports, and suggest the presence of a deck at their level running almost, if not quite, from end to end of the ship, covered fore and aft by the castles and in the waist by the hatches.

On the bow is seen an immense hawse hole. The anchor is stowed in the fashion of that day with its crown at the 'loof' the positions of the crown and ring show what a small structure the forecastle was apart from the forestage.

On the ship's side in the waist are what may be skids, though they are somewhat vaguely drawn.

The bowsprit is stepped entirely in the forestage; from its position it does not come in board at all. The spritsail is shown furled as though the yard were lying fore and aft beneath the bowsprit, but the yard is not shown. The two ropes hanging in bights between the middle of the bowsprit and the forestage, are possibly the spritsail sheets.

The foremast is right forward, apparently before the stem and therefore stepped in the forestage. This position, however, is almost certainly due to careless drawing, for a foremast with a top and topmast would hardly find enough support save in the ship proper. The shrouds, of which there are not many, come within the bulwarks. The stay leads to the bowsprit.

The foresail is halfmast high or a little more. The lifts, one sheet and one bowline are clearly shown. The sheet appears to lead through a hole in the forecastle bulwarks. The bowline comes from high up the leech of the sail and leads to the bowsprit before the forestay. A bridle is hinted at rather than certainly shown. The foretop is small, and shows little detail. The fore-topsail yard and the furled sail are shown without any gear but a pair of 'yard ropes' leading slackly from the yardarms to the top. The topmast head bears a small pendant.

The mainmast is stepped amidships, and, as at the present day, the mizen mast is nearer to it than the foremast. Shrouds of an uncertain number are shown, set up outboard. The maintop covers the eyes of the rigging. The mainstay leads to the forecastle, and from its position may well have been set up to the stem. The mainlifts are clearly shown.

The mainsail is mastheaded. The robands, bowlines and sheets are shown. As in the case of the foresail, the bowlines are high up the leech. They have a single bridle and lead to the bowsprit, at least the lee bowline does, the weather one seems to lead to the fore rigging. We know, however, and two other ships in the picture agree, that the lead was to the bowsprit.

No bonnets are shown and there are no braces or other gear. The maintop is large and contains the usual javelins. The topmast appears to have shrouds. The stay, probably owing to a mistake in drawing, comes from half way up the mast, but leads in a natural manner to the foremast head.

The cockbilled maintopsail yard is seen. Its importance is secondary to the great swallow tailed pendant that is flying from the mast. In none of the ships in Fig. 57.1, it will be noted, is the pendant in the maintop flown from the masthead. Can this be an early example of half masting, or does it denote a salute or a signal, or was it the usual practice?

It is remarkable how many parts of a ship once served for duties other than those to which they have come to be put. The bowsprit was first introduced to carry a grappling iron, or perhaps first to supply a good lead for the bowlines, and only after many generations became a sail carrying spar. In our own times the mast has ceased to have any propelling function. So with topmasts. There is no doubt that the first use of a topmast was to bear a flag in the top, and the phrase continued in use till long after the days when the flag 'in the top' was commonly flown from a staff above the topgallant mast. Here we see the new use of the topmast as a mast well established, but still subordinate to the old use as a flagstaff.

The topmast head is confused and indistinct. Of the other maintop-masts in the picture, one bears a cross and the others little square black objects that may be flags or may be some form of crow's nest.

The mizzen mast is small. It has shrouds, but no stay. It also bears a swallow-tailed streamer not quite at the masthead.

The mizzen yard is inside the shrouds. It has no lift and what gear is shown is somewhat difficult to understand. There is a pendant from the after yardarm, at the end of which, judging from Fig. 57.2, we may suppose there is a block. Through this block is a rope, of which one end leads to the outligger and the other inboard. Is this fitting a vang, the smiting line, or the sheet? It can hardly be the sheet, because the pendant would prevent the mizzen from being sheeted home if it were. What, too, is the pendant and whip hanging in bights between the outligger and taffarell?

The gaskets of the mizzen are passed where the robands secure the sail to the yard. Is this a mere convention of drawing, or were the furling lines long ends of the robands?

The ship in the right hand top corner closely resembles that just described, save that in common with the other ships in the picture she lacks a fore top and topmast.

The ship in the middle sailing into harbour shows very well the peculiar appearance of the curved stem and long overhanging forestage that must have been familiar to every seaman's eye between the middle of the fifteenth and middle of the sixteenth centuries and probably for much longer.

This ship's topmast rigging is carelessly drawn, and whether it is her topsail yard hanging downwards and resting on the top rim aft, or a flag, or whether the doubtful object is due to a mistake of the artist is uncertain. The position of her spritsail yard is also peculiar; perhaps it is intended to show that she is stowing it before coming into port. She has a mizzen lift, which seems to bear no weight, and is strikingly reminiscent of the 'yard tackle' of a Thames barge.

The ship riding under the cliff with two anchors down suggests rather than shows her forebraces led to the mainstay in the fashion soon to

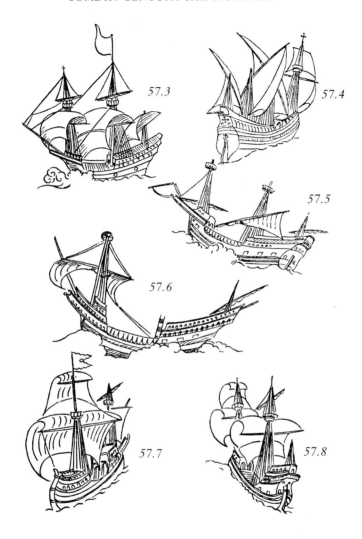

become universal which was to last till the first quarter of the XVIII century was passed. She seems to have lifts to both of her mizzen yardarms. The ropes hanging in bights from the main yardarms are probably the braces, which the artist in a moment of forgetfulness has drawn to look like the topsail yard ropes and which lead from the yard arms to the top.

The ship towing out has her yards pointed, and the towrope apparently leads from the hawse hole.

The boats show some carelessness on the part of the artist, who has in one case put all the oars on one side. The boat towing the ship out is more carefully shown, but faint lines can be made out on her starboard side suggesting that her oars were wrongly drawn at first.

Each boat is steered with a 'scull,' and it may well be that this practice gave the name of sculling to propulsion by a single oar from the stern.

Passing to the ship in Fig. 57.2, we find the same general features. The forecastle is unusually high and its shortness gives the ship an ancient look. Parts of the rigging suggest inaccurate copying; the rope leading forward from the main yard-arm is certainly meant to be the bowline. The topmast too is provided with a backstay to the mizzen mast but no stay, and this also suggests an oversight. These and the fact that the main rigging is apparently set up under water deprive such features as the topmast abaft the masthead and the deep main bonnet, if bonnet it be, of their value as evidence; but the 'bowline comb' on the bowsprit is interesting and so are the main puttocks.

To sum up. The great interest of these pictures lies on the advanced development that they show. At the beginning of the XV century few ships seem to have had more than one mast and yet here in a MS. probably of about 1450 or so we find at least one ship shown as rigged almost after the typical XVI century fashion.

The light of our knowledge of the XV century is dim, but by it we seem to see traces of a development unequalled save by that of the age in which we were born.

From Vol V, No 1, §§15–20 (*July 1919*)

58

A SIXTEENTH-CENTURY
SEA-MONSTER

By R Morton Nance

When compared with the usual forms of shipping that one associates with the Sixteenth Century, the monstrous type here illustrated seems strange indeed; and were Bruegel our only, as he is our chief, authority for its strange features, we should be justified in rejecting it as a sea-nightmare of that demon-loving artist; but others, less imaginative than he, have also preserved its memory.

Van Yk, a Dutch writer (1696), copies some ships of Bruegel, calling them carracks; Jal also engraves one of these, questioning if 'carrack' might be its name, and there leaving it. From the available evidence it would seem, however, that the carrack differed from its fellow ships or *nefs* only in being greater, of deeper draught and with higher upper works than these. Such was the case in 'W.A.'s' earlier 'kraeck' certainly, and if one is right in assuming that certain ships, with the colours of Portugal and lying in oriental ports, in the *Orbis Civitates Terrarum* of Braun and Hogenburg (1572), are indeed carracks, the same holds true of these also.

The name 'galleon' has also been applied to these vessels, and in one respect fits better, for they sometimes carry Spanish flags, and in many cases they bear upon their round bows the galley-beak or spur that was, at the date of Bruegel's designs, probably a feature of the galleon. In Braun's volume, cited above, are some Portuguese vessels that would seem to be early galleons (Fig. 58.13). They are longer, better armed, and less castellated than the *nefs* that enrich the same pages, and instead of the overhanging mediaeval forecastle of these, they have the round-fronted forecastle and beaked bow of a Venetian galleass, precisely as these are seen in Martin Rota's print of the battle of Lepanto (1572) or in the galleas (copied one may guess from a Lepanto *ex-voto*) that Bartolomeo Crescentio gives in his *Nautica Mediterranea* of nearly fifty years later (Figs. 58.15 and 58.14). Beaked ships like these are seen also in the Madrid tapestries (and in the original designs by Jan Vermayen from which they were slightly altered) that commemorate the siege of Tunis (1535), and at

58.1
58.2
58.3
58.4
58.5
58.6
58.7

this siege a Portuguese galleon is recorded to have been present. But such beaks were by no means confined to the galleass and galleon; caravels thus armed are shown both in the tapestries above-mentioned, and also in the *Orbis Civitates Terrarum* (Fig. 58.11). The latter, too, gives us a small beaked sailing vessel, galley-rigged, but with broadside guns, possibly a zabra (Fig. 58.12) while in its northern views we have, besides ill-drawn beaked ships at Goricum, Riga and Königsburg, an excellent specimen of our beaked sea-monster type at Stockholm (Fig. 58.6). The idea of crossing the sturdy round-ship or *nef* with the galley in order to produce the perfect ship was much in men's minds at this period, and under its influence the shipyards of Europe, our own included, were producing many hybrid forms, so that we need not at once conclude that these ship-rigged, galley-nosed mongrels are Spanish galleons. Judged by the scanty and poor Spanish and Portuguese drawings of their own galleons and by the sea-fight pictures of the Dutch, who certainly had an eye for ships, they would seem to have differed very little in form from the fighting ships of other nations by the end of the sixteenth century. Ships and galleons all alike had adopted the shelving, narrow poop and harmless, but beautiful, beak-head of the period. Their assimilation was complete in all but size and proportion: and yet we find associated with them these strange ships for which we seek a name.

It will be seen that our authorities for the existence of this type of ship are all, if not Netherlanders, at least northern draughtsmen. The Spaniards never seem to have had ships enough of their own to supply their requirements, and while Flanders had a ship left, their mutual relations were such that the ship would be at Spain's service. It may be worth while, then, to consider the possibility that these ships, with their Dutch-looking, round bows, may have hailed from Flanders. Fig. 58.8 lends a little colour to such a view. This ship stands in the foreground of a low-relief carving of Antwerp city, c. 1490; her high bow, her simple sterncastle, and the strengthening cleats, or skids, on her sides, are not in themselves unusual for her period, but when combined with the stumpy forecastle and back-curved stem, they mark her out from other ships of her time, and, allowing for the trend of the changes that took place in ship-fashions during the half-century between this and the ship (Fig. 58.1) of Bruegel, we find some striking points of likeness which may be worth following up. The mediaeval aftercastle has become a poop; the forecastle, modest before, has now almost vanished; the stem is even more curved; the bow skids are still there, while those at the stern have increased until they give the poop its strongest note of character. The waist, too, has its skids that strengthen the sides beneath the battery that is there. The placing of the ordnance, and the incongruous beak join in suggesting that both are later defensive additions to a ship of tried usefulness as a trader.

The form of merchant ship that we have learnt to consider typical of the Netherlands is the round-sterned *flûte* or fly-boat; but although the name itself seems to be ancient, we hear little or nothing of *flûtes* during the first years of the sixteenth century, and during this period the hulk seems to have been the typical trading ship of the northern counties. Antoine de Conflans, writing at this time of the ships then in use, tell us nothing of *flûtes*, but of hulks he says that great numbers of them, of from two to six hundred tons burden and more, came in fleets from Russia, Norway, Denmark, Friesland, Holland, Zealand and Brabant. The hulk (called *hulk* or *holk* by the northern peoples and *oulque, hourque, urca,* and *orca* by the Latins) is constantly referred to during the century as a large merchant ship. Thus we read of 'Hulkes of Dantsick,' 'Easterling Hulks,' 'Hulks of Flanders,' and Crescentio even writes of '*Urche Inglese,*' referring to the ships of our sea-rovers. By the middle of the following century, however, the hulk seems to have vanished, leaving but a suggestive name that soon became applied to the dismantled remnant of a ship, to the obsolete ships preserved in heraldry and in church windows or, from similarity of sound probably, to ship hulls, to hookers and even to hoys; while the place formerly held by the hulk was everywhere filled by the flute.

This displacement of hulks by flutes will be found to synchronise remarkably with the rise of Holland and its trade and the consequent ruin of the hulk-owning ports of Flanders and the Baltic; it seems, therefore, not unlikely that the capacious flute was a new Dutch conception, an enlarged, ship-rigged barge contrived to carry as much merchandise as possible with the smallest possible crew, typical of the businesslike methods of the nation that had wrested practically all their trade from the owners of the hulks. We find indeed, that the names 'flie boat' and 'hulk' are occasionally used as synonyms by by sixteenth-century authors, which seems to oppose this theory, but as being northern merchant vessels of similar use and both less ornamented than ships they might well be confounded. The pictorial evidence available gives us no *flûte*-like vessels of countries other than Holland during the century. The ships that we may tentatively call 'hulks' are, on the contrary, well represented. Stockholm, as pictured in *Orbis Civitates Terrarum*, provides us with two varieties, one beaked, the other with a slightly projecting forecastle (Figs. 58.6 and 58.16). Antwerp gives us two more, one a stern view. These are taken from the title page of a navigation book published at that city in 1580 (Figs. 58.3–4). Again, we find the type represented in Adam's charts of the Armada 1588. In these prints the ships are drawn with great attention to character, a fact which increases the value of those selected as evidence. Firstly, we have a beaked vessel, her large mainsail decorated with the ragged-staff saltire of Burgundy (Fig. 58.7). Next is an English ship (Fig. 58.10), her bow is not unlike that of our 'hulks,' but there the

resemblance ceases. It is allowable to suppose that this may be a portrait of the fly-boat *Yonge*. Lastly, we have the ship (Fig. 58.5) with her main topsail bearing the device of a haloed figure. The Saint Andrew's cross behind hints at his name, but, lest this should not be sufficient, beneath saint and saltire runs the legend 'S: AND:.' Why should the artist have been thus careful, if not to identify a particular ship? Of ships named for

Saint Andrew there were three in the Armada, a small zabra or patache of two guns; a larger vessel, originally Scottish, of twelve guns, but still classed as a patache or zabra; and, lastly, the hulk *Santo Andres*, of 14 guns, 400 tons, 28 mariners, and 150 soldiers. The guns, as listed, could not obviously have included the many small breechloaders, that at this time defended the cage-works; deducting then the four of these that are in the poop, we find four great guns low in the hull and two more, carried as they had been prior to the introduction of port-holes, in the waist; doubling these and adding the two that would certainly be in the stern ports, we have the exact tally of guns. The large poop would lend itself well to the stowage of troops and, apart from the false idea of size that is given by the figures of sailors introduced, the tonnage would seem to be in proportion. It seems then not unlikely that we have here a fairly faithful portrait of the hulk *Santo Andres*. Most of the guns in this, as in our other examples of the type, lie so perilously near the water line that it is difficult to see how their shot, as we read of the galleon's missiles, could have flown high over the English ships during the Armada fight. In rough weather indeed, the greater number of their big guns would be out of action, and one is forced to admire the greater discretion of Raleigh's 'Easterling hulkes, who were wont to paint great red portholes in their broadsides where they carried no ordnance at all.' It will be seen, however, by a reference to our illustrations (Figs. 58.1, 58.4 and 58.6) that usually no guns are shown in the broadside amidships and beneath the waist-battery, and it may be that Raleigh intended only to say that such a gap in the line was filled with painted ports.

The persistence of this antiquated type to the days of the Armada was remarkable, but there is good reason to suppose that it may have lasted for many years longer. Fig. 58.9 is taken from a *Mercator's Atlas* of some decades later. It may be merely a bad copy from an earlier original, some of Bruegel's gallies being recognisable in the same collection of maps, yet it seems to have developed beyond our other specimens in respect of the abandoned waist battery and the completed and raised line of guns. She still has the broad continuous poop with upright skids, and in appearance her beakless bow brings her nearer again to the fifteenth century ship of Antwerp. (Fig. 58.8).

Parallel with these 'hulks' we have, in Bruegel's works, in Hoefnagle's designs for the *Orbis Civitates Terrarum*, in some old maps and even in the design used as cover for this journal, a closely related type that combines the poop of a 'hulk' with the bows of either galleon or *nef*. The galleon combination is well shown in Figs. 58.17, 58.18 and 58.20, all from Mercator, the last two from a map dated 1631, and the nef bow in Fig.

58.19 from the view of Messina in *Orbis Civitates Terrarum*. Those drawn by Hondius in *Mercator's Atlas* seem to be the last recorded specimens of ships with the heavy skidded poop, and already, in 1631, the beaked bow would seem to have finally disappeared.

Apart from changing fashion, an explanation for the extinction of this school of shipbuilding may be sought in the history of the period. The defeat of Oquendo in the Downs (1639) was a heavy blow to the naval power of Spain, but yet, one would think, not a sufficient cause for this disappearance had the ships been Spanish; on the other hand, the merciless opposition of Holland in trade as well as war had already by this time brought ruin to the port of Antwerp; and when, by the treaty of Münster (1648) its implacable foes closed the Scheldt to traffic, the end had come. Had these ships been Flemish hulks they must, if not already extinct, have then vanished.

These vessels, apart from the doubtful question of their identity, for it must be owned that the 'Flemish hulk' may yet prove, on further evidence, to be something quite different, have many points of interest. The mediaeval character of their hulls has already been touched upon; with this they have, too, a tendency to preserve the mediaeval proportions of mast and topmast, while their rigging shows a variety of curious details. Among these, the furled mizen top-sail in Fig. 58.1, its sheet leading to an outlicker on the half-top, its ship-style lift contrasting with the galley-fashioned vangs of the mizen yard and, in Fig. 58.6, a galley or mizen-style half-top on the square-rigged fore-mast are especially noteworthy.

From Vol II, No 4, §§97–104 (April 1912)

¶ 59   THE HULK

I think that Mr. Nance has established that the ships represented in his drawings, published in the April No., (see 58) are hulks. There is no doubt that throughout the 16th century the hulk was the large merchant-ship of the northern nations. Mr. Nance cites passages in support of this thesis, and other quotations could easily be added, *e.g.*, from the naval papers illustrating the war of 1545, published in L. & P. of Henry VIII (Rolls' Series), and also from N.R.S., 'The Spanish War, 1585–87,' edited by Mr. Corbett. In the last-named collection there are many advices which speak of great fleets of hulks, often mentioned as being of large size, in the Spanish ports, and especially in the Tagus, *e.g.*, p. 52, 'there is in Lisbon upon (*i.e.*, about) 80 sail of hulks from 100 tons to 800 tons, of Holland, Zealand, and Hamburg.' Elsewhere (p. 64) mention is made of three score 'hulks and flyboats,' the flyboats being obviously of the same class, though not of the same type, as the hulks, but smaller. At the end of the 16th century when a flyboat was very large she was termed a 'double flyboat,' and the fact that she needed and received a special name showed that she differed in type from the hulk. We know, especially from Hollar's drawings, what the flyboat looked like in the middle of the 17th century; and we may perhaps infer that she was in the main of similar build and appearance, though smaller, from 50 to 100 years earlier. If so, Mr. Nance's suggestion that Fig. 58.10 may represent the flyboat *Yonge* will not stand. With the pictures of hulks before us we are likely to wonder the less that a more rational type of ship should have been developed in order to supersede them. The flyboat was less high charged, and entirely free from the weak 'clench-work,' which forms so prominent a feature of the hulk, and she must have been much more seaworthy and sea-kindly than her predecessor.

By 'L.G.C.L.', from *Notes*, Vol II, No 5, §156 (*May 1912*)

¶ 60   A SIXTEENTH-CENTURY SHIP OF LÜBECK

The *Schifferhaus* at Lübeck is noteworthy for possessing, besides its many ship models, an old painting, the portrait of a once famous ship of that city, by name *Der Adler*. The painting itself is too faded for satisfactory photographic reproduction, but the accompanying drawing, made with some care from a photograph, will give a fair idea of the original. We are happily able to give some particulars of the ship in question, gleaned from the archives of Lübeck and other sources by Captain Georg Bendfeldt, President of the *Schiffergesellschaft*, and kindly handed on to us.

This vessel, *Der Adler*, was laid down in 1566 by the burghers of Lübeck, then at war with Sweden as Denmark's ally in the Northern Seven Years' War, to replace their flagship *Morian* lost in a storm off Visby, together with 13 other ships, two of Lübeck and 11 Danish. At that time the largest ship yet built at Lübeck, and in all probability the largest ship in the world, she cost her proud builders the sum of 32,000 marks. Her main dimensions were as follows:—

Length over all, 220.5ft. Length of keel, 122 ft. Beam, 49 ft. Depth at stern, 71 ft. Height of mainmast, 118 ft. Length of mainyard, 116 ft.

She had six decks and two deckhouses (poop and forecastle?) Her stoutest cable was 24 in. She carried 500 soldiers and 400 seamen, while her 75 great guns required 150 gunners. In another document her guns are enumerated as follows:—

In Lubeck Erbaut 1566, Renovatum 1608, & 1621 & 1631.

60.1

Cast guns (probably brass):

8 'Kartaunen' firing iron shot of 40 lbs.

6 'Halbekartaunen' firing iron shot of 20 lbs.

26 'Feldschlangen' firing iron shot of 10, 9 and 8 lbs.

Wrought iron guns:

28 'Steinbuschen' (or 'Hagelbuschen'), firing stones of 30, 20, and 10 lbs., with 56 'Kammern' (breech chambers.)

20 'Kleine Steinbuschen,' firing stones of 3 lbs, with 20 'Kammern.'

20 'Quartierschlangen,' firing stones of 5 lbs., with 20 'Kammern.'

40 'Quartierschlangen,' firing stones of 1½ lbs., with 80 'Kammern.'

Besides many muskets, etc.

She carried 6,000 iron shot large and small, 300 bar and chain shot, 1,000 stone shot, 10 *lasts* of powder, and 1 *last* of hail shot (*Hagel und Schroot*). Her total armament was accordingly 40 muzzle loaders and 108 breech-loaders of various sizes, some with one breech-chamber per gun, some with two.

Her name, *Der Adler*, is associated with the double-headed eagle, emblem of Lübeck in particular and of the Hanseatic League in general. This spreads itself repeatedly upon her pendants, her pavesades and in other prominent places, notably the large shield above the rudder head with the ship's name and the date 1566 written over it; in this case only the eagle is crowned. With this eagle badge the white and red colours of Lübeck share the honours. Taking various shapes on pendants, top awnings and shields, they appear again in stripes on the ensign and the planking of the cage-work, and fly in their usual flag form from the four mastheads.

An inscription on the frame of the picture runs:—'Lübeck erbaut 1566, renovatum 1608.' This is placed symmetrically in the middle, but has been added to in latter years with the dates, 'und 1621. und 1631 (*or* 1681.*)*' These later dates cause a difficulty, since it seems very doubtful if *Der Adler* was still in existence as late as 1630. Nothing is heard of her or any other big ship of Lübeck during Wallenstein's attempt to form an Imperial Navy in the Baltic, and a ship of this size recently repaired would almost certainly have been employed, or at any rate, mentioned at some time in the course of the Thirty Years' War. *Possibly* the later dates refer to a restoration of the *picture*, not of the ship, but this is merely a conjecture.

The original inscription may perhaps imply that the painting dates from 1608, but though as a 'great ship' she may have anticipated developments to some extent, there are some details that would suggest a later date, certainly a date long after 1566. The difficulty of deciding such a point is not lessened by the general faultiness of the drawing, of which the reverse perspective, which causes the lines of the stern to curve outward where they should be hollow, may be taken as an example.

Still the painter shows considerable knowledge of sea-warfare in his detail of sheer-hooks, bowsprit-grapnel, and, in the tops, darts and top-armings. The running rigging, too, although apparently dashed in at random, to be made fast here and there afterwards with a spidery crowfoot, may for the most part be identified with actual detail of the time. The rounded stern-gallery with its guns; the beak-head, this a little muddled in drawing; the two tiers of guns in the waist and the elaborate mast head crosses are all noticeable, but not impossible features for 1566; but the backstays, set up with deadeyes, seem extraordinary even for 1608, and the bobstay tackle is another somewhat startling detail for so early a date. Even more striking, however, are the sails, for each of these has besides the customary bonnet at its foot, a row of reef points with, below it, a row of eyelet holes running across its head. These reef points are visible even upon the mizzens and also on the sail of the boat beneath the stern. Are we to condemn these modern-seeming details as prophetic errors of the painter; or must we believe that in 1566 or at latest in 1608, they were to be found in a great ship of Lübeck?

By 'R.M.N.' and 'R.C.A.', from *Notes*, Vol II, No 5, §§152–53 (*May 1912*)

℈ 61   SIXTEENTH-CENTURY SHIP OF LÜBECK

The details of the armament of the *Adler*, laid down at Lübeck, in 1566, as quoted by R. M. N. and R. C. A. (see 60) are interesting. 'Kartaunen' are 'curtows' undoubtedly; and 'Schlangen' may presumably be identi- fied, as far as derivation goes, with the English 'slings.' If this supposition is right, it would appear that the English word 'sling,' as a gun name, is corruption of the German root, which means 'serpents.' This seems all as it should be, seeing how much in favour names of serpents were for different types of mediaeval cannon. It should be noticed, however, that in calibre the German 'schlangen' do not correspond to the English 'slings,' which were quite small pieces; but that the 'feldschlangen' are approximately equivalent to English 'demi-culverins,' and the heavier kind of 'quarterischlangen' to English 'sakers.' 'Steinbuschen' seems to be 'perriers'; and the application of the word 'busch' to this type of gun, definitely stated to be wrought not cast, may probably refer to the bundle or faggot of iron rods which were welded together. I do not remember to have seen any other mention of 'chambers' for guns throwing even 10 lb. shot, let alone 20 and 30 lbs. as here described.

By 'C.L.', from *Notes*, Vol II, No 7, §§215–16 (*July 1912*)

℈ 62   NAMES ON THE STERNS OF MEN-OF-WAR

The drawing of the German ship *Der Adler*, in the present volume of The Mariner's Mirror, (see Fig. 60.1) shows her name on the stern. Possible date of original picture, 1608, but see the Note accompanying the drawing.

By 'W.S.', from *Answers*, Vol II, No 11, §350 (*November 1912*)

BIG SHIPS IN HISTORY

By R C Anderson

There are many references to be found here and there to ships of a remarkable size for their epoch. As a rule definite figures are somewhat scarce, and even when they are given it is often difficult to make comparisons, because of the variations and uncertainties in the methods of measurement. Still it is possible to piece together a certain amount of information, and this I have tried to do in the following article.

The first mention of actual dimensions that I have found dates from the beginning of the sixteenth century; before this I know nothing more definite than that various ships were of 1,000 tons, obviously a round number merely, though early tonnage measurement was very probably not quite so unscientific as is generally supposed. The English *Regent*, for instance, a ship of 1489, is said to have been of 1,000 tons, and was in all probability the biggest ship of her time.

The first figures available, those for the Scottish ship *Great Michael*, of 1506, are somewhat startling. She is said to have been 240 ft. long over all, and 36 ft. broad withinboard, while her sides were 'ten foot thick in the wall and boards, on every side so slack, and so thick that no cannon could go through her.' She was lost at sea in 1512. Probably she was the cause of the building of the *Henri Grace à Dieu*, launched in 1514, and described as of 1,000 or 1,500 tons. No actual measurements are to be found for this ship or for her French successor, the *Grand Français*, of 1,500 or 2,000 tons. This latter ship had, however, five masts with four tops on the mainmast, the uppermost so high that a man in it would appear from the deck to be no bigger than a fowl, while her length was such that a ball could hardly be thrown from one end to the other. Like the *Great Michael*, she was unlucky; in fact, she never reached open water and was wrecked in harbour in 1533.

A year before this there had been launched a very large Swedish ship, the *Stora Krafvel (Great Caravel)*. For her we have exact authentic dimensions. She was 179 ft. long over all, 157.5 ft. exclusive of the beak, and 134 ft. on the under side of the keel, the 'tread'; her beam was 41 ft., her draught of water 11ft., and her total depth at the stern 39 ft. Her mainmast was 130 ft. long and 18.5 ft. thick at the bottom, with a mainyard of 105 ft. Her sides were 6 ft. thick; not quite so thick proportionatley as those of the *Great Michael*, but still pretty stout. Another Swedish ship, the *Mars* of 1563, burnt in action in the following year, was perhaps a little bigger. Chapman, the great Swedish naval architect, reckoned that she must have been 160 ft from stem to stern, without the beak, and 41 ft. wide. She was, however, undoubtedly surpassed by the *Adler* of Lübeck, built in 1566, for this ship was 220.5 ft. long overall and 122 ft. on the keel (presumably the measured keel, not the tread), while her extreme beam was 49.1 ft. (see 60). She must have drawn much more water than the *Stora Krafvel*, since her depth at the stern was 71 ft. Her mainmast was shorter than that ship's, 118 ft., but its yard was longer, 116 ft.

English ships at this time were comparatively small, especially in beam; the broadest Elizabethan ship, the *Triumph*, measured only 40 ft. in beam, while the greatest keel-length was the 110 ft. of the *White Bear* and *Merhonour*. Under these circumstances, the Portuguese *Madre de Deos*, captured in 1592, appeared particularly remarkable. In length she was about the same as the biggest English ship, being 100 ft. on the keel and 165 ft. over all, but her beam of 46.8 ft. was a great increase on anything previously seen in this country. It is uncertain how she compared with other Portuguese and Spanish ships, the 'great San Philip,' for example, but probably she was nearly if not quite as large as the largest of them.

The *Madre de Deos* was never used by her captors, but it is perhaps allowable to trace her influence in the great increase of dimensions that took place in English shipbuilding in 1610, when the *Prince Royal* was launched. This ship was 43.5 ft. in beam, 115 ft. on the keel, and probably about 210 ft. over all. She was soon surpassed by the *Sovereign of the Seas* of 1637, 232 ft. long over all, 128 ft. on the keel, 48 ft. in beam and 76 ft. from her keel to the top of her stern-lantern; roughly of the same size as the *Adler* of 1566. The *Sovereign* seems to have marked the greatest extension of the beak; subsequent ships exceeded her in keel or gun-deck length by more and more, but her over-all length was not beaten until a century later.

Extract from Vol III, No 2, §§43–44 (February 1913)

❡ 64   THE GUNS OF THE *ADLER* OF LÜBECK

In the July edition of the 'M. M.' for 1912 (see 61), C. L. notes that the English 'sling' and the German 'schlange,' though apparently identical in derivation, did not correspond in size. He also notes that the 'feld-schlangen' were roughly equivalent to 'demi-culverins,' and the larger 'quartierschlangen' to 'sakers.' Now if we suppose that the 'schlange' fired a shot four times the weight of that of the 'quartierschlange,' or in other words 20 lbs., we see the close correspondence between the 'schlange' and the 'culverin.' At the same time we may note that the word 'culverin' was derived form the French 'couleuvrine' or 'cou-leuvre,' an adder. Perhaps, therefore, the German 'schlange' was simply a translation of 'culverin,' or its French original. It is well known that foreign words are very seldom adopted in Germany, but are nearly always replaced by a German equivalent.

By 'R.C.A.', from *Notes*, Vol III, No 5, §153 (*May 1913*)

ℐ 65   THE *ADLER* OF LÜBECK

With regard to the note on the picture of this ship in the *Schifferhaus* at Lübeck (see 60); the inscription. 'Renovatum 1608 and 1621 and 1631' must refer to the picture not to the ship, for she was accidentally burnt before 1600. The crew of the *Adler* is given as numbering 900 men; this is wrong, as can be imagined for a vessel of that size; an authentic list in the state archives of Lübeck gives her crew as 672, including 352 soldiers. This appears more likely.

By L Arenhold, from *Notes*, Vol III, No 7, §222 (*July 1913*)

ℐ 66   THE *ADLER* OF LÜBECK

Captain Arenhold suggests that it is unlikely that the *Adler* carried as many as 900 men. (see 65) A good many ships of the period seems to have carried as many or even more. Danish accounts give the three Danish ships *Jegermesther, Samson* and *Hannibal* as having 1,100, 1,100 and 943 respectively; they also give the *Morian* of Lübeck 1,000 men, while estimates of the crew of the Swedish *Mars* range from 800 to 1350. Apparently the *Adler* was bigger than any of these, so there seems nothing very improbable in supposing that she carried 1,050 men as stated in the account given to R. M. N. and myself—the 150 gunners were additional to the 500 soldiers and 400 sailors, not included among them. It seems to me that the ship, when carrying the 672 of Capt. Arenhold's authority, must have been under-manned, at least according to the practice of the time.

By 'R.C.A.', from *Notes*, Vol III, No 8, §25 (*August 1913*)

¶ 67   THE *ADLER* OF LÜBECK

My statement as to the crew of the *Adler*, 672 men, seems to be doubted by R. C. A., (see 64, 66) who gives her 1,050. I can only say that the number I have given is based upon documents in the old library in Lübeck, so that if the ship is 'under-manned,' the responsibility is not mine. It may interest the readers of the 'M. M.' to know how the crew of this great vessel of 1560 was composed. There were:

 2 gentlemen of the Town Council.
 2 captains.
 4 skippers.
 3 mates.
 1 clergyman.
 1 clerks.
 2 sergeants of police.
 2 policemen.
11 carpenters.
87 bussenschutten (musketeers).
10 ark knechts and boys.
12 schiemanns (non-com. officers).
 5 quartermasters.
 2 sailmakers.
 5 musicians.
 7 barbers.
 5 better servants.
 9 servants (trabanten).
14 cooks.
 4 chief boatswains.
88 sailors.
 9 dregers.
34 boys (powder and cabin).
——
320

In addition to these there were the soldiers:—

 1 captain.
 1 ensign.
350 men.
——
352

Total crew, 672.

It would be very interesting to learn the number of the crew of similar vessels of that period. An English list of 1584 gives:—

	Tons.	Men.	Guns (all sizes).
Henri Grace à Dieu	1000	700	122
Peter	600	400	90
Christopher	400	246	53
Unicorn	240	140	36

A list in Fincham's 'Shipbuilding' gives 100 years later:—

	Tons.	Men.	Guns.
Sovereign	1141	600	100
Fairfax	745	260	52

Witsen gives the crew of De Ruyter's flagship, *Seven Provincen,* of 80 guns as 425 men and 50 soldiers, or 475 in all.

These numbers seem very reasonable. The greater numbers given by R.C.A. are these which are traditional, but they must be treated with caution.

It would be of great interest to learn more about the numbers of the crews of other great vessels of the 16th century; presumably there are MS. lists still in existence in the different countries.

By 'L.A.', from *Notes,* Vol III, No 9, §284 (*September 1913*)

¶ 68   THE *ADLER* OF LÜBECK

The details which L. A. gives of the crew of this ship (see 65 and 67) are very interesting but he does not tell us whether they represented her official complement or merely the actual number of men on board on some particular occasion. If, as I suspect, the latter is the case, it may well be that at other times she carried the 1,050 of the account given to Mr. Nance and myself, in other words, that she was undermanned when carrying the 672 of this list. The French *Cordeliere,* in 1512, carried 1,250; the Swedish *Stora Krafvel,* in 1535, had 1,300. The *Adler* was probably a bigger ship than the *Henri Grace à Dieu,* and she certainly carried more and heavier guns. Even by the standards of a much later age she was a very large ship, while at her date, hand to hand fighting, and therefore small arms, played a very important part in an action. The conditions of a century later had been altered so much by improvements in rig and the growth in importance of pure artillery fighting, that it is hardly worth while to compare ships of the two dates. However, the *Royal Sovereign* carried, according to Pepys' official list, 815 men (not 600), while the French *Soleil Royal* and *Royal Louis* carried 1,200 amd 1,100 respectively. The *Zeven Provincien* was, of course, a comparatively small ship, and Dutch crews were always smaller than those of ships of the same size in other fleets.

By 'R.C.A.', from *Notes*, Vol III, No 11 §345 (*November 1913*)

69

THE NODAL CARAVELS OF
1618

By H S Vaughan

The voyage of the two brothers, Bartolomé and Gonzalo Nodal, from Lisbon to Magellan's Strait, including the circumnavigation of Terra del Fuego, was performed in 1618–19. It was remarkable not only for its success in exploration, but because the two little caravels, practically sister ships, in which it was conducted, never parted company and never lost a single man from misadventure or sickness.

These vessels, *Nuestra Senora de Atocha* and *Nuestra Senora del Buen Suceso*, were of 80 tons each, were provisioned for 10 months, and carried crews of 40 Portuguese seamen. In the 'Sailing Directions' to their remarkably concise narrative of the voyage (*Hakluyt Soc.*) the brothers say:— 'They made such a pair when sailing that in all the rains and fogs we met with they were never separated one from the other. It follows that with ships of that kind the quickest voyages can be made.'

The accompanying figure is a combination sketch made from the four representations of the vessels which occur in the narrative of the voyage, two of these being on the chart of the edition of 1621, and two on the title-page.

The type might be described as an early four-masted barquentine, lateen-rigged on all three after masts. I do not recall other instances of this rig, but perhaps the publication of this note may evoke further evidence.

De Courbes was the engraver of the chart and title-page, and although between the four representations there are slight variations, and some little difficulties as to perspective, etc., I think it may be assumed that the engravings show the principal details of rigging correctly, and, certainly, that the type was an actual one. The enormous lateen yard and sail on the mainmast must have proved, one would think, very unwieldy, and although this is not stated in the narrative, it may perhaps be inferred from references such as the following:—

'On Friday, 28th September, in the afternoon we found that the mainmast was sprung, from rifts caused by the rolling of the ship.

Fig. 69.1 A caravel of 1618.

Nothing could be done that day because it was already late, so it was left until the next day, meanwhile shortening sail.'

'At dawn, 29th September, the mast was very well fished with spare spars.'

'19th December, 1618. Late in the afternoon the Captain's ship carried away her mainyard, and it was God's miracle that three men were not lost who were aloft and fell head foremost on to the broken part of the yard.'

But, for the rest, Bartolomé de Nodal says, in his letter to the King, dated the first of December, 1618:—'The ships were the most efficient that can be imagined, strong, and the sails so fitted that the spread of canvas was the same in both ships. I was well content and could find no fault, except that the ships were flush and wanting in freeboard, so that the sea was always washing over the deck even in fine weather. But the new bulwarks remedied this, so that we could pass through any sea.'

The remark as to the bulwarks refers to the alterations which were carried out on their arrival at Rio, consequent upon the representations of the Flemish and Portuguese pilots, who 'declared that under no circumstances could the caravels leave the port without having their freeboards raised.' . . . 'They all agreed that the vessels could not go to sea in their present state, having great openings and the decks being very low, as indeed was the case. Though the caravels may have been the best in the world when they sailed, they now had the decks much exposed. They had come in fine weather, but with any rolling the sea would easily find its way over the decks, and the crew would be much incommoded. For they had no chests nor change of clothes.'

'Fore course and mizzen,' seems to have been the usual sail carried in bad or doubtful weather, and this is mentioned frequently in the log: probably the big mainsail was only set in fair weather.

In all the four figures the caravels are shown head to wind; fore course and foretopsail being the only sail set. The sheets are apparently 'flown,' and the yards braced up.

Under date 24th June, 1619, there is the following entry in the log:— 'We hove to, *taking in all sail except those on the foremast.*'

From Vol III, No 6, §§171–73 (*June 1913*)

70

CARAVELS

By R Morton Nance

Amongst the caravels that I have brought together on the accompanying pages there are hardly two that are exactly alike in both build and rig; yet one easily recognises two or three prevailing types, and of these the most common is that with a square-rigged foremast, to which the Nodal caravels, described by Mr. H. S. Vaughan belong. (See 69).

Caravels of some sort were common in the fifteenth century and even earlier; but these seem not to have had a square-rigged foremast, although, like most lateeners, they probably set a square storm-sail or running-sail on this mast occasionally, and thus paved the way for the later development, and Jal was (or so it seems to me) on firm ground in following Crescentio and deciding that καράβι in Greek, rather than such words as *carré* and *voile* or *quadrada* and *vela* in Romance languages, first gave the caravel her name. It is not necessary to go to Greece, however, to find other forms of this name for a ship, for in France the coracle, with a slight change of sound, becomes a *corable* and a similar word exists in Spanish. Slavonic tongues give us *korable* and *korabie*, while Arabic and Malay offer *ghorâb* and *ghourab* (the 'grab' of English writers) as possible origins of the word caravel. Besides the strong doubt as to whether the earlier caravels had any square sail from which they might have been named, there is another as to whether the words describing such a sail would have been put together in what to Portuguese ears would be the topsy-turvy form of *caravela*, rather than as 'vela quadrada' or even 'velacara.'

An early lateen caravel with two masts is 'said to have been 'drawn by Columbus as a portrait of the *Pinta*. It is at least a reasonable vessel, although perhaps a little later than the claim that it is the work of Columbus would make it (Fig. 70.18). A contemporary print of the ships of Albuquerque at Aden, 1513, shows what may be another two-masted caravel, but, if so, she stands alone amongst caravels in having her sails of nearly equal size instead of becoming smaller or larger by half than their forward or aftward neighbour, respectively. The shape of her bows, too, so much like those of ships in Breydenbach's *Journey to Jerusalem* or

Schedel's *Nuremberg Chronicle*, seems typical of the Mediterranean, rather than of Portugal (Fig. 70.19).

A three-masted caravel of entirely lateen rig is given, in two poses, in the *Orbis Civitates Terrarum* (Figs. 70.16 and 70.17), and, but for her third mast, she is very like the supposed *Pinta*. Hondius, in *Mercator's Atlas*, 1606, has drawn two other lateen caravels that with their two masts are even more like her (Figs. 70.20 and 70.21), one of the caravels drawn by le Testu, too, is a three-masted lateener without square sails (Fig. 70.27).

A slight advance towards the caravel type of the Nodal picture, where a short foremast carries a square sail, but has neither round-top nor topmast above it, is shown in several pictures, one the frontispiece to *Arte del Navegar* (Fig. 70.22) another in *Orbis Civitates Terrarum* (Fig. 70.24) and others in *Speculum Nauticum* (Fig. 70.26), and a print engraved by H. Cock and (I am convinced, wrongly) attributed to Peter Bruegel (Figs. 70.23 and 70.25). Probably these were vessels intermediate in size and importance between the lateeners and the larger full-fledged caravels such as those of the Nodals.

Coming now to these caravels proper, we have first a group of three, taken from various sources, but all representing the caravels that went to Tunis with the Emperor Charles V, in 1536. Of these Fig. 70.4 is taken from one of the designs with which Jan Vermayen commemorated this expedition. This gives us a very clear notion of the build and rig of a war caravel. Her hull astern is that of an ordinary ship of her time, but her round, beaked bows suggest the 'Flemish hulk.' Her lateen-rigged main-mast carries at its head a galley-style half-top, but her square-rigged foremast has a ship's round-top, armed with darts. Her fore-topmast is stayed aft by means of a crow-footed craneline, to blocks upon which lead the fore-topsail braces. Under the bowsprit is a spritsail, the bona-venture sheet leads to an outlegger astern, and between the bonaventure and the counter mizen we see a great awning that, decorated with the Portuguese emblem, an armillary sphere, sweeps down the quarter and trails its border in the sea. It is possible that Fig. 70.5 represents the same vessel. She is, however, taken from quite a different source and one probably less to be relied on—a silver trophy, made in Antwerp to celebrate the Imperial triumphs at Tunis and now exhibited at the Louvre. This caravel also has the sphere-painted, draggle-tailed awning of Fig. 70.4, and her general rig is similar, but here the resemblance ends, for besides the additions of a second awning, Portuguese and Spanish banners, and a pavesade, we have more permanent differences. The bow, for example, has a high forecastle like that of a galleass, and several guns are shown. The third Tunis caravel (Fig. 70.1) shows only her bow, but this

is interesting as being more like that of some later caravels and unlike those of the 'hulk' and galleass. This is a mere suggestion of the form of a ship in one of the famous Madrid tapestries for which Vermagen made the cartoons.

Our next caravel is from Jollivet's Map of Normandy, 1545, and shows us a beakless bow, even more bulbous than that of Fig. 70.4, but this is the only feature that distinguishes her in build from the square-rigged ships of the same map, and her rig adds nothing to what we have already learnt.

Braun's *Orbis Civitates Terrarum*, c. 1560, gives us some fresh details in the caravels (Figs. 70.2 and 70.10), where we get in the four-master (Fig. 70.2), fore-topsail bowlines and a counter-mizen stay, a lift to the lateen mainyard and a craneline or backstay to the mainmast, where one would suppose that it would be very much in the way; while in the three-master we have a craneline leading from beneath the fore-top and lifts to both lateen yards.

The drawings of le Testu give five caravels including the lateener already mentioned. One of these has already been illustrated in the MARINER'S MIRROR (see 57.4), another showing the beaked bow and, in the fore and main masts, the forward rake that is given so frequently to the masts of lateen-rigged craft, is perhaps even more typical of the Portuguese caravel of 1555 (Fig. 70.12).

Ortelius, in a map of 1570, gives a caravel (Fig. 70.6) that, with her variously raking masts, her long beak and well-proportioned sails, seems to show that her designer had a very good idea of the peculiarities of the type, but in Jacques Devaulx, 1583, we have another sailor-artist who, like le Testu, drew ships with more than a landsman's love and knowledge. His caravel (Fig. 70.8), was chosen by Jal as a typical specimen, and has been used over and over again by his imitators, but the long dhow-like bow that she shows was evidently not a constant feature in caravels, at least of the larger sort. Another that he has drawn (Fig. 70.13) hides the bow and gives no new detail; it does, however, strengthen the evidence given by other pictures, and the same may be said for the caravel from Pine's engraving of one of the House of Lords tapestries (Fig. 70.3), or that in Fig. 70.9, which appears on a Dutch Armada medal.

In our last example of the caravel proper (Fig. 70.11), a *Portugische cravelle*, as recorded in a Dutch account of the voyage of Jori's Van Spilberghen to the East Indies in 1601, we have something quite new, one would imagine, in 1617, the date of the book, that is a spritsail topmast with its little yard; while the great forward rake of the mainmast, the other masts being upright, although no doubt correctly observed, is unique in this series of caravels. This mainmast, like that of the Tunis caravel (Fig. 70.4), still has a half-top, but this is not set abaft the masthead in imitation of that of a galley, but before it, to allow of the yard being brought upright abaft the mast in changing it over, a fashion borrowed from the mizen mast of a square-rigged ship of the time. These, however, are but trivial differences after all, and the Dutchman's caravel would at once be recognised as being of the same rig as the vessels that sailed to Tunis.

Quite otherwise was it with the *caravela redonda*, or square-rigged caravel, which is sometimes mentioned in old records. This has been described by a modern writer, who, unfortunately, gives no reference to the source of his information and of whose name I have kept no note, as a vessel 'with square sails on the main and fore masts and lateen sails on the bowsprit and mizen.' Without better authority one might, after the vain attempt to conjure up an image of this cross-bred caravel, refuse to believe in it. Ortelius, however, has had the happy thought to decorate a map with, perhaps, the only picture of a *caravela redonda* in existence (Fig. 70.14). Here we see her with all sail set, running with her lateen sails spread *a oreilles de lièvre*, and we understand that the fore lateen was actually set upon a fore-raking mast and that a true bowsprit with its square spritsail might be carried as well.

The restored side view of such a *caravela redonda* (Fig. 70.15) shows a sail plan very like that of a full-rigged ship of her time, but with the addition of a lateen sail that is practically a great jib, spread by means of a mast-supported yard instead of a stay. Having gone thus far, one wonders that the *caravela redonda* was allowed to disappear, when her triangular headsail might, by borrowing the idea already acted upon in Holland at the time, have been so easily made to run upon a stay, thus making her the handiest square-rigged vessel yet invented, but evidently she was never popular with sailors and soon went to a limbo, from which Ortelius alone helps us to bring her back.

It is surprising that while caravels are so frequently named in sixteenth century writings as sailing in Northern seas, our own included, there yet should be so few pictures of them in which they are not directly connected with Portugal. The long-standing confusion between the 'carvel' of Normandy and elsewhere (which was simply a big carvel-built square-sailed boat used chiefly for fishing) and the lateen caravel may account for many references to English caravels. Manwaryng's description of the caravels that carried Newcastle coal (or is it Smith's) may also be explained by assuming that a printer's error has mixed up his definition of 'cat' with that of the word next above it in his dictionary:—'caravel,' but Tobias Gentleman, in *England's Way to Win Wealth*, 1614, also names caravels as sailing from Harwich for Newcastle coals, and there still remains some reason to doubt whether the lateen caravel, with or without a square-rigged foremast, was not in fairly general use in the North during this period, although, curiously enough, a map of Normandy, the land of 'carvels,' is practically the only source whence a possibly non-Portuguese caravel appears amongst those that I have collected and wherever flags are shown on them these are invariably Portuguese (Figs. 70.2, 70.5, 70.8, 70.11, 70.12, 70.14, 70.19, 70.21).

From Vol III, No 9, §§265–71 (*September 1913*)

Index

Page locations in *italic* denote illustrations.